Presented by

THE NOTTINGHAM ASSOCIATION
OF UNIVERSITY WOMEN

IN MEMORY

OF

ELLA STEWART

who will always be remembered
for her vitality, originality
of thought, and devotion to
the Association.

The Face of France

The Face of France

by

NESTA ROBERTS

HODDER AND STOUGHTON
LONDON SYDNEY AUCKLAND TORONTO

For my god-daughter Frances, in the hope that
this book may foster the love of France kindled by
her first visit.

PROLOGUE

MARSHAL MOUTON STANDS on his pedestal, looking out over the square whose scale is altogether disproportionate to the needs of a town like Phalsbourg. Was it reaction against a mildly ridiculous name that inspired him to a career so valiant as well as so persevering that Napoleon said of him: 'My sheep is a lion'? More likely it was the climate produced by the facts of frontier geography, which sent boys into the army as, in mining villages, they used to go down the pit. Alsace-Lorraine has been a battlefield for the past 2,000 years; Celts against Romans at the beginning of the period, French against Germans towards its end, a variety of other combinations in between. The vastness of the square becomes understandable when you know that it was conceived, not as a country market, but as the *place d'armes*, the parade ground of a garrison town. Phalsbourg was founded in the second half of the sixteenth century as a stronghold of the Palatinate, barring the way from Strasbourg to Paris, and fortified by Vauban after it had been taken over by France in the seventeenth century. Discounting the big neo-Gothic church,

5

which is a comparatively recent addition, its centre cannot have changed much since. The good brownstone *mairie* and the flat-fronted houses roofed with russet tiles which surround the *place* must look much the same today as they looked a century ago when André, a locksmith's apprentice who was fourteen, and his seven-year-old brother Julien shouldered their bundles and, in the thick mist of a September night, slipped out through the Gate of France to march into legend.

Into legend rather than history because the boys were not tender sprigs of the 'nursery of heroes' that was Phalsbourg, but the central characters of a book which, for more than sixty years, was to be for successive generations of French school children at once a reader, a course in history, geography and practical affairs and a manual of civic and moral instruction. Beyond even all that, *Le tour de la France par deux enfants*, first published in 1877 and still in print, has an extra dimension that makes it something more than a text-book. G. Bruno, an *Académie française* laureate, who was its author, was concerned above all else to give French children a better knowledge of their country, 'so that they may love it still more and be able to serve it even better'. That country was no mere nation-state as the term has been understood by other peoples in other times. It was the mystical concept of *la patrie*, and, when Bruno was writing, the concept needed re-gilding. France had been badly shocked by her defeat in the Franco-Prussian War, when, after the painful disillusionment of learning that an army which had been believed invincible was ill-organised and under-equipped, and fortresses which had been thought impregnable were ready to capitulate, came what the prudent regarded as the terror of the Commune and peace terms which involved handing over to Germany Northern Lorraine and the greater part of Alsace. The last was a serious economic loss, but patriots saw it not so much as a matter of iron mines and metallurgy and textile factories going to increase the wealth of Germany as the rape and selling into slavery of the elder daughters of the house.

6

What better models could there be for the young citizens of the newly established Third Republic than two brothers from martyred Lorraine who escaped over the frontier and made an adventurous journey round France in the course of fulfilling the wish of their dying father that they should grow up as Frenchmen? Both the escape and the travels called for some ingenuity on the part of the author since, after the annexation of Alsace and Lorraine, those who wished to keep their French nationality were allowed to leave without any drama. Tens of thousands did so : in Alsace alone, during the period following the settlement, 160,000 people exercised their option. But the application of a minor had to be made by a guardian who, normally, would be a member of his family, so M. Bruno solved his problem by arranging that the only living relative of the orphan brothers should be an unknown and, as it proved, elusive uncle, who had to be tracked from Marseille to Bordeaux. From that city uncle and nephews took the north-east passage, via Britanny and the Normandy coast, to regain Phalsbourg, where the formalities had to be completed. The whole journey seems to have taken about eight months (M. Bruno's calendar is a little vague) and was studded with almost Pauline perils, of storm and tempest, fire and shipwreck, as well as drunken driving — of a horse.

In all of them André showed exemplary resource and courage, coupled with a Swiss Family Robinson sententiousness, and Julien gave a virtually continuous object lesson in the art of making friends and influencing people. For eloquence they rivalled each other, taking into account the seven years' difference in their ages. If, when they fell into each other's arms after crossing the mountains and reaching French soil, it was André who cried : 'Beloved France, we are thy sons, we will strive to be worthy of thee our life long!', it was Julien who celebrated their arrival at the farm in the *Orléannais*, where they settled, by clapping his hands and crying : 'I love France!' till the echoes took up the chorus. The language may seem a thought high-flown by contemporary Anglo-Saxon standards, but it must be remembered that, in the France of 1871–2, the model for prose was still Victor Hugo, who, a year or two earlier, when the war was not yet lost, had pulled out all the stops for an 'Appeal to the French' which contained lines like : 'Lille, take up thy musket!' 'Marseille, sing thy song and be terrible!'

Traces of the style persist even today in French public oratory. What of other aspects of the Republic whose portrait emerges from Bruno's book, clear and sharp and detailed as a daguerrotype? One hundred years on, would its lines still be recognisable? Idle speculation grew into serious interest in the question, finally into a determination to seek the answer by following in the tracks of André and Julien. Some modifications there would have to be. Crossing the Vosges on foot and by night, for instance, would be merely pedantic, since the *Deux Enfants* had done so only from necessity and, throughout their pilgrimage, had never walked if there was any alternative. Again, there seemed little possibility of doing a large part of the circuit by sea, even if M. Bruno did not lay himself open to the suspicion that he made his heroes take ship because he got bored with chronicling the detail of travel overland and wanted to sketch a broad panorama.

Otherwise the conditions of the original tour could be reproduced faithfully enough, beginning with making no advance arrangements for transport and lodging. Luggage restricted to what one could carry would mean a strict minimum of clothes divided between two small grips, but a bedside book was allowed because Julien, along with his school exercise books, for which one's notebooks would be the equivalent, had an edifying volume about the great men of France, from which he was given to reading aloud. My choice, after some thought, was Châteaubriand's *Memoires de l'outre tombe* as being (in the *Livre de Poche* edition) light as well as lasting and sustaining. Equivalent finances were less easy to determine. The two boys started out with forty francs wrapped in a piece of carefully folded paper which André kept in his waistcoat pocket.

At the beginning of their journey a kindly neighbour added two five franc pieces to their treasure. The franc of 1871 was still the Germinal of April 1803, whose official rate against the pound sterling was 25.122, but what would it buy? The author is imprecise on this point, saying only that the occasional meal or night's lodging for which the boys had to pay was 'not dear'. The one positive clue offered is that André and Julien made a profit of fifty centimes per head on twenty-one pullets which they sold in the market at Mâcon, but even here we are not told what they had paid for the pullets in the Bresse, only that they had got them cheap as a bulk buy. Supposing the profit of fifty centimes to have represented one-third, or even one-quarter, of the wholesale price, it does not seem that Henry IV's wish for his people of 'a chicken in every pot' can have been very near fulfilment in the France of 1871. Certainly the meals which the boys shared in cottages and farm houses consisted largely of potato salad, cabbage soup, cheese and dry bread; an omelette, or fish caught in the river was not daily fare.

The monetary problem was finally solved by a decision to follow the example of the boys in spirit rather than letter by, like them, taking such funds as one could raise, in the knowledge that the sum would have to be spun out pretty thin if it was to last as many weeks as the original tour occupied months.

Which is why, on this April evening — a September start had been impossible to arrange — one is eating *truite au bleu*, the cheapest item on the menu, in the least ambitious of Phalsbourg's restaurants. All around diners who are evidently locals are speaking the Alsatian dialect which is not quite German and not at all French and eating steak and chips or *choucroute*, on a weekday evening at that. Change there, at any rate, and, now that the working day is over, change irrupting into the seventeenth-century calm of the *place* in the shape of rather small ton-up boys who are making a half-circuit past Marshal Mouton at a speed which is humiliatingly out of scale with the noise they are kicking up.

Change, too, beyond the Gate of France, surviving remnant

of Vauban's fortifications, where one prospected this afternoon. The road leading out of it has been named La Rue du Tour de la France par Deux Enfants, but, except for a well-set kitchen garden on one side and a fine old barn with a rippling tiled roof on the other, there is nothing along it which André and Julien would recognise. They would be as greatly bewildered by the long-legged girls in track suits bouncing a ball as they stream out of the modern secondary school as by the tennis club next to it. Further out there is an industrial zone where you can buy a prefabricated *'fermette'*, one of those rural playhouses where today's French townspeople flock at weekends. The lorries, loaded with cars coming from Sarrebourg and beer coming from Strasbourg, thunder past between fields that are the shallow green of a Dürer landscape and studded with cowslips. From here the famous 'blue line of the Vosges' is not blue at all, but more an affair of meadowland rising and merging into the dark green of forest. Tomorrow, when one must get to the other side of them to reach Épinal, the first halt on the journey, they may seem more formidable.

1

SUPPOSE THE BROTHERS had stayed at home? After all, in spite of an exodus which, like so many emigrations, drained Alsace-Lorraine of more than it could spare of youth and talent and energy, three-quarters of the population did stay where they were. The question is prompted in the morning by the sight of a neat van labelled A. Horn, *Serrurier* — locksmith — driving along the far side of the *place* which, now, is tessellated with market stalls. If André had finished his apprenticeship at Phalsbourg it might be his great-grandson driving that van and, supposing him to be not much more than thirty years old, he would have been born and grown up a Frenchman. Whereas his great-grandfather, if he had lived to a ripe enough age, would have experienced four changes of nationality between 1871 and 1944 — French to German, French again from 1918–40, German for the next four years, then back to French after 1944. His grandfather would have been lucky if he escaped being conscripted into the German Army during the First World War. During the Second World War his father, as one of the

130,000 young men from Alsace-Lorraine who were called up by the Nazis, would have been sent to the Russian front, unless, even more poignantly, he had been forced to serve on French soil. There were twelve men from Alsace-Lorraine in the detachment of *Das Reich* Division which perpetrated the massacre at Oradour-sur-Glane, in South-West France, in June 1944, when the entire population of 642, men, women and children, was wiped out. How could they avoid it when the alternative was deportation, or even execution ('Not everyone has a vocation for martyrdom', they said in Alsace afterwards), and when vanishing into the Resistance meant reprisals against the families left behind? Between the wars, though, now they were French, young men from Alsace-Lorraine doing their military service often found that their comrades from the other side of the Vosges called them 'the Fritzes' and might carry clannishness to the extent of appropriating all the beds on one side of a barrack room, leaving the Fritzes and their dialect on the other. Even after the Second World War, the troubles of those reluctant conscripts, who came to be known as the *'malgré nous'* — in spite of ourselves — were not over. Towards its end those serving on the Russian front deserted to the Soviet Army by their thousands, only to be received, not as allies, but as some kind of Germans and bundled into concentration camps whose régime had little to learn from the Nazis. Those who survived to come home found themselves in a no man's land. Rejecting the Germans, rejected by a considerable section of French public opinion, twenty-five years after the end of hostilities they were still battling for their right to the compensation and disability pensions paid to French deportees to Nazi Germany. Clearly there would have been complications about remaining in Alsace-Lorraine, which would perhaps not have been outweighed by the fact that one inheritance of nearly fifty years of German rule was a legal and administrative system a good deal simpler than the infinite complications of the Napoleonic Code.

The immediate problem is how to get out of it. The brothers

were given a lift in a farmer's cart to St. Quirin, the last village before the 1871 frontier, which was their starting point for their crossing of the Vosges at, or near, the Col du Donon, by a path which brought them down to the valley of the Plaine, safely in France. Between 1940–4 that same path was to be one of a number of classic escape routes; today, high above the valley whose people earned a gallant reputation for helping escapees on their way, there is a monument to the Fugitives and 'Passers' of the Donon. But short of hiring a car, which is against the spirit of the enterprise even if the exchequer would stand it, there is no means of getting to St. Quirin from Phalsbourg. In fact there is no means of getting anywhere useful from Phalsbourg except back to Saverne, which was where I started yesterday. Since it is the centre for a number of bus routes it will surely offer some way of reaching Épinal, even if not via St. Quirin and Celles, where the brothers spent their first night in France, so I catch a bus full of well-built women with market baskets who have cast away their winter coats and are baring their arms to the early sunshine with an abandon that would make Parisians foresee doom in the shape of *une angine* at the very least, and more probably *une pneumonie*. We run down from the plateau on which Phalsbourg stands, past houses whose every yard has its log-pile and whose red-brown roofs pick up the colour of the sandstone rocks above. A radio in the bus plays juicy German music and, outside its windows, marked footpaths disappearing into the fir woods are a reminder that we are near enough to the border for walking for fun, a concept which is not Gallic, to be an approved pastime.

At Saverne there is no help to be found either at the bus station or the railway station. 'Épinal!' they say at the latter. 'Now, if it were Paris it would be easy,' and you sense a little of the bitterness of the people of an outlying province for whom it is easier to get to the capital than to move about within their own borders. Talk about decentralisation has become fashionable in recent years, but between the idea and the reality is still a mortal way when the power rests with Paris, and the money comes from it, and successful careers converge on it. After two or three increasingly complicated projects for links between road and rail, it becomes evident that the most feasible way of crossing the Vosges is to turn one's back on them and take a train to Strasbourg and another train to Colmar. From there, in the morning, there is a guaranteed bus service which crosses the range by the Col du Bonhomme, a good deal south of Donon, to arrive at St. Dié, which is at least on the road to Épinal.

Once you have accepted the absurdity of going to Birmingham by way of Beachy Head in this fashion, the idea becomes appealing; an unexpected bonus to the journey which was not to have included the Plain of Alsace or the guide book villages among the vineyards on the eastern slopes of the Vosges. The country is tentative with spring, but even on the way to Strasbourg there is a thick dusting of green on the birch trees while, higher, there is still no more than the bronze sheen of the twigs against the inky conifers. The train runs between woods of anemones, then beside a careful patchwork of allotments, then along a river bank with the rods jutting out over the water like shafts of light, and you think that the essence of France could be symbolised by a picture of an elderly man with a fishing rod strapped to his bicycle pedalling slowly past a vegetable garden where another elderly man is setting early potatoes, then reject it as being hopelessly outmoded, finally to admit it as being permanently valid but, as is the way of symbols, representing only one facet of the truth.

At Strasbourg, as always, one has the sensation of stepping out of the train into another country, strongest, obviously, when the train has come direct from Paris, but perceptible even now. The country is not Germany, though there might be grounds for thinking it around the place de la Gare. Late nineteenth-century Germany, like Mussolini's Italy, had a railway station culture which has left its mark here and there along this border strip — Metz is a notable example — and at Strasbourg they built on the largest scale. Nor is it a matter solely of architecture; atmos-sphere counts for as much. *Gemütlichkeit* sets in at the station buffet, where every table has its miniature hat rack hung with pretzels to go with the golden streams of beer, and the bill of fare has a solid foundation of pork and pastry. But German it is not, so it is the more baffling that it should not be French either, even though the cathedral, whose single spire thrusts up its 142 metres of stonework as intricate as an ivory carving, has had the status almost of a sacred relic for France during three German wars. No thanks to the fathers of the First Republic that it was still there in 1871 : the Revolution, which saw the wrecking of much of the sculpture of the West Front, was for lopping it in the name of *Égalité*. It was a local citizen who devised the saving formula of keeping it standing in order that it should be crowned by an outsize Phrygian bonnet — Strasbourg had already established its particularity by being at the same time staunchly republican and staunchly Catholic.

The truth is that the city, like the region in which it stands, is at once both and neither, which is to say that it is Alsatian; French in its sympathies and profoundly Germanic in its language and culture. It might have been better if Bismarck had carried out the idea of making Alsace a neutral state which he considered in 1871. His reason for entertaining it was that the strong French elements which would long persist in a region 'whose interest, whose feelings, and whose memories bind it to France' would be likely, whoever was its sovereign, to make it side with France if there should be another Franco-German war. Would neutrality have given a more generally recognised identity to a people who, today, often complain of being disregarded, misunderstood and sometimes even of being 'colonised' by the French of the interior? Unlike the Basques and the Bretons, the Alsatians do not use dynamite to draw attention to their discontent : it is not even certain that a majority of them would support autonomy, but there is no mistaking the depth of feeling about what Alsatians look upon as neglect, when it is not active discouragement, by the French authorities of the dialect which is their daily language. The problem is one in which, for generations, politics have been tangled with linguistics. Even the young heroes of the Tour of France are never represented as speaking dialect. How could such ardent French patriots be tainted with speech which recalled the hated invaders? But, as Phalsbourg lies east of the linguistic frontier, and they were the sons of a carpenter, it is most unlikely that they would have spoken anything else at home. Three-quarters of a century later, after the speaking and teaching of French had been forbidden in Alsace-Lorraine during the German occupation of the Second World War, it was understandable that both dialect and German should have been forbidden in the infant and primary schools of the region for some years, but it remains sad, for the dialect provides so firm a basis for German that the people of Alsace-Lorraine have a vocation for bi-lingualism. The situation in the schools has improved since then, but Alsatians resent the fact that wholly German language newspapers are still forbidden — twenty-five per cent of the editorial content must be in French — and claim that there is a deliberately 'French' policy both in the posting of civil servants and in broadcasting. Not that you would think the latter could matter greatly when viewers and listeners can take their pick of Swiss and German stations, and would be likely to do so quite apart from language, since the French State radio and TV service is not precisely at the top of the European table.

The Colmar train runs through the smiling Plain of Alsace, with theatrical castles crowning the heights on the right and, between crystal showers of fruit blossom, an occasional glimpse of a tin stork perched on a rooftop or a plaster stork standing on one leg on a lawn. They might equally well be the equivalent of decoy ducks or resigned substitutes for the real thing. It is sad about the storks of Alsace. Traditionally they have been regarded as the emblems of the province, eagerly awaited and welcomed when they arrived in March, bringing good luck on their wings according to popular belief, and so faithful to last year's nesting places that, in the spring after the Liberation, villages wrecked during the fighting of the previous months saw the birds returned to build on what might have been one of the few roofs still standing.

Even then, however, their numbers were dwindling, though the war was in no way responsible. Gradually over the past fifty years, for reasons which ornithologists have so far been unable to explain, the migrations which, every spring, bring something like 50,000 pairs of storks from Central and Southern Africa to nest in Europe, have been displaced to the north and east. Alsace, moved by genuine sentiment as well as recognition of their value as a tourist attraction, has made efforts at repopulation rather like those adopted by development authorities trying to draw industries to problem areas. It has built artificial nests, in the hope that they will be tenanted, it has even transplanted a population, importing nestlings from Algeria and rearing them in Alsace, in the hope that instinct will bring them back to nest there next year. As yet there has been no announcement of spectacular success.

Bismarck, from whom the storks have temporarily distracted one's mind, said also that Alsace would not be conquered by artillery; it would have to be bought, piece by piece. The transactions are going on briskly these days. From the lakes of the Moselle, in the north of the province, to the valleys of the Jura in the south, more and more property, both land and houses, is passing into the hands of Germans looking for holiday homes, who are ready and able to pay a price so inflationary that locals are often crowded out of the market. On a larger scale, in a country where feelings are likely to be even more acutely exacerbated by history, it is the story of Welsh cottages which are occupied by English holidaymakers, and, in the one case as in the other, the trouble is economic rather than national. Having rich neighbours is often a strain.

If the Germans, and, equally, the Swiss, cross the frontier westward because they can pay the price, the Alsatians cross it eastwards, where they can command the price. Daily, 12,000 of them, with a preponderance of younger skilled workers, go over the border to German factories and 15,000 to Swiss. In both, conditions are better and higher wages are improved still further by a favourable rate of exchange. The travelling is made as painless as possible by factory buses which tour the villages of Alsace to pick up their employees, sometimes getting to the far side of the Vosges. Perhaps the true problem is the artificiality of a political frontier running down the centre of the Rhine, when, on both its banks, there is an affinity of language and culture, and when there is so little to distinguish a village on the German side from one on the French side, or the life of a farmer or a timber worker in the Vosges from his counterpart in the Black Forest. You can understand why many in Alsace set their hopes on a political Europe, in which regional autonomy would be a reality and their province would be thought of as the centre of a continent's industry rather than in terms of its distance from Paris. As they are fond of telling you in these parts, sixty-five per cent of the Common Market's purchasing power lies within a radius of 500 kilometres from Alsace, and when the canal linking the Rhône and the Rhine, due to be completed by the end of 1981, is opened, Mulhouse will be at the halfway point of a direct waterway from Marseille to Rotterdam. There is a foretaste of that future in the existence of the Grand Canal of Alsace, running parallel with the river between Basle and Strasbourg, which will be a section of it. It is wider than Suez and has made ports of towns as far from the sea as Mulhouse and Colmar.

What will development on the scale envisaged do, not merely to the Rhine, which is already sufficiently polluted to have any surviving *Lorelei* down with dysentery, but to a region which, up to now, has been largely successful in reconciling advanced industry with rural calm and unfossilised folklore? Colmar, which would be a strong starter in any contest for the most beautiful town in France, is a good example. True, it is just far enough north to be clear of the potassium workings centred on Mulhouse, with their accompanying mess, but it is still a manufacturing city, living by engineering and textiles and machine-made tools among a good deal else. The market gardens, renowned for their magnificent asparagus, come up to its walls, the vine-covered hill slopes are intimately near and the impression you take away is not of modern technology but of the timbered houses of the centre, where the fifteenth and sixteenth centuries are not merely encapsulated but transposed warm and living, into our own day. That they exist at all is a prodigious piece of luck. The 'Colmar pocket' was the last point of German resistance in Alsace, where the ravaged villages in the area testified to the fierceness of the fighting in the winter of 1944–5 and helped to make Alsace sixth in the list of French departments for the extent of the war damage it suffered. Colmar escaped because when the French and American troops commanded by General de Lattre de Tassigny had closed the prongs of their pincer movement at Rouffach, about fifteen kilometres to the south, a section of the French Fifth Armoured Division, under General Schlesser, which was given the honour of first entering the town, made a bold dash without any preliminary bombardment and took it intact on February 2nd, 1945.

By so doing they saved, among other treasures, one of the few museums whose settings are so perfect that you would want to visit them even if they were empty — the San Marco in Florence is another. Unterlinden, too, is in an old conventual building, a thirteenth-century Dominican house renowned as a nursery of saints and mystics which, during the Revolution, suffered the idiocies and indignities inflicted upon so many churches and religious establishments, being by turns barracks, stables and workshops before being turned into a museum in 1849. During the intervening years damages and dereliction have been lovingly restored, and it would be easy to linger indefinitely in the sandstone cloisters surrounding a green garden where, a little later in the year, the scent of blossom from the lime trees, which do indeed hang over the museum, will drift down to mingle with the faint but enduring odour of sanctity. In fact, anybody whose first visit seems likely to be their only one would be wise to linger at least for a few minutes while they decide how best to apportion their time, for Unterlinden is not one museum but several, and it is important to avoid so dissipating your attention between them that you take away no lasting impression. There are Gallo-Roman remains, there is an absorbing section of local history and folk art, which includes porcelain stoves so magnificent that to light a fire in them would be sacrilege, there is a collection of Alsatian Primitives, notable for the work of Martin Schongauer, who brings a happy earthly innocence to heavenly matters and there is the Grünewald altarpiece, which is a collection in itself. It belonged originally to the monks of the Antonite Order who, at their monastery at Issenheim, not far from Colmar, cared for the victims of the *'mal des Ardents'*, a plague akin to ergotism which was endemic in the holy and horrible Middle Ages. Grünewald lived in the monastery for four years, from 1512 to 1516, cloistered with the monks and their patients, while he executed his masterpiece and it may not be over-fanciful to believe that some of the pressures of an enclosure which might have provided a subject for Bosch can be felt in a work whose contemplation is a peculiarly draining as well as a memorable experience. It is superbly displayed in what was the chapel of the convent, with the great golden altar which it adorned set in the apse. Is there anything else you can look at after that? For myself, one exhibit only, and that poles apart from Grünewald. In the room devoted to the minor arts there is a polychrome wooden statue which, in its own fashion, never fails to move me as deeply. The Palm Donkey, which dates from the late sixteenth century, is a figure of Christ mounted on an ass, the ass itself mounted on the wheels which allowed it to be drawn in the Palm Sunday procession. Is it the calm, broad lines of the figure, grave and certain as plainsong, or the naïveté of the proportions, or the concept of the Incarnate Lord astride a child's toy which makes it unforgettable?

Something of all of them, perhaps. It remains printed on your mind as you walk back through the park where the fountain, as on other visits, is not playing. Only countries like Italy, where it is scarce, are prodigal with water; places with an average to high rainfall often tend to be stingy. It is the principle of the poor helping the poor, which is one of the moral maxims propounded by André in our book.

The hotel is the unfashionable one which, in true French style, works downwards from the dining room, which is admirable. There is a tart of young pink rhubarb at dinner; only on this eastern side of France is rhubarb ever served in restaurants. Afterwards you settle over coffee in the bar where everything that in Paris would be of tile or metal or plastic, is made of wood, so that the edges of the companionable clatter are softened. The local paper gives ample space to soothing news items like the regretted retirement of a police officer who gained the esteem of one and all just by being loyal and conscientious and amiable, or a wedding at which the bride's father, who was treasurer of the town sports club, got up a football team from the assembled relatives to play the club's veterans, who beat them 3–2, in spite of the entire wedding party shrieking encouragement from the touchline.

There are forty-two obituaries, set out like display advertisements, and thirty-two of them mention that the deceased was fortified by the sacraments of the Church. Since one of the others records a death in the Congo, with few details available, and the subjects of two are stated to be Protestants, that leaves only seven certainly *non-pratiquants*. But when you are beginning to feel, drowsily, that time here has run back to fetch the age of gold, you turn the page and read that, at Montbéliard, the patron of a bar was shot by a customer whom he refused to serve, and he is dead, and at Sarrebruck, because of a family rivalry, a boy of seventeen knifed another of the same age, and he is dead, and at Pontarlier a young wife whose husband was 'more threatening than usual' jumped out of a first-floor window and she is dead, and all that was just one quiet weekend.

The bedroom is strait and the bidet lacks a tap, but there is that summit of comfort, a *plume*, cosy as a fleece, weightless as a cloud. I start on Châteaubriand — 'As it is impossible for me to foresee my end, and as, at my age, the days accorded to a man can only be days of grace . . .' — with the pleasure, born of the knowledge that the store is so bountiful, with which one embarks anew on Proust, but the *plume* prevails over thoughts of mortality. Just as I am pitching into sleep I remember the detail about Colmar which has been eluding me all day. It was the birthplace of the sculptor Bartholdi, and while every schoolboy, if he is French, knows that Bartholdi carved the great Lion of Belfort from the living sandstone of a hill above the town, surprisingly few know that he created also the Statue of Liberty whose light beams over the entrance to New York harbour, and even fewer that the statue was the gift of France to the USA.

A ESPINAL. Par C. CARDINET, Imprimeur Iuré de Son Altesse, & Marchand Libraire 1664.

2   IN THE MORNING there is a man fixing what looks like a torn-off scrap of some black stuff to a flagpole over the post office. Nobody is taking any notice and only when I glimpse a headline on a newspaper stall do I learn that the President of the Republic has died in the night and realise that the fluttering rag is mourning crape.

'*Tiens!* But he wasn't ill!' says a woman planted before the spread-out pages of the current edition which newspaper offices in France obligingly stick up in their windows. It is so astonishing that you have almost said aloud : 'But of course he was ill! Everybody knew he was ill!' before remembering that 'everybody' is the inbred little Paris world of politicians and diplomats and journalists. To look about you is to be reminded that, in spirit, it is even further distant than the 446 kilometres which separate it from Colmar. Here people are going tranquilly about their own concerns, they all look as if they got enough sleep — not even the children have rings under their eyes — and nobody pushes.

The bus for St. Dié leaves by the northern suburbs then swings west to pass the mouth of the broad Munster valley before starting to climb. There is more than coincidence in the echo of Ireland. They were Irish monks who Christianised this part of pagan Europe and, with time, the *monastère* which they built in the valley 1,300 years ago was slurred and softened to the present Munster. The cheese came later, but it still has a respectable ancestry, having been made in the farms on the eastern slopes of the Vosges since the sixteenth century. Munster is rich and soft and nobly pungent, a cheese for addicts rather than dilettante tasters: if you cared to paraphrase you could say: 'Camembert for boys, Livarot for men, Munster for heroes.' The tourist board tells you that the thing to drink with it is the full, fragrant Gewürtztraminer, one of the aristocrats of Alsatian wines, which, like the so-called Tokay d'Alsace, or *pinot gris*, is made from black grapes, whereas the rest, *muscat d'Alsace*, riesling, *pinot blanc* and sylvaner are made from white, which is to say, shades ranging from heady gold for the first to cool green for the last. It is a good enough match, but the ideal marriage with Munster is beer (strong German is even better than the lighter Alsatian) and a scatter of caraway seeds eaten with it enhances the flavour. In Lorraine, on the western side of the range, the farm cheese is Gérômé, which spends four months maturing in a cellar while the crust turns biscuit colour and the inside becomes creamy, and to this a little caraway, or, alternatively, fennel or cumin, is sometimes added in the making.

The regimented vines, marching up the slopes in close order, begin almost at once, as satisfying a sight as a wheatfield in stook. Did corn and wine and oil come to stand for peace and well-being not only because they denoted plenty, but because the ranked sheaves and the vineyards and the terraced olives were the visible assurance of order and civilisation? In Alsace the vines have made their own civilisation. The 'wine road', running north among low hills from Thann to Marlenheim, which we cross at Kayserberg, about a third of the way up, zigzags between a string of idyllic villages, small towns, rather, for they have an

24

urban energy and coherence, whose quality derives from the fact that each is an organic community, living by one industry like a fishing village of the past century. There have been vineyards here for 1700 years : today 10,000 families live wholly by them. It is a quality industry; Alsace is at the far pole from an area like the Languedoc, with its mass production of *ordinaire*, and the fact seems to be reflected in the elegance and gaiety of the little towns. Some are reconstructions; much of this area, buildings and vineyards alike, was devastated in 1944–5. Others escaped without a scar, like Riquewihr, the most perfect, where one steps through an arched gateway on to the cobbled street of a sixteenth-century city — the title is not invalidated by a population of no more than 1,400 — with timbered façades, galleried inner courts and the stone of wellheads and fountains blooming into luxuriant carving. Kayserberg, where pilgrims can divide their attention between the Tokay d'Alsace produced in the neighbourhood and the house, now a Protestant church, which was the birthplace of Albert Schweitzer (it is a dizzying mental exercise to try to project oneself from this German fairy-tale setting into Lambarene) is bigger but hardly less attractive. It is on the Roman road over the Col du Bonhomme, for long the main line from Southern Alsace into Lorraine, and you go through the language barrier almost as soon as you are out of it, the dialect stopping well before the 1871 frontier. The road climbs gently, then more abruptly, with lordly views down the valley of the Grande Meurthe; beside it a small boy holds out for sale a bunch of the first *coucous*, the small daffodils that sheet the valleys in April and find their way to the markets in tight posies. The river has that peculiarity of several which rise in the Vosges of changing direction during its course. The Moselle is another. Both seem headed for the Paris basin, both take a sudden turn north-east and the Meurthe joins the Moselle to flow into the Rhine at Coblenz.

The col is 949 kilometres up, with, just beyond it, the statutory picnic site, with wooden tables and benches and a panorama. Then we run down through mountain pasture, but it is still too early for the cattle to be out, making the hillside chime like a belfry as the bronze clappers sway to their movement. Traditionally they go up to the alp on St. Urbain's day, May 25th, and stay till Michaelmas. The cowherds go up with them, carrying their cheese-making equipment, and settle in chalets which, once, were made of wood, with flat roofs weighed down by boulders, but these days are stone built. The interior plan of two rooms, one for the cheese-making, the other for everything else, including sleeping, persists.

St. Dié, where one changes buses, owes any international fame it may enjoy to the fact that it was here, in 1507, that the name America was first used for the continent which Columbus had discovered fifteen years earlier. It was recorded in the 'Cosmographiæ Introductio', a preface to Ptolemy's Geography, produced there by one of the earliest printing works to be set up in Lorraine. In France, deservedly, St. Dié is regarded as an outstandingly successful example of post-war town planning. When the Nazis were forced out of it in November 1944, they adopted a scorched-earth policy, turning between 10,000 and 15,000 people out of their houses and destroying most of the public installations. Luckily the charges under the towers of the cathedral did not go off, though the rest of it was badly damaged. There is time to walk up the broad rue Thiers, whose regular, three-storey buildings are so agreeable to the eye that, tomorrow, somebody may call this a noble street, but for the moment we will be satisfied with 'fine', to admire the clean red sandstone of the rebuilt portion of the cathedral and the perfect placing of a lime tree to the right of the façade. Only, since the lime tree is alleged to be 700 years old, and the façade and towers are eighteenth century, perhaps they were placed in relation to it. Then I buy a frugal *pain chocolat* for my lunch at a rather grand baker-confectioner's shop whose window is full of chocolate trains and motor cars in readiness for Easter (St. Dié has engineering works, as well as textiles and timber, so you cannot expect its infants to stay with Pascal eggs and fish) and eat it in the sun beside the Meurthe, telling myself that now I am unquestionably on French soil but unable to evolve any ritual to celebrate the fact.

The Épinal bus climbs through dark woods to the Col du Haut Jacques, with its commemorative pillar to 'The Forest of the Vosges and its Resisters'. There is a clean smell of resin and sawn wood; then, as we begin the descent, the scenic railway prospects down the valley of the Blanche Fontaine. Coming into Épinal by farm cart from the direction of Celles-sur-Plaine, André and Julien would have missed that splendid introduction to the town. At least when they left it, going south in another farm cart, they would have been spared the melancholy parting impression of the American cemetery at Épinal-Dinozé. Its 5,600 graves of US servicemen killed in the east of France in the Second World War are no more than a handful beside the obscenity of slaughter of the 1914–18 battlefields, now draped with legend and ticketed for tourists, but enough all the same to remind one what a histrionic little war was that of 1870 compared with those which were to follow. The histrionics are so impressive that one tends to overlook some of the positive results. They included the transformation of certain towns in 'French France' by an injection of skill and capital from Alsatian emigrants. Belfort, whose population went up from 8,000 to 40,000 between 1870 and 1900, is the most striking example, but Épinal enjoyed a similar development. It was the arrival of textile manufacturers from Alsace which gave what had been no more than a lively little market town a thriving cotton industry to back up the timber trade and the furniture and paper-making which are native to forest regions.

Not that you would go to Épinal for lace and calico and strips of embroidery, or even to buy a pair of the sabots carved from a single block of wood which used to be daily working wear here. Today, the one surviving maker explains, though local people sometimes wear them for gardening on muddy days, they are sold largely to tourists with a taste for bygones, who pay up to twenty-five francs a pair for their souvenirs. In Italy, he goes on, returning holidaymakers use them as sugar basins, which seems one degree further out than the vogue for propping a wheel with no cart attached against the front porch. Épinal's fame rests on its *images*, and the extent of that fame can be gauged when you learn that an *image d'Épinal* has two meanings, the literal one, of a sheet of vivid prints, and the metaphorical one of an idealised, tuppence coloured version of an event or an individual. The prints are folk art in the true line of medieval carving and glass painting, though their purpose was humbler and their form impermanent to the point of fragility. As a centre of paper-making the town was a natural growth point for, and, purely by chance, it seems, is now the only surviving centre of a craft which, from the seventeenth to the second half of the nineteenth century, flourished in many places in France, from Toulouse to Beauvais, from Lille to Le Mans, each with its distinctive character. The holy pictures which proliferated in the first part of the period were cheaper versions, and, to a degree, *vulgarisations* of medieval illuminations, though an example like the Crucifixion, of Claude Cardinet, from seventeenth-century Épinal, gives the *vulgarisateur* a claim to stand as an artist in his own right.

They were believed to protect a household as an amulet protects its wearer; the guilds ordered *images* of their patron saints; the pictures were pinned above hearths to watch over the family and in stables to watch over the beasts. The models were painted engravings on copper imported from Paris, but the craftsman, mostly unknown, who cut the woodblocks and, between working on sacred subjects, designed playing cards and dominoes, were not mere copyists but interpreters, who gave a good deal of expression to their own fancy and left their personal mark on their work. Like ballads and broadsheets, the prints were sold by pedlars whose turnover was high, since the *images* were flimsy and, exposed as they were to a good deal of wear and tear, had to be renewed frequently.

The Revolution ended the market, if not, perhaps, the secret longing for holy pictures, and production stopped at almost all the centres. Except for Rennes, all those which survived were on the eastern side of the country, Nancy, Metz, Strasbourg, Besançon, Montbéliard, as well as Épinal, and it was Épinal which led the nineteenth-century revival when a group of print-makers, of whom the most remarkable was Jean Charles Pellerin, found a new theme in the triumphs of Napoleon Bonaparte. Given the prevailing climate this, perhaps, should be counted as a sacred rather than a secular subject, and, in time, the prints were to suffer the fate of the earlier holy pictures, since, after the Restoration, they were declared seditious, and were liable to confiscation. But secular *images* there were, among them one aimed at bad payers captioned : 'Credit is dead !' which was nailed on shop counters as a warning to customers. Épinal made a speciality, too, of soldiers in full dress uniform, to be mounted on cardboard and cut out, which, with children, rivalled in popularity the series of classic fairy-tales.

In 1951 the Director of French Museums, evidently more sensitive than his predecessors to the appeal of these naïvely vigorous illustrations, decided that they merited a museum of their own. Épinal, by then the one town in France where they were still produced, was a natural choice, and the Natural History section of the Departmental Museum was transferred into a Museum of Popular Prints. Six years later it had the good fortune to acquire a private collection of almost 3,000 items, and so was able to call itself international. Today what you can study in the building set among flower beds on an island in the Moselle is social history and national differences as well as the development of an art whose earliest example here is a fragment of a fourteenth-century Crucifixion. What you see also, I realise as I climb the hill leading up to the *château*, is the birth of the strip cartoon, even if the descent of Popeye and Andy Capp, Varoomshka and Charlie Brown from ancestors as diverse as a Gothic Way of the Cross, or a broadsheet depicting the Dreadful Shipwreck of the Colville West Indiaman with the Loss of all her Crew, or a late nineteenth-century Greek Madonna and Child, purely Byzantine in character, is not immediately obvious. The link between them is one of the essential qualities of folk art, as distinct from folk crafts, like corn dollies or those geese moulded out of *rillettes*, with a dab of lard denoting the white feathers on their heads which you see in French delicatessen shops, the reduction of a situation to clear and manageable proportions, with the emotions, and so the expected responses, as unequivocal as the colour and line. An *image d'Épinal*, in fact.

Seen from the terrace of the *château*, the town itself, cupped in wooded hills, threaded by the bright skein of the river, itself looks like an *image*, so fitting a background for André and Julien, whose virtues were most certainly larger and more brightly coloured than life, that, consciously or not, M. Bruno was matching like with like when he made them spend a month here at the outset of their journey. It was not a rest period. They lodged with a widow, once a schoolmistress, now earning her living by sewing, who stopped the clacking of her treadle machine only to read them lectures on the virtues of industry and thrift. In fairness to good Madame Gertrude, she represented the reward of saving, not as the prospect of setting up for yourself in a corner shop, but as the ability to help those worse off than yourself, and put her precepts into practice by adding two five franc pieces to the cash resources of the young travellers. Julien went to the local school, where, inevitably, he was top of the class. André was taken on by the local locksmith, who, at the end of the month, gave him a valuable addition to that stack of papers, then as now necessary for life in France, an exemplary reference officially stamped by the mayor.

It is that working stint of Andre's, and the fact that he had packed the tools of his trade in the bundle slung over his shoulder, which makes one feel that M. Bruno, though he does not acknowledge it, got the inspiration for his book from a tradition, centuries old in France, which was flourishing at the time when he wrote, the *Tour de France* of the *Compagnons du Devoir*. The *Compagnonnage* was an élite of highly skilled craftsmen in various trades whose fraternity, born of the need to protect the individual worker against the power of the corporations, became committed to what was nothing less than a quest for perfection.

In the stories of its founding history and legend are tangled. According to legend, the fathers of the *Compagnons* worked on the building of Solomon's Temple, and the obvious resemblance to Freemasonry is found again in the surviving rites. Somewhere between legend and history are the stories of the *Compagnons*' going to the Holy Land with the Crusaders as an engineering corps. They built the bridges and fortifications necessary to the campaign and, in return, were initiated into skills which they transmitted to later generations. It is certain that they took part in the building of the French cathedrals; a twelfth-century manuscript refers to the fact, but written records are scarce, as may be expected when every branch of the fraternity, at the end of its working year, destroyed its archives by burning them and swallowed the ashes — they were mixed with wine to help them down. A manuscript of 1480 shows a squad of *Compagnons* marching on to a building site, tools in hand, wearing round their hats the ribbons which remain a part of their insignia, though today they are often worn in the buttonhole.

By that time the *Compagnonnage* had developed into an association able to give very considerable protection to its members in the labour market, countering what would otherwise have been the monopoly powers of employers, with Church and State at their head, by strikes, or by 'blacking' certain workplaces, or even towns. That militant past, even more than the clouds of myth, accounts for the secrecy with which the *Compagnonnage* cloaked its doings, which extended to giving members *noms de guerre*. Usually these were made up of a man's place of origin and what was considered to be his most notable characteristic — *Normand La Fidélité* for example. Occasionally it was a Christian name followed by the place of origin, as Guillaume *Le Normand*.

All that made up the trade-union aspect of the fraternity, a function which was largely usurped by the development of the modern unions. The perfectionism was, of course, allied to it, since their skill was the one bargaining counter which the craftsmen possessed, but it was also a preoccupation in its own right. To enter the *Compagnonnage* was not a matter of paying a union due and being admitted to membership, it was to embrace a way of life. There were three orders, *Aspirants*, *Compagnons* and *Compagnons finis*, to each of which candidates were admitted by an elaborate initiation ceremony, after presenting a *chef d'oeuvre*. The *Tour de France* was undertaken by *Aspirants* and *Compagnons*, who packed their tools and their small belongings into the *'malle à quatre noeuds'*, the trunk with four knots, as they called the big kerchief slung over their shoulders, and set out to tramp from one town to another, selling their skills and adding to them as they travelled. The parallel that comes to mind is that of the Wandering Scholars of the Middle Ages, with the *chef d'oeuvre*, in its own medium, fit to rate with a doctoral thesis. A carpenter, or a mason, or an *imagier*, as the stone carvers were called, might be on the road for five or six years, sure of finding support, lodging and friendship from his brothers of the fraternity. There can hardly be a notable building in France to which the *Compagnons* have not made their contribution.

The remarkable feature of a tradition which, by rights, should have died with the nineteenth century, extinguished by an age of mass production and plastics, is that they are making it still. Numbers, inevitably, have dropped steeply, but in the present decade there are each year about 1,500 *Aspirants* or *Compagnons* moving from one town to another in the course of making the *Tour* and gaining mastery in their trade. There are even signs of a resurgence of interest among the young men; some are calling for a revival of the strict traditions of the fraternity, including the wearing of gold earrings which symbolised a *Compagnon*'s commitment to his craft and its ideals. In earlier, bloodier days, those who disgraced the *Compagnonnage* had their earrings torn out and a good deal of the ear lobe with them.

Even more surprisingly, *chefs d'oeuvre* are still being produced, comparable to the monuments of ingenious workmanship to be seen in some of the museums of the *Compagnonnage*. In our day a *Compagnon* may spend up to 9,000 hours, spread over four years, on his master work. Some of these pieces, notably those of the carpenters and joiners, are carried out for the joy of meeting challenges and demonstrating superlative skills — 'Think of a problem and solve it' — some are contemporary and practical : recent *chefs d'oeuvre* have included a tricycle for the handicapped and a design for a car chassis.

So that if, looking down from the terrace of the *château* at the Basilica of St. Maurice, one envisages *Aspirants* and *Compagnons* arriving on foot, singing as they marched, to work on its eleventh-century beginnings, the meditation need not end with a sigh for a vanished past. The rectangular block topped by a low round tower which lies to the north-east, on the other side of the Moselle, is the new church of *Notre-Dame au Cierge*, built to replace an earlier church, wrecked by bombing in the spring of 1944. The booklet telling the story of its building, which was completed inside two years, between November 1956 and October 1958, names the craftsmen who worked on it, the carpenters, and the stonemasons, the locksmith and the wrought-iron worker, as well as the glass painters and the enamel workers, who produced the blue blaze of the great east window and the remarkable west door of enamel and copper, bearing the emblems of the four Evangelists. It is likely enough that a *Compagnon* or two were among them, their pride and mastery not diminished because, these days, they make their *Tour de France* on a Honda, or in a hard-working little Renault.

33

3   IT WAS ON the way from Épinal to Bésançon
that André and Julien met the Demon Drink. They were
marching bravely just south of Vesoul when it began to rain
and they contracted with a passing carter to get them to
Bésançon by nightfall for fifteen sous, which they handed over
in advance. Madame Gertrude might have done better to have
cut down on her teaching on thrift in favour of a warning on
the unwisdom of such a proceeding, adding a few hints on how
to recognise at ten paces that a man has drink taken. As it was
the brothers learned both lessons the hard way. The price they
paid seems moderate enough by today's standards, though the
misadventure gave André the opportunity of pontificating in his
best manner : 'What a horrifying and shameful vice drunkenness is !' All that happened when the driver, having topped up
at a wayside *cabaret,* passed out with the reins in his hands was
that the horse first stopped thankfully for a breather then started
off again at a pace staid enough to minimise the dangers of its
rather erratic course. Such perils would have seemed derisory to

the modern successors of the pair of *gendarmes* who finally piloted boys, horse, cart and comatose carter safely into Bésançon. Recent *gendarmerie* figures on the relation between road accidents and alcohol showed drunken driving to be directly responsible for eight per cent of the total number of road accidents resulting in death or injury which produce so horrifying a casualty list each year in France. That is a conservative estimate, limited by the word 'directly'. The statement more usually put forward is that alcohol is responsible for — a purist should perhaps read 'implicated in' — one-quarter to one-third of all road accidents.

The mere thought of it makes one glad to be doing the journey to Bésançon by train, until I remember a piece of research carried out by a doctor who found that, of 55,000 employees in one sector of the national railway company, thirteen per cent were confirmed alcoholics. It is small comfort to remind oneself that the 55,000 were described as *cheminots*, which means railwaymen in general, rather than as specifically *mécaniciens*, or drivers.

Except among hard core reformists that kind of gloomy facetiousness seems to infect most discussions about the problem of alcoholism in France, though few subjects are less inherently funny. Apart from its share of responsibility for road accidents, alcohol has been listed as the third national cause of death, after cardio-vascular ailments and cancer. It accounts for about forty per cent of the country's already grossly inadequate hospital budget and, in Paris alone, it costs each year roughly the price of a teaching hospital.

Why France, one ponders, as the train sets out at a reassuringly sober speed for Bésançon by way of Belfort, which is once more to go forward by going backwards, or eastwards, but there is nothing practicable that will take me directly south through Vesoul. Why should the people of a country which, the world over, is the symbol of the good life have an annual intake of twenty-eight litres of pure alcohol for each adult, which is twice that of Germany, three times that of Britain or Belgium, four times that of Sweden or Denmark, and means that two million people in France drink two litres of wine a day, most of it gut-rotting *gros rouge*? The obvious explanation, that France is a wine-producing country, will not hold, unless you restrict it to meaning that the wine lobby would block any radical reform, which is true enough. Italy, equally, is a wine-producing country, but the consumption of the Italians is forty per cent less than that of the French. It collapses completely when you look at the geographical break-down of the figures for alcoholism. The black spots are not the wine-growing areas of the south-west, or the Mediterranean, or the Rhône Valley, but those which a regional development board would rank high for grant aid. Drink, 'the quickest way out of Manchester', is for many of the French, women as well as men, the quickest way out of Britanny, the Nord-Pas-de-Calais, parts of the centre. Broadly, the difference is that between the Meridional and the Northerner, with the Loire as the traditional dividing line, which suggests that climate and regional temperament are at least as important in the equa-tion as poverty. The old joke about individuals who are born two whiskies below par can apply to groups who find communica-tion and spontaneity difficult without artificial aid; surely there is a link between the emotional illiteracy of many Scots and the national drinking pattern. Perhaps one should take into account, too, the effect of the peculiar constraints which, even today, still hedge the education and upbringing of the French young who, once they are adult, may react with curious explosions of violence which can be nearer the surface than you think in the least likely people.

At Belfort there is time only to step across the platform into the waiting connection, so I am cheated of another pilgrimage to the lion, which I can never see without a prickle of pride, even though, for a foreigner, it must be vicarious pride. Like Sedan, up north, which is dominated by the biggest fort in Europe, Belfort is a frontier stronghold, but, where Sedan is remembered as the place where Napoleon III signed the capitulation of 1870 and the Germans made their break-through towards the sea in 1940, Belfort earned its fame, and its status as a free territory, as the place where, in 1870–1, they were held against heavy odds.

'Make it impregnable', was Louis XIV's order to Vauban, whom he commissioned to improve the defences of the town that commanded the thirty-kilometre gap between the southern end of the Vosges and the northern end of the Jura which, from earliest times, had been Europe's natural invasion route. 'Never surrender!' were the instructions to the commandant of his garrison of the Comte de la Suze, whom Richelieu appointed Governor of Belfort. Both got lasting obedience. Belfort resisted sieges in 1814, 1815, and, most gloriously, in 1870, when a garrison 15,000 strong, under a colonel of sappers, Denfert-Rochereau, faced 40,000 Germans with 200 pieces of heavy artillery which sent shells over at the rate of 5,000 a day for eighty-three consecutive days. The city held out for 140, surrendering on February 8th, 1871, only on the express orders of the French government, which had concluded its own armistice three weeks earlier. The garrison marched out to receive full battle honours and to have the more lasting satisfaction of knowing that they had played their part in enabling Belfort to escape the fate of Alsace-Lorraine. Bartholdi's great lion is one of the relatively few giant monuments — it measures twenty-two metres by eleven — which achieves grandeur without being grandiloquent. From its station on the rock above the town it mounts guard in perpetuity over the gap, looking out over a panorama of the Vosges whose nobility matches its own and makes the replica in the *place* Denfert-Rochereau in Paris seem tamed and shabby merely because of its surroundings.

The leather seats of the second-class coach to Bésançon are so comfortable that you wonder why anybody should ever travel first until you reflect that, in most countries which have got beyond trains with slatted wooden seats, a large number of first-class tickets are bought to bolster the ego rather than cushion the coccyx. In France the various rebates operated by the SNCF, the national railway company, allow quite a few categories of

37

citizen to travel first-class for the price of second, so enjoying the pleasures of conspicuous consumption while still remaining solvent. Good luck to them if they feel it is worth it, and not to be smug just because, in matters like that, my own ego is buffered like the Michelin man.

After Pontarlier the rocks turn white as we get off the sandstone, and the cows, some of whom at this low altitude are out at grass, turn red and white. Lacking other evidence, you could get a fair idea of your whereabouts in France from the type of cattle which are ruminating over the hedge even today, when the spread of certain beef and dairy breeds is just about nationwide, and mixed breeds are more and more common. Not that such mobility is an exclusively modern phenomenon; a farmer's wife who gave André and Julien a night's lodging in Lorraine had a Breton cow because that hardy breed gave a good return for its feeding costs.

Bésançon is superb, with the glowing rooftops of the old town drawn up in a loop of the Doubs like coins in a bag, a rocky height plugging its mouth to make a natural stronghold. Raise your eyes to the hills across the river and they are affronted by the sight of new apartment blocks stacked up the slopes like egg boxes, so it is best to keep them firmly on the sunlit stream, its banks dotted with fishermen, calm as porcelain figures, or the solid villa residences set in gardens inhabited by the *notables*, the worthies, of what considers itself to be essentially a *bourgeois* town. Takes pride in it, too; a project for establishing a hostel for young women who were considered to be in danger of falling into prostitution, or, conversely, to be in the process of being reclaimed from it, was defeated by the *notables*, who held that such an establishment was not *digne*, not fitting for their town. The promoters of the scheme seem to have missed their chance of asking the *notables* whether they thought prostitution, full or part-time, was any more *digne*.

Typical of the prosperous villas are the houses of two doctors, one of whom inhabits a small greystone mansion, the other a small greystone *château*. Doctors do quite nicely in France, and, like members of other liberal professions, have certain opportunities for tax-evasion if they wish to take them, though it would be wrong to set the standard of the mass by that of a handful of Paris surgeons in private practice, whose earnings equal those current in big business. The weekly magazine *Le Nouvel Observateur* once established a table of earnings in France which put these men at the head of the list, with bankers and manufacturers and property dealers. But both country doctors and GPs in Paris, whose practices are made up of insurance patients, were still comfortably in the top third of the list, with an average income comparable with that of a successful architect, a notary or the editor of a major provincial newspaper. The well-established striptease artist who figured in the same section was unlikely to be typical of her profession, one in which, in any case, the period of peak earnings is likely to be brief.

Bésançon does not look like hopeful terrain for stripteasers, nor even for sex-shops, which, within the space of two or three years, have sprung up in the most improbable places in France, judging, at least, from the windows of the Grande-Rue, once a Roman road, now the main street that goes through the historic town as clean as a cheese-cutter, heading for the cathedral and the *Citadelle* above it. There is nothing more bizarre than the notice of an institution offering classes in both yoga and karate. Something for everybody, and can it be that both are taught by one deeply schizoid instructor? Otherwise, there is information about practical things like a collective taxi running every hour on Sunday mornings, which in itself tells one a good deal about the domestic life of the *Bisontins*, dividing their weekends between attendance at mass and visits to or from Aunt Philomène, and shops with displays of equipment for tapestry work and rug-making, suggesting long, quiet evenings behind those seemly façades. One of them, on the right-hand side of the Grande-Rue, is that of Victor Hugo's birthplace, though Hugo was a *Bisontin* only by the chance that his father, a general of the Empire, happened to be stationed in the town when he was born. It might have been more just, as well as more likely to stir a response from succeeding generations, if the little *place* leading from the Grande-Rue to the rue de la Convention had been named, not after him, but after the brothers Louis and Auguste Lumière, inventors of the cinema, who were born at No. 1 in the *place*, respectively in 1864 and 1862.

The Cathedral of St. Jean has an astronomical clock, as befits the centre of the French watchmaking industry, but I tell myself that it can hardly be any more remarkable than that of Strasbourg, which I know, and press on up the hill. It is no day to be spent in cathedrals. The weather, all gust and glitter, is hallucinating for the place and the time of year — the Jura, like Ireland, owes the vernal green which is one of its charms, to an abundant rainfall. The top priority is to make the circuit of the parapets forming the outer defences of the *citadelle* which crowns the ridge above the town. It is a catwalk slung between heaven and earth, with diamond-bright views over the town and the sinuous curves of the Doubs, a river that covers 430 kilometres on the way from its source to its junction with the Saône, though, overland, the distance is only ninety. After that there is the indulgence of a whole long, vacant afternoon, to be divided between wandering about the green slopes inside the walls, visiting the small zoo where the peacocks parade and red flamingoes perch like stylites on the pillar of a single leg, and inspecting the complex of museums which now occupy the building of Vauban's fortress.

You have to be selective about local museums; so often a walk round the town on market day and a session in the most popular café will give you more relevant information about a place, not to say far more memorable items for your mental snapshot album, than boning up on dates among the showcases. Two reasons make this one, or rather these, outstandingly worthwhile. One is a collection of marionettes constituting an animated *crêche* from a so-called mechanical theatre of the late eighteenth and early nineteenth centuries. These days *santons*, the little pottery crib figures introducing characters from daily life, the fisherman, the vegetable seller, the baker, into the Nativity scene, are known far beyond their native Provence, and also beyond the Paris shops which devote whole windows to them at Christmas. The *crèche* of the Franche-Comté, with its carols sung in *patois*, its subsidiary characters as stereotyped as those of a Punch and Judy show, and its procession to the manger in which all the local figures, from the Cardinal to the chimney sweep and the blind man and his dog take part, is relatively unknown even in France. A long half hour spent studying them set one dreaming of a revival, surely not impossible at a time when puppets are established as an element of popular theatre.

The second reason is that, between them, the folk museum and the agricultural museum which has been set up in the old riding school of the fortress, encapsulate as is rarely possible a way of life which, for today's children, must seem to belong to archaeology rather than to history. It has become a cliché to say that, in the past fifty or the past hundred years — the period can be varied without affecting the general truth — France has changed more than in the previous three centuries, if not the previous four or five. The cliché takes on reality when, in the agricultural museum, you see a wooden ploughshare which was not changed for an iron one until 1850, and this in a province where iron has been worked since the Middle Ages, and which supplied first the Revolution and then the Empire with armaments. It was in the same decade that farming in the Franche-Comté embraced the Machine Age. The precursor of today's battery of reapers and binders and threshers and combine harvesters is here in the enormous '*manège*' installed at a farm in 1858 at a cost of 680 francs. It was powered by four horses treading an eternal round, and it was capable of carrying out all the processes of an oil manufactory — corn oil, not olive. 'All changed, changed utterly', you think, then you come upon a photograph of an ox team ploughing, with the information that not only oxen but cows also are still worked on farms here and there in the Franche-Comté.

To find the clock museum you have to go to the Musée des Beaux Arts, down in the town. Surprisingly for a place which is the home of the *École Nationale Supérieure de Chronomètrie*, it was not established until around 1970. It will be interesting to see in due course how a State institution has dealt with the most recent chapter in the history of the clock and watchmaking industry which employs more than 35,000 people in the region, an attempt at something which the public persisted in seeing as workers' control, though authority was equally insistent that it was nothing of the kind.

Bésançon made clocks as early as the end of the seventeenth century, but the real development began in 1793, with the arrival in the town of eighty Swiss watchmakers, political refugees from Geneva. In sound protectionist fashion the local men were for hanging them, as the surest way to stamp out competition, but it was a period when the government was still experiencing a rush to the head of ideas about brotherhood, and generosity and similar impracticalities. It advanced money to the immigrants to set up a factory and start a national school of clock and watchmaking, to which the Republic sent 200 apprentices each year. The bread so cast on the waters came back thickly buttered. Clockmaking established itself in many other towns in the Franche-Comté, and the factories provided outwork for the mountain villages. There was a slump around the turn of the century, when that kind of cottage industry failed to stand up to the Swiss — across the border this time — but after the Second World War Bésançon was able to complete once more on fairly level terms.

It became a centre of national interest in the spring of 1973, when Lip, the model watchmaking factory of the region, announced its forthcoming closure, which would mean the redundancy of more than 1,300 men. Fred Lip, the head of the firm, was an egocentric character whose flamboyance had run to having the great hall of the factory decorated with murals depicting scenes from his own career, and whose commitment to top quality production was such that he would not consider meeting the demands of the market by making cheap watches. Gradually the firm's share of French sales dropped from twenty

42

per cent to five per cent. In 1969 the Ébauches Swiss Watches group bought a controlling interest in Lip; in 1973 the firm went bankrupt. There were suggestions that Fred Lip had been guilty of mismanagement, or at best lack of foresight, whose price was now to be paid by men who had a strong loyalty to their own factory and an aversion to working elsewhere, even if they could have found jobs in their own trade, which was unlikely. Also they believed that the situation could still be saved and the firm made viable.

On April 17th, 1973, Bésançon awoke to a situation which was new in its experience, not a strike but a work-in. The Lip men had occupied the factory and were continuing production. Two major trade unions were involved, the powerful *Confédération Générale du Travail*, whose executive, though not its membership, is predominantly Communist, and the less rigid *Confédération Française Démocratique du Travail*, a breakaway from a confessional union which continues to be marked by what its opponents call woolly Leftist extremism, its friends intelligent progressive idealism. In practical terms that means that if CGT and CFDT officials are involved in negotiations with employers, the former are likely to concentrate on pay and the latter to talk also about working conditions. It was a CFDT leader, M. Charles Piaget, who was the inspiration of this action, but the movement was essentially that of a group who were acting spontaneously, rather than that of union members who were being called out.

Bourgeois Bésançon, which would have shuddered at violence, could sympathise with steady workmen who wanted only to go on working. More remarkably, their campaign caught the imagination of the nation. It must have been an unpleasant surprise for the government when one of the opinion polls, with which the authorities regularly take the temperature of the electorate, produced a sizeable majority who felt that the most important item in a given list of current events was the conflict at Lip. After two months of orderly and industrious occupation the men were turned out of the factory by a detachment of the so-called 'riot police', the *Compagnie Républicaine de Sécurité*, a mobile force used for emergencies of all kinds. What was no doubt expected to be the end of the battle proved to be hardly more than the beginning. Funds were not a problem. The men had managed to smuggle three-quarters of a million pounds' worth of watches out of the factory. The rumour that they were hidden in the Bishop of Bésançon's garden was never substantiated, but its currency indicated the sympathetic attitude of the Church. The watches were sold directly and the proceeds used to make a uniform payment of 1,400 francs a month to all the workers, a sum which was approximately half as much again as the national minimum wage. In an artisan industry the closing of the factory did not necessarily mean the end of production. As M. Piaget pointed out, watch parts could be made and assembled on a corner of the kitchen table, as they had been in the past, provided you had the skills and the tools. The men, who had both, made them, and met daily at a local cinema to get campaign news and instructions from M. Piaget.

The history of the next nine months was a mixture of the predictable and the astonishing. There was the inevitable political exploitation of the dispute; there was apparently division and indecisiveness and certainly clumsiness on the part of the government and there was disagreement between the CGT and the CFDT on acceptable terms for a settlement. On September 30th, 1973, a demonstration in support of the Lip men brought 30,000 people to Bésançon from every part of France. There were fears beforehand that the town would be sacked and the citizens robbed, if not raped, and 12,000 CRS were imported in readiness. The great march took place as planned without incident, possibly because the police had the sense to keep out of sight, leaving crowd control to the tough trade union stewards.

Over the succeeding months some of the original 1,300 found jobs elsewhere, but an irreducible band around M. Piaget held on. On March 11th, 1974, the Lip factory opened again under the control of a holding company, the *Société Européenne d'Horloge et d'Équipement Mécanique*. On that first day only

140 men and women clocked in, but the agreement which had ended the dispute provided for the progressive re-employment of the rest, sometimes after government-sponsored training courses.

The first couple of months after the re-opening showed a will to make certain changes in styles of management, as well as introducing new manufacturing projects, but the most startling novelty was to be found outside the factory. Ten weeks after the end of the dispute many of the men who, during it, had met daily at the Lux cinema to discuss tactics, were still meeting there once weekly. They heard from M. Piaget and his colleagues how their fellows were getting on, what progress the trainees were making, who had started work again, the kind of news you would look for at an Old Boys' meeting. But they got also information about the firm and a run-down of general industrial news, including the movement of wages and prices and the progress of strike movements in other parts of the country. Underlying it all was a recognition of the need to keep alive the spirit of community which they had forged over eleven months, from April 1973 to March 1974.

'We have learned that we can't do anything unless we stick together and act collectively,' said a man after one of those meetings.

In the long run, that lesson on the possibilities of what the workers called 'collective self-defence' is likely to prove more important than the material gains of the 'work-in'.

4   'I AM NOT *raciste*,' says the woman at the hairdresser's at Lons-le-Saunier. She starts winding a too-short strand
of hair round a too-large roller, giving it a sharp tug as though
the roots were extendible before stabbing home a blue plastic
pin. 'I have never been *raciste*. All people have the right to live.
But these Algerians! I know what they are like — I have had to
put up with them. When I had to go into the clinic last year
there was this Algerian woman in my room. The dirt! The
filth! France is full of foreigners. De Gaulle opened the door
and they came pouring in here to undercut our own people,
and take all the jobs and get the best apartments and live off
our social security. All those Portuguese! If the next government
doesn't make a change there will be trouble ahead!'

She ties a mauve net in a bow under my chin and transfers
me to the drier. 'And we have to pay too much in taxes. It is
the little people like me who suffer.'

Round the chair I have just left, her kewpie doll of a daughter, in a miniscule tartan skirt worn waist-high like a pelmet, is

sweeping up the hair clippings with a toy dustpan and brush, grunting seriously as she works. I have already learned that she is twenty-three months old and that she is called Clytemnestre, which is another item for my collection of the improbable names which the French sometimes give to both their children and their pets. In my *quartier* in Paris I know three dogs who answer respectively to Balthasar, Quasimodo and Bémol (the musical flat sign), and yesterday's paper had an item about an accident in which one of the victims, sadly, was a small boy named Goliath.

Clytemnestre's mother is a dramatic brunette, somewhere in the thirties; at first glance you are struck by how tough she looks under the pancake make-up, at second by how tired. Her husband, divorced or not, has cleared off, leaving her to cope alone with Clytemnestre as well as the business, and she had this operation, which would have meant finding somebody to look after the shop while she was in the clinic, and the *impôt* has gone up, and she is involved in some negotiations with the *sécurité sociale* involving mountains of forms and endless visits to the office, and in a last nervous flicker of energy she has turned up the drier too high before hurrying over to the next customer.

It is not every day that you can hope to find such a case-book demonstration of the roots of racial prejudice. The French always claim that they have none, above all that they have no colour prejudice, and in the past they did indeed accept Black immigrants, and particularly passage migrants, happily enough, whether they were the handful of intellectuals from Francophone Africa who moved among their peers at the Sorbonne or the *École Normale Supérieure*, or the American writers and musicians whom Paris considered chic, or the quiet, well-conducted young men from the French West Indies who got jobs in the post office or the lower ranks of the civil service whom landladies referred to amiably as '*mon petit antillais*'.

Then, in the latter part of the Gaulliste era, came the bid to transform France into a modern industrial nation, with the accompanying demand for cheap labour, and the unskilled and unorganised and undemanding came flooding in; Algerians, whose history of emigration to France began before 1914 and now increased rapidly after the gap of the Algerian war, Italians, Spaniards, Portuguese, Yugoslavs, Turks. You could trace the rising prosperity of the less highly developed European countries in the composition of the immigrants. Italians and, later, Spaniards, lost their place at the head of the list, to be replaced by the Portuguese, many of whom came in illegally, sometimes to escape military service in Africa, sometimes merely to escape the poverty of a mountain village. Beyond them were the Africans, smuggled into Europe by 'passers' in conditions little better than those in which their forebears were shipped across the Atlantic, to embark on a working life at least as arduous. The difference was that, technically, they were free men, but there is nothing like social and economic misery for adulterating the concept of freedom.

By the early 1970s, seven per cent of the total population of France was made up of immigrants, and in areas like the Paris region, the Rhône Valley or the Moselle it was more than twelve per cent. The Algerians, numerically at the head of the list, were at the bottom of every pecking order. Beginning with the lingering political rancour which was a legacy of the Algerian war and the OAS violence in France, everything worked against them, even their supposed advantages. As former French nationals, even if the mainland had thought of them as second-class citizens, they could get a job in France without a work permit, though, after 1968, they needed a medical certificate and a permit from the Algerian Employment Office before they could leave their own country. Consequently they were thrown on the labour market with no guaranteed job or lodging, and often with rudimentary skills, to be natural victims for unscrupulous employers, and to live in shanty towns or sordid and exorbitantly priced lodgings. Mostly they worked on building sites, where the national casualty rate was three fatal accidents a day. Immigrants of all nationalities, indeed, are found predominantly in exhausting and/or monotonous jobs, where pay and prestige are alike low. Eight per cent of France's total working population is immigrant, but they make up twenty per cent of unskilled labourers.

Here were all the conditions needed for the release of latent xenophobia, and it has surged out. The immigrants, it is said, and, above all, the Algerians, introduce disease into France, and have a higher crime rate than the native born. An observer has noted that when a theft or an assault is committed there are usually witnesses who have seen 'a sallow man, or men, of North African type' near the scene of the crime, of which, later, a blond Norman or Picard may be convicted. If the offender really is Algerian there can be a frightening wave of violence, extending from himself to his guiltless fellow countrymen, as happened at Marseille after a mental patient, in a sudden crisis, fatally stabbed a bus driver and wounded five passengers.

Finally, the accusations continue, the foreigners are quite unnecessary to the economy of the country; all they do is take the bread from the mouths of Frenchmen and drain the resources of the social security.

In truth it is the immigrants who have made possible the rapid development of recent years. The jobs they take are those which French workers refuse, and doctors have testified that the amount of disease they introduce is far outweighed by that which they pick up after their arrival in France, particularly TB and VD, to which the conditions of their life makes them peculiarly vulnerable. They make fewer demands upon the social services than the French, and, remarkably for a population with so high a proportion of single men, their crime rate is not above the national average. But facts are powerless against convictions, and the two most surprising facts, that the proportion of immigrants in the population of France today is little higher than in 1931, when it was six point six per cent, and that ten per cent of French citizens are of foreign descent, are the most powerless of all. What they have to combat is the emotional intensity of the Poor White syndrome, as a break-down of attitudes according to social class has shown. It is the members of the liberal

49

professions who are least tinged by racialism; the small shop-keepers who are the deepest-dyed. How can it be otherwise when, between the growth of supermarkets and the introduction of VAT, they feel threatened from all quarters, even if the mass have not the additional personal reasons for feeling insecure and victimised which motivate my hairdresser.

The only surprise is that so virulent a reaction should be found at Lons-le-Saunier, where foreign faces, if not unknown, are still a fairly unobtrusive minority. It is an unexpectedly elegant little place, making much of itself, as one says of those blood ponies whose bearing makes them seem bigger than they are. Sitting on a café terrace in the place de La Liberté one has the impression of being in the heart of a town with more than the actual 20,000-odd inhabitants. There is an impressive clock tower, the last surviving bit of the old fortifications, and a curve of arcaded greystone houses in the rue du Commerce, built in the sixteenth and seventeenth centuries by highly individualistic citizens. The irregularities of the terrace would have appalled Nash, but it remains most satisfactory to the eye. As in some small towns in the Home Counties or the Cotswolds, the dress shops are surprisingly unprovincial, and, unlike most of the small towns I know anywhere in England, the bookshops are remark-ably good. Possibly that is due to the fact that the Jura, like Scotland, has long been a well-educated region. Dole had its own university before the French conquest of the Franche-Comté, and even before the Revolution every village had its school.

Originally the prosperity would have been founded on the salt deposits, which have been worked hereabouts for 2,000 years. Now only the works at Poligny is still operating. Some of the other small towns have converted themselves into spas and tourist centres, like Lons-le-Saunier, where you can cure, or any-way treat, your rickets, and swim in a pool fed by a spring which the Romans used, as well as making expeditions into the attrac-tive surrounding country. But there is also a whole complex of thriving smallish industries in the region, some of them testifying to the initiative and adaptability of self-contained communities. My favourite example is Oyonnax, where they started making combs as a cottage industry in the fourteenth century, all that forest ensuring an inexhaustible supply of raw material. After 400 or so years they began to make the combs of bone, so capitalising the other end of the cows which they milked between stints of harnessing them to the plough, later of tortoiseshell, later still of cellulloid and all the synthetics that came after. Today Oyonnax is a European centre for the manufacture of plastics in every conceivable form, from radio parts to those bristling bouquets which decorate the reception desks of every other hotel in France.

None of it seems quite the right background for the native of Lons-le-Saunier whose statue — Bartholdi again, but on the human scale this time — stands on the promenade de la Chevalerie. Rouget de Lisle, author of the 'Marseillaise', must be the definitive case of the creator who has been overwhelmed by his creation, that peerless Drury Lane national anthem whose only possible rival in its line is 'John Brown's Body'. As can happen with perfection, it came into being almost fortuitously. The Army of the Rhine, garrisoned at Strasbourg, wanted a marching song. Rouget de Lisle, an engineer captain known to have a talent for verse and music, got down to producing one overnight and, so the story goes, appeared at breakfast with the words and music of a 'War Song of the Army of the Rhine'. It was April 1792. Four months later the song had travelled as far as the Mediterranean : it fuelled like octane spirit the detachment of volunteers from Marseille in the forced march that brought them to Paris in time for the assault on the Tuileries on August 10th. The War Song got a new title : it was known as the Hymn of the *Marseillais*. The newborn Republic had 100,000 copies printed for the use of its armies and generals came up with unsolicited testimonials like : 'Send me a thousand men or an edition of the "Marseillaise",' or : 'Without the "Marseillaise" I would be ready to fight against odds of two to one; with it I would fight against odds of four to one.'

By 1795 it had been officially adopted as the national anthem, which did not prevent rulers from banning it as being too revolutionary periodically through the nineteenth century. Napoleon Bonaparte was the first of them, but he found it expedient to resurrect the 'Marseillaise' during the retreat from Moscow. Similarly, Napolon III, who had previously rejected it, ordered the whole nation to sing the 'Marseillaise' on the day of the outbreak of the Franco-Prussian War. This seems to have been the only recorded instance when it failed to have its accustomed galvanic effect. For generations the aristocracy and the *haute bourgoisie* felt that it smelled of gunpowder and barricades, an attitude which lingers even today. New to France, I found it comically incredible that, at a public occasion, my neighbour, a member of one of the oldest families in France, should remain mute while his national anthem was sung, saying : 'I do not like it. It is a revolutionary song.' Shamed understanding came to me later, when another friend, whose *ancien régime* background had not prevented her from coming to terms with her age, said : 'You know, one doesn't feel quite the same about it when the *"sang impur"* that was to drench the soil of France was your great-grandfather's.' With such exceptions the 'Marseillaise' was accepted as the anthem of all the French by the end of the First World War, as the *tricolore* was accepted as their flag. The same war saw Rouget de Lisle's ashes transferred to the national necropolis of heroes, the Panthéon, which was one of the most ironic episodes in the story of the young officer, a favourite of pre-Revolutionary salons, whose later life was to be a catalogue of banishment and poverty and debtors' prisons. The saddest of all is the postscript, the four volumes of his songs, not a word or a note of which are likely to be heard again, which are preserved in the museum of his native town. It seems inconceivable that such a man should have written a refrain that is terrible like an army with banners, and in one sense he did not. The Revolution wrote the 'Marseillaise', but somebody had to hold the pen.

The morning threatens to be penitential, because the only

means of getting to Les Rousses, high on the French-Swiss border, which is my next stage, is by a bus which leaves at six forty a.m. In the event there is nothing but well and fair, largely because the previous evening develops into an unexpectedly harmonious prelude to it. The dining room of the hotel which was chosen merely because it faced the station is, like Lons-le-Saunier, elegant in the best sense. I go to sleep full of meltingly light apple tart and well-being that survives even my making a mistake over setting my alarm clock, so that I am out in the street on an empty stomach at six ten on a hunting morning, with a big, cherry-red sun coming up through the mist over the hill but, as yet, no warmth in its splendour.

Eventually, we climb up to the plateau, where your breath steams and sparse meadow alternates with chocolate plough-land, with, here and there, the bones showing through in out-crops of rock, in a very local bus. An old lady slung with baskets like a mule with panniers who is going in to St. Laurent to do her shopping addresses a small boy in the next seat as *'mon lapin'* my little rabbit, and says to a girl who comes aboard a stop or two further on: 'You'll be getting married this year, then?' When the young woman says no, she and her fiancé have to have a place of their own and some furniture before they can even think of it, she comes back with: 'Ah, bah! Marriage isn't about all that!' 'No,' the girl agrees, 'but after all you've got to have a bed and a kitchen. I'm not thinking of a *salon.'*

Morez is extraordinary, strung out along the bottom of what is more a crevasse than a valley, with the River Bienne rattling through it. An improbable place from which to send spectacles to every part of France, but here is another example of Jurassian initiative. At the end of the eighteenth century one of the wrought-iron workers who had practised their craft in the Franche-Comté since the Middle Ages turned his skill to making spectacle frames. In a surprisingly short time an industry which began with those gargantuan gig-lamps had introduced pince-nez to the market: today Morez turns out the better part of twelve million optical lenses a year.

53

It is as cold as an icehouse and I am hollow with hunger. The Hotel de La Poste provides an Italianate sort of breakfast — a vast jug of hot milk with a tiny one of coffee to splash into it — to the tune of a vacuum cleaner purring round my feet and the chilly tinkle of the river outside the window. It is still only nine thirty-five a.m. when I finish, which leaves another hour and a half to patrol the floor of the chasm before getting my bus. On its walls — it seems inexact to speak of slopes — there are incredibly hideous concrete edifices; down below you can follow the march of progress from a street market at one end to the latest in *supermags* at the other. The first sells jeans appliquéd with flowers like those currently worn in Saint-Germain-des-Pres : on the other hand, a glance around verifies that the granny prints piled beside them are still bought and worn almost exclusively by grannies rather than by the young. Nostalgia is no fun in places where the past is still so near that people may think you are rooted in it. The supermarket has a bar and there is a rocking horse to amuse the children, but the cars parked outside it are all small and the stock not calculated to give a great deal of ammunition for condemnation of the excesses of the consumer society.

The ride to Les Rousses is terrifying, the bus negotiating progressively sickening curves over the abyss as we rise to 1,100 metres. In spite of the altitude there is so little snow — it is patchy even on the tops — that it is hard to take seriously the dictum of the natives that in the mountain you get eight months of snow and two of gales, but apart from that, the weather is idyllic. A century ago one virtually battened down hatches for those eight months, and farmhouses in the Jura are still built low, so as to offer the least possible resistance to the wind, with wide overhanging roofs covering dwelling house and stable and hay stored in the loft serving for insulation as well as feed. Snug beneath it, the whole family used to switch to its winter economy, the women knitting, the men, in these parts, making watch springs and decorating watch cases at least as often as they worked at the traditional wood-carving. There are remote valleys and lonely farms where things have not greatly changed, but the chalets which are springing up on all sides of Les Rousses are not farmhouses. This is the full blossoming of the post-war civilisation of leisure — quiet mountain holidays in one half of the year, winter sports in the other — and one of the sharpest thorns among all these roses is the fact that I have to hump my two bags the whole length of the main street, passing a number of the kind of hotels at which I could not possibly afford to stay, before finding, in the lane leading up to the church, the comfortably shabby one which had been there before any of them.

From the churchyard at the top of the lane you can look across to the hills three kilometres away, where Switzerland begins, but only the eye of faith can divine the Lake of Geneva beyond them, near as it is. One has to be content with the lake of Les Rousses, spread out blue as a flower at one's feet, and the knowledge that the church is that rarity, an unnatural watershed; the rain that trickles down the northern slope of its roof flows into the North Sea, that down the southern slope into the Mediterranean.

The path leading down to the lake, which turns out to be a considerable distance from one's feet, winds among the alps where purple and white crocuses are filling the gaps where the snow is melting. The next day, when I walk up to the snowline, it is between banks stained blue with violets, and primroses are gleaming new-minted between the dry beech leaves of a copse. Here is a later spring than the opulence I saw in Alsace last week : in a country like France you could have six months of spring if you followed it from the Mediterranean to the high alps or the Pyrénées.

The snow can come back any minute, crocuses notwithstanding, a woman with whom I walk the last few hundred yards into the village tells me. She never notices the flowers herself; you don't look at what is there all the time. The changes are what you notice, the way people who used to live in a very modest way are making money to throw out of the windows these days.

55

What do I think they charge for a *deux pièce* apartment in the height of the winter sports season? While I am wondering whether to add something to or take something away from the Paris equivalent she says: 'Nine hundred francs *lourds* (current value) a week, a *week* do you understand? And you know that very smart hotel by the bus stop?'

I do, it was one of those I had trudged past heavy laden without even imagining I could afford to stay at it.

'Well, five years ago those people were running a plain little *pension*. What with that and the money the young people get when they go over the border to work in Switzerland ... And look at all these new houses everywhere.' She doesn't know where all the money comes from, she concludes.

I have my own taste of high life by drinking lemon tea and eating fruit cake at one of the largest and newest of the hotels after getting back. The pretty girl who brings it to me is wearing Andalusian frills and flounces, ready, presumably, to click her castanets when, later in the evening, one of the dark young waiters picks up the guitar which is lying on the piano. Spanish you well might think — I do not hear them speak — but while I am on my second cup I overhear her recalling to a local customer at a neighbouring table that two or three years ago she used to play with the boys in the junior school football team.

Before it gets dark I walk as far as the *fruitière* which is the pride of that section of Les Rousses which does not live by or off tourists. Contrary to the sound of it, a *fruitière* is not an establishment for processing cherries and mountain strawberries but a co-operative for the production of those solemn wheels of Comté cheese (a type of Gruyère) which are one of the mainstays of the economy of the Jura. The exigencies of hill farming, in which small men have to battle against large odds, encourage team work even in a people in whose national ethos it has as little a part as the French. Back in the thirteenth century the farmers in the high alps of the Franche-Comté were already producing cheese by this method. There seems no record of the size of a Comté at that time. Julien, when he visited a *fruitière* here, was impressed by the sight of cheeses weighing twenty-five kilos. Then the maximum daily yield of a milk cow was seven litres. Today it is ten — that's what cattle cake will do for you — and the Comtés run at forty-eight kilos, which is the solidification of 600 litres of milk. The mere thought of them, stacked peacefully in the *cave*, where they may spend as long as six months maturing, is a steadying counterpart to the Andalusian flounces.

After dinner I take a stroll before an early bed — tomorrow's bus, too, leaves before the break of day in order to catch a connecting train at Morez. The street is all but empty. There is a largesse of stars but during the couple of hours for which I have been indoors an iron cold has crept down from the hills that bulk enormous against the sky. It is easy now to believe that the snow may return. Suddenly the extravagances of the local property market, and the nonsense of tarting up for the holiday trade, and even the herd of reindeer that are a tourist attraction in a neighbouring valley are reduced to their proper scale.

5

THE HOTEL AT Bourg-en-Bresse charges thirty-
six francs a night, with another seven francs for breakfast, and
for that sum I got dinner, too, 11,000 metres up. But the price
here includes glory as well as relative luxury — relative only
because the breakfast coffee turns out to be, if anything, slightly
below the lamentable average standard; for, along the corridor
from my room, is a door labelled: '*Chambre de l'Empereur*'.

Napoleon III says the chambermaid, but surely nowhere
would be labelled in perpetuity after him, and the dark green
and brazen solemnities glimpsed through the half-open door
suggest a more august occupant. There is no opportunity of check-
ing at the desk as the receptionist, though amiable, seems permanently busy, so I keep my illusions while wondering yet again
at the capacity of the French, perhaps even more than other
nations, to get excited about the wrong people. Up at Les
Rousses where, this morning, I was one of a group waiting for
a bus to Morez in the shivering six a.m. dusk — some of its
members were white collar workers, which raises another aspect

of living in the mountain — we were overlooked by a bust whose legend read : 'Pasteur's country starts here.' Pasteur's country is the world, but, to the end of his life, the great man kept his love for his native Jura and, during his annual holidays, kept also the approachability of the local boy whose father had been a sergeant major in the Imperial army before returning to his original craft of tanner. His birthplace at Dole is now a Pasteur museum, as is the house at Arbois, further south, where he spent his boyhood, but I have yet to see a textbook which presents Pasteur to schoolchildren on the scale of Vercingétorix, still less Bonaparte. M. Bruno gives Pasteur a page and a half in the supplement which he added to his book in 1904, but Vercingétorix keeps the two and a half devoted to him in the original edition.

The run down from Morez to Bourg is a monument in itself, a feat of engineering that has you catching your breath as the train weaves in and out of tunnels between great shoulders of hills and crawls across viaducts above valleys where the mist is still packed like damp wool. The plain of Bresse is in another hemisphere, the meadows spread with cowslips as thick as butter, and Bourg itself, with urns of winey polyanthus at street corners and a little park full of pansies and intensely blue forget-me-nots, exudes prosperity and good living. The prosperity is still based on poultry, though this is a country of stock-rearers and pig-breeders also; anyone who sees the gargantuan *nature morte* of the Christmas fair when, after plucking, the pullets and capons are dipped in milk to turn their flesh to pearl and alabaster, is likely to feel that there are enough birds here to keep Europe in roast chicken. Wrongly of course : supply is so far short of demand that many French *restaurateurs* put on their menus *'poulets de Bresse'* which have never tasted a grain of the maize or buckwheat of the Ain on which the genuine product is fattened for the last few weeks of a life which is otherwise free-range. There is a poultry room at the local museum, filled, not with stuffed birds, but with figures and pictures of them, from some rather nasty Venetian glass to a lithograph of a rooster in a splendid scarlet rage.

Hallucination sets in when the visitor to Bourg hears Big Ben measuring out the quarters, morning, midday and night. It is a relief to learn that the chimes are real, and that they were modelled on Westminster. They come from the tower of Notre-Dame, which is interesting to those with a taste for religious curiosities because it contains one of the first Black Virgins which travellers coming into the region from the east are likely to meet; the cult flourishes mainly in Central and South-Western France. This one is a very fairly typical example, richly robed in black and gold and enthroned on an altar where the number of *ex votos* testify to the devotion she commands. A certain testiness in the wording of a notice, stating that the altar is mid-nineteenth century, the statue 'allegedly thirteenth', but so much restored that it is impossible to say, testifies to the lack of enthusiasm of the more *avant garde* elements of the Church in France for some aspects of folk devotion. One can see their point while sympathising with the folk, which has already been deprived of much of the comfort of incantatory prayers. Naked faith, like naked truth, can be chilly, just as the real explanation why these virgins are black in skin as well as garments is less picturesque than any of the fanciful ones. These include suggestions that the dark Virgins were an allusion to the Song of Songs ('I am black but comely'), or were statues of Isis, brought to Europe by Syrian merchants or Crusaders and 'baptised' into the Church. The truth seems to be that Byzantine icons, the silver of which was oxidised, found their way to the West, where the black was believed to be original and was imitated. Alternatively, smoke and grime may have darkened statues of wood or stone, and the tradition that they had 'always' been black would soon be established. Certainly some of the figures were originally pale-skinned. When the famous eleventh-century Black Virgin in the Church of Notre Dame at Dijon was restored in 1945, natural flesh tints in medieval polychrome were found under a coating of black or dark paint. The restorers re-blacked the statue for the sake of 'tradition', but later, truth prevailed and it was once more cleaned.

The real miracle of Bourg is not the Black Virgin but the Church of Brou, just outside the town, whose perfection is sheltered by a lagoon of green lawn from the traffic roaring past it towards Nantua. An even greater miracle is the fact that the building should have survived intact through four and a half centuries, during which it was imperilled by both Wars of Religion and the Revolution. The church was built by one queen in fulfilment, however belated, of a promise made by another. In 1480 Margaret of Bourbon, grandmother of Francis I, vowed that if her husband, Philip Count of Bresse, recovered from injuries suffered in a hunting accident, she would build a monastery to replace the existing modest priory at Brou. Philip did recover, but Margaret herself died before she had time to do more than lay the charge of carrying out her intention on her husband and her son, Philibert le Beau.

They may have intended to fulfil it, but, twenty years later, Philibert in the meantime having married Margaret of Austria, they had not yet done so. Then Philibert died suddenly and Margaret, widowed for the second time at the age of twenty-four, saw his death as a direct visitation from heaven for the failure to carry out her mother-in-law's vow. When, in 1506, she put in hand the work on the new monastery, it was with the double purpose of keeping that vow by proxy and ensuring that the soul of her own husband should rest in peace. She was never to see more than the plans of the church, which was completed in nineteen years, between 1513 and 1532. When the work began she was living in Flanders as Regent of the Low Countries and the Franche-Comté, and left everything to a master mason she found there. It was an era of general practitioners, but Van Boghem, who was at once architect and mason, contractor and works manager, must have been a phenomenon even for his time. He completed the whole job in twenty-six years, but Margaret died two years before it was finished.

The cruellest part of the story, because of its inherent

61

absurdity, is that she should never have occupied the two little oratories, set one above the other and linked by a staircase, built for her north of the choir, so that, as was customary for royal or noble personages, she could fulfil her religious duties in the utmost comfort, with a fire in the grate, a carpet under her feet and a squint through which she could keep an eye on what was going on at the altar.

With such a history you would expect all the resonances at Brou to be tragic, but from the moment one sets foot in the church the mood is exultant. The milky stone of Revermont, never cleaned since it was quarried because it was never marred, gives off a glow of light, crossed by dazzling shafts of colour, vermilion, sounding crimson and gentian blue, from the windows which were the work of local, not Flemish, glaziers. The beautiful Philibert and the two Margarets lie at the East End, their effigies cut from blocks of marble that did the last stage of their journey from Carrera in carts which, despite being drawn by nine horses apiece, covered no more than six kilometres a day. All around and above them is a profusion of decoration in which stone has been given the intricacy of ivory carving. The whole effect, while being stupendous, is also gay and triumphant, so that the intimations of mortality conveyed by the tombs of Philibert and his wife, on which the occupants are represented both as they appeared in life and in their winding sheets, are not so much banished as set in their appointed place in the re-assuring scheme of things. Mortality, it seems clear as you go out into the sunshine that strikes like June rather than April, while other visitors stream into the church, is 'rotting to flowers and fruit, like Adam and all mankind', and, if you are very lucky as well as very deserving, having as your memorial here below not a church like Brou but perhaps a tablet like that on the outside wall of the church which I am now contemplating. It commemorates Thomas Riboud, born in 1755, a historian and economist, who, when he died at the age of eighty, had been *Procureur Général*, a *Syndic Départemental*, a *Représentatif du Peuple* and a *Membre de l'Institut*, and had founded the *Société d'Émulation de l'Ain,* the *Société Litteraire de Lyon* and the *Bibliothèque de Bourg.* More than all these, in 1791 and again in 1793, when the Revolution indulged a rage of destruction, he was responsible for saving Brou, which should make him a *notable* of all *notables,* those local worthies who have so fitting a sense of their own importance in French provincial life.

If only the tablet told you how he managed it, I think as I stroll back to the hotel, with those phantom chimes laying out their bronze rods of sound about my head. If only, too, there were some more logical way of getting myself in the morning from here to Nevers, which, as the crow flies, is a mere 150 kilometres than taking a train to Mâcon, a bus from Mâcon to Chalon-sur-Saône, and, after that, heaven knows what through and over the wooded hills of the Morvan. When André and Julien went that way in a carrier's cart the logs were still floated down the Cure and the Yonne till the latter joined the Seine, which carried them on to Paris, and at Mâcon there were vineyards where they trod the grapes in Virgilian fashion.

For myself, when the train drops me there after crossing the opulent plain of the Bresse, which leaves an overall impression of cows in clover, white Charollais appearing more and more often among the black or red pied, it turns out to be a tantalising stop. There is not enough time to go to see the house in the rue Beauderon-de-Senecé where Lamartine was born, even if he were one of my favourite poets, and it is too early in the day to eat the local *specialités* of *quenelles de brochet* or *coq au vin,* still less to drink Pouilly-Fuissé, which for a good many visitors are in themselves reason enough for coming here. So I sip a black coffee in the station buffet, next to a man who is ordering a *'petit blanc et un Vichy',* the French equivalent of that Victorian tipple, hock and seltzer, and consider the respective attractions of the two possible bus routes for Chalon. There seems everything to be said for the one which crosses the range of hills west of the town just at the point where the white wine meets the red, then turns north for Cluny and follows the valley of the

63

Grosne until it joins that of the Saône a few kilometres south of Chalon.

On the way out of town you would skirt on the right the vineyards that produce the Mâcon *blanc*, while southwards stretch the granitic slopes of the Beaujolais country. 'Three rivers flow through Lyon', says the kind of geography one does not learn at school, 'the Rhône, the Saône and the Beaujolais.' More of the last flows through Paris alone than is produced in a year from that strip of sunny hillside where the districts can be told off like titles of honour, St. Amour, Juliénas, Chenas, Fleurie, Chiroubles, Morgon, Brouilly, Moulin-à-Vent, and if a reputable *vigneron* were to taste some of the Beaujolais that flows through London and parts north and west he would be liable to have a stroke. The genuine article, particularly when it is drunk young and tasting of the grape, very nearly justifies the literary flapdoodle it tends to provoke.

It was the Romans who planted the first vines here, but it was the monks, 1,000 years later, who extended and improved their cultivation, clearing forests and terracing hills, and it was Cluny, founded in this valley in 910, which was the centre of the work, as it was the centre and powerhouse of the whole of the great rekindling of art and learning and civilisation that illumined Europe towards the end of the first millenium AD. Cluny was sacked by the new Goths during and after the Revolution; today it is half a shell, half a survival that houses one of the *Écoles nationales d'Ingénieurs Arts et Métiers*, but ten kilometres north of it the road passes a new monastic centre. The stark Church of the Reconciliation, 'like a warehouse rather than a church' say traditionalists, was built by German Christians in 1962 for the Oecumenical Community of Taizé, which has introduced monasticism into the Protestant Church. Every year Taizé attracts the young in their thousands for what critics sometimes write off as prayerful pop festivals. It is an opinion that seldom survives experience of one of them.

That route gives glimpses also of the Renaissance *Château* of Cormatin and the eleventh-century church tower at Chapaize.

Unfortunately the bus which follows it does not leave until after lunch, and if I want to get off from Chalon before night it seems advisable to start earlier than that. So, perforce, I settle for the duller way up the Valley of the Saône, leaving Mâcon by the *quais* beside the river and the splurge of suburban development, with tulips and forget-me-nots at the crossings between blocks of new buildings, a motel, a restaurant calling itself *la Vieille Ferme* — proof positive that it is not — and nursery gardens which, in the country, often succeed in being depressing. In truth it is all most worthy; it is my own perversity which makes me respond more vividly to a flock of brown goats in a field near St. Oyen, and the yellow that is beginning to warm the jade of the young corn, and the tremendous romanesque church of St. Philibert at Tournus, and the golden rooftops and plenitude of space at Sennecey-le-Grand.

The banners say they are having a *Joyeux Carnaval* at Chalon, but not now. Sometimes I feel that being on the road like this is one long sequence of arriving at places where a party has just finished or has not yet started. This one is well over; Chalon, quite conventionally, has its carnival at *mardi gras*, when people wear outsize masks called *Goniots*. More remarkably, twice a year, in February and June, it has had since the Middle Ages a fur fair which attracts trappers from every part of France and, at the June fair, from other European countries also.

If you ask why Chalon you are told that, set as it is on the magnificent waterway of the Saône and at a crossing of land routes, Chalon is the Crewe Junction for the whole of Europe, a fact recognised by Julius Caesar, who had his central stores there when he was conquering Gaul. Things have changed since, because it looks as if it is going to take me all the rest of the day to get to Nevers. One train to Chagny, change; another to Montchanin, change. Then on, at what sometimes feels like a walking pace, through the Creusot basin, whose varied industry is so dove-tailed into the landscape that the memory you take away is of lakes and forests, in which, more often than one cares to see, the native oak and beech and birch and hornbeam are

65

being replaced by conifers. Even Le Creusot itself, where the coming of the Schneider works in 1836 rapidly brought up the population from 3,000 to 30,000, leaves an impression of flowers and apartment blocks for executives rather than of the steel town where the sledge hammer was invented five years later.

One drowsy little station succeeds another almost indistinguishable from it; one square woman in a serge skirt and an acrylic jumper, with a copy of *France Dimanche*, which is published on Wednesday, turned back at the page headed *Le Calvaire de Madame Pompidou*, gets out and another, her twin, down to the copy of *France Dimanche* gets in; at St. Julien there are kingcups; at Montchanin there is a young soldier from the Antilles to be shaken awake and got aboard his connecting train; near Luzy there is stone quarrying. Time is suspended and it seems entirely appropriate to be reading yesterday's newspaper, bought at Bourg-en-Bresse, which, as it happens, is rich in the kind of perennially interesting information that is independent of date-lines. An official of the local association of *charcutiers* assures his brother members that, despite the growth of supermarkets, *charcuterie* is a *métier* with a future, because a civilisation of leisure will be raring for ready-to-eat pork products. A M. Léon Dilas, now aged seventy-four, who is in practice as a *sourcier*, or water-diviner, is said to be able to divine also whether a child in the womb is boy or girl — though by then there doesn't seem much that could be done about it — and a Madame Mignot, from Mezerat, who has been a well-borer for twenty-six years, says diviners are never wrong and it is much easier to employ one than to have a geological survey, even if the *sourciers* cannot be exact about the depth of the water. The *Société Crématiste de l'Ain* makes clear that cremation is also a *métier* with a future, because towns are outgrowing their cemeteries, and municipalities are refusing to sell their neighbours a few hectares of land for so fundamental a purpose. In Marseille, the article goes on, there are towers eight or ten storeys high, packed with coffins, which are known as *Cathédrales de Silence*. That, surely, is French for Whispering Glades, but

66

the profane call them '*HLM des morts*' (skyscrapers for stiffs). There is an '*odeur détestable*' in the corridors, and soon, doubtless, zinc coffins will be obligatory and it is the families who will have to pay . . .

I have just learned that the *Société Crématiste* has its own journal called — what else — *La Flamme*, when the train comes to the forty-seventh, or it may be forty-ninth, stop of the day, and lo !, it is Nevers.

6   SOMETIMES, IN A mood of counting my blessings, I try to imagine what it would be like to be the kind of expensively packaged traveller who accomplishes a world tour without ever divagating from the path that leads from the gilded cage of one Hilton to the next, and always I end chanting songs of thanksgiving. The mood awakens the moment I cross the doorstep of the hotel at Nevers, once more chosen because it is the one nearest the station and I badly want to put down my two bags. It is of the kind that is becoming rare even in the less fashionable corners of provincial France, enormous and ramshackle without being in the least scruffy, with undulating corridors down which you could drive a gig, and rather low bedroom doors that creak and are set faintly askew.

My room is the diametric opposite of the glossily orthodox tourists' caravanserai; it is huge and threadbare with living, an entirely personal place, with unexpected pieces of furniture like a rather elaborate writing desk, and a nineteenth-century footstool and three small tables as well as two beds, one amply double, the other rather exiguously single. The last is not un-common in country France where, once Paris is well behind you, beds may come in graduated trios, as for the three bears. The bathroom opening out of the bedroom is on the same scale, with scalding water, plentiful, if worn towels and none of those minatory notices about not washing your smalls, when what else do they think travellers want a private bathroom for. Everything is comfortably clean, which means that the linen and the por-celain — well, vitreous enamel — of the bathroom are irreproach-able and you would quite possibly find some dust on the skirting boards if you were silly enough to crawl round looking for it.

I unpack contentedly before going across the road to have dinner at the station buffet because the hotel has no dining room and it is too late to hunt for somewhere more alluring. Actually there is little need to do so. Like the vast majority of modest restaurants up and down France, it succeeds admirably in creat-ing in a public place that air of homeliness which is sometimes less evident in domestic settings. Each customer is, for the moment, seated at his or her own board and involved in an amiable conspiracy with the waiter in the interests of supplying his strictly individual needs.

The involvement of the couple on my right seems, however, to be less than amiable, or perhaps it is just that the female half of the pair is permanently short on amiability. If the rings can be believed, they are engaged; he is non-descript and correct, she high-coloured and over-pitched. I catch myself looking at her with a disapproval that must be obvious, noting and condemn-ing the discordant jangle of bracelets, on her left wrist, shudder-ing with distaste when, to the waiter's enquiry whether the pair want a small or a large carafe of wine, she replies before her escort can get a word out : '*Une grande. J'ai soif*', then, when it comes, empties three-quarters of a glass at a breath. It was Colette who said that water was for thirst, wine for taste. As the young woman works her way through a fish coquille, fol-lowed by a pork chop, followed by crême caramel, followed by coffee, managing the while to keep up a continuous stream of what is less conversation than irritable recital and comment, I realise why I am disliking her so much. This is the Frenchwoman gone wrong, the pouting earthly innocence of all those little girls in Renoir's paintings peevish and overblown, the sensuous relish of Colette debased into greed, the characteristic firmness and good sense twisted into hard aggression. I pay my bill and walk back to the hotel in a spatter of light rain, brooding rather sadly on 'lilies that fester'.

My room restores me almost instantly. Later, when I draw back the curtains and look out over the *place* from three floors up, there is another Frenchwoman to think about. The lights are still on in the station buffet, but the *place* has emptied with that suddenness which means that, in provincial towns, there is little division between early evening, when everybody is about, shopping or taking an apéritif, and late evening, when nice people, not called out by urgent affairs, are at their own hearths.

In the void, half a dozen youths and one girl, with two bicycles disposed among them, are indulging in that larking about which is the human adolescent's equivalent of courting flights in birds — and the relative elegance of the displays should keep us properly humble. What does a girl who is out with six boys after ten p.m. in provincial France grow up into? You might be very wrong if you said the town tart; it is just as likely to be an excellent mother of four, but it does provoke speculation about what it means to be young in towns where, after about nine o'clock at night, the most vivid signs of life are the lights and the comings and goings around the railway or bus station.

In the morning I am brisked into action by a harassed but still friendly chambermaid, who explains that there are only two of them for all the bedrooms and an American invasion is expected later in the week. The Americans will not like my room. I suffer a proprietary pang at the thought of voices from Wisconsin, Milwaukee and Salt Lake City making disparaging comments about the patch under the writing table where the carpet is almost worn through, or the plug of the bidet which does not quite fit, while over-looking the rare patina of the whole.

Whether they will or will not like the town is irrelevant. Nevers, which does not live by its tourists alone and has the self-confidence of an ancient city set in a province which, for centuries, has been a continental crossroads, exhibits noticeably the very French quality of not giving a damn whether you like it or not.

It is one of those places whose reality by far exceeds all one may have learned of them beforehand. To know that it is built on a slope above the river, that the cathedral of St. Cyr and Ste. Julitte is one of the very few in France with two apses, fore and aft, so to speak, that for nearly four centuries, up to 1708, the Duchy of which it was the centre was ruled by the Italian princely family of Gonzague, whose realm embraced Mantua as well as Nevers, gives one no idea of the view of the terraced roofs of the old town as one looks up from the river, or the sheer mass of the basilica, where every style of architecture from the tenth to the sixteenth centuries is represented (and recently they found a sixth-century baptistry under the present church), or the golden walls of the Ducal Palace. The palace symbolises the inter-penetration of nations and cultures that so greatly enriched Renaissance Europe. A plaque on one of its towers commemorates those princesses of the Gonzague family who became Queens of Poland. If Nevers, to this day, is known for its *faience*, it is because Louis de Gonzague, when he became Duke of the Nivernais in 1565, imported with him from Italy a large number of artist-craftsmen who passed on their skills to local workers. Within two or three generations, these had grown away from their original models and evolved their own, entirely French style.

It seems typical of a town whose economy is based largely on having a number of irons in the fire that, if you are so inclined, you can make here two wildly unrelated pilgrimages. Nevers is where they keep the Charollais Stud Book, the Debrett of the race of white beef cattle which constitute by far the most important resource of the farmers of this region. Pig-rearing is secondary to it. Child-rearing remains a flourishing subsidiary in the poor hill country of the Morvan, which does not mean

71

that peasant farmers have large families, but that wet-nursing, which, in the nineteenth century, ranked as a major industry, continues in another form. At a period when it was customary for families of substance to put their children out to nurse — only a few nights ago I was reading Châteaubriand's expressions of affection for the countrywoman who reared him — the Morvan was a nursery for Paris, many of whose citizens spent the first months of their lives there. Occasionally the *nourrices* of the Morvan themselves went to Paris to provide breast milk for infants whose parents did not wish them to leave home. Today it is the *Assistance Publique* of Paris which continues the practice by placing young children committed to its care in carefully selected and supervised foster homes in this region.

The second pilgrimage centre of Nevers is on the same side of the town as the Charollais headquarters. In the chapel of the *Couvent St. Gildard*, far removed in more than space from the holy honky-tonk of Lourdes which, over the past century, has benefited by her visions materially as well as spiritually, Ste. Bernadette, miraculously or otherwise preserved from corruption, lies in a glass tomb rich with gold and enamel and lavishly decorated with birds and flowers. She entered the religious life here in 1867, under the name Sister Marie-Bernard, and died when she was thirty-five.

Down by the river stands a new glass palace, in shining reproach to last night's six young men and a girl, who, it now becomes evident, if they spent their evening in the place de la Gare, did so from choice, not from the lack of any alternative. It is a good example of the *maisons de culture* which were one of the most interesting ventures of post-war France. Monsieur André Malraux, when he was Minister for Cultural Affairs, decided that one way of enlivening the flat calm of the provinces in a country where art, music and theatre, like every other department of life, tended to be centred on Paris, would be to set up a number of cultural centres with directors who would act as regional animators.

The centres vary in size and character — that at Grenoble,

which was opened in the year when France staged the Winter Olympics, is probably the showpiece, but a town as dissimilar as Amiens has a fine one — and, inevitably, their way has not been all roses. Sometimes there has been difficulty in reconciling the aspirations of a director, shared, no doubt, by M. Malraux, with the tastes of citizens who crave for light opera, sometimes in convincing those same citizens that a given director is not a dangerous *gauchiste*, or that, even if he is a Leftist, he may still be an excellent man at his job. But the worthwhileness of the policy may be judged from a glance at the programme which the Nevers *maison* is offering during the current month. There is a production of Giraudoux's *Sodome et Gomorrhe*, a folk evening with Steve Waring, Roger Mason and the Blue Grass Connection, three films in a cycle of *Cinéma Fantastique*, Joseph Rusillo's Ballet and an evening of varieties. This in a town 232 kilometres from Paris, with a population of 41,000. Also the *maison* is open every night of the seven except Monday and it has a café-restaurant with a terrace over the river.

The river is the Loire, the noblest as well as the longest — 1,012 kilometres — and most varied in its course of France. Here, just before it receives the Allier, coming down from the mountains of Auvergne, and leaves the upper part of its course, it is dotted with wooded islets. This was the point, as a tablet on the Tour Goguin nearby records, at which the pilgrims to Santiago de Compostella, who passed through Europe in their thousands, made the crossing. Down the river, when roads were rudimentary, went not only the logs from the forests of the Morvan but virtually all the produce of the area between Roanne and Orleans. The current took barges and lighters down stream at some speed; before the days of steam, battling up against it was such slow, hard going that often the crews preferred to break up their craft after they had unloaded, sell the timbers, then walk home and start again.

Today, below the red granite bridge, a dredger is worrying away at the sandbanks which, in summer, all but block the course of the Loire. Nearer the shore, two men are fishing from

73

perilously small boats with a minimum of freeboard. Both are elderly, both are overweight and dangerously high-coloured; it is likely that neither can swim a stroke. Such a sight, which is repeated all over France where there are a few square metres of water, always impresses me by its contradiction of the general national tendency to avoid anything like athletic excess or physical danger.

If I had a boat, the glittering current would take me, in its own time, downstream to La-Charité-sur-Loire, with its six-teenth-century hump-backed bridge and its great eleventh-century church known as 'the eldest daughter of Cluny'; beyond, it touches the Puisaye, which is Colette's country. There I could make my own pilgrimage to St. Sauveur, to lay a votive ball-point on the doorstep of the house in the rue des Vignes where 'Claudine' spent her childhood. Since I have no prospect of acquiring one, and my road leads in the opposite direction, I leave the Loire in time to lunch off a lamb cutlet and that purest of country pleasures, *fromage blanc*, served in a bowl made of the local earthenware, before catching a train for a town where a sacred monster far different from Colette, though they were contemporaries and acquaintances, spent part of her youth.

7 IT IS THE Goncourt prize-winning novelist,
Édmonde Charles-Roux, who, in an absorbing biography of
Chanel, has recorded that it was at Moulins that the designer
who, more than any other, epitomised the first half of the
twentieth century, took the first tentative steps in her parallel
careers of *grande couturière* and favourite — the archaic word
seems the only one that will fit — of a series of the rich and
notable. She was a gifted little dressmaker, fresh from a convent
orphanage, no conventional beauty but striking in her unorthodox fashion, and already a formidable businesswoman in bud.
Moulins, far from being a soggy provincial centre, was a gay
little garrison town, teeming with aristocratic young cavalry
officers who still wore breeches of *garance*, the vermilion that
went out of the French Army's uniform during the First World
War. The social climate as well as the décor had a hint of light
opera. It would be difficult to imagine a more favourable launching pad, and Chanel was never to look back.

Moulins is still elegant and gay, prosperous as you would

expect of a town set in an area of fat farmland, hiding a variety of industries behind a façade of trees and flower beds and fountains. Heading for the cathedral, pausing on the way to watch a swan oaring gently across a patch of water in the little park, noting that a visiting ballet company is in the town, that an opera company from St. Étienne is doing the *Barber*, and that there is a race meeting next week, I think, not for the first time, what an agreeable life you could lead in many a small French town once you had stopped being bedazzled by Paris. Granted, this small French town — the population of Moulins is little more than 27,000 — had a good start. During the fifteenth century, when the Duchy of Bourbon was at the height of its power, it was the seat of a court of almost royal splendour.

You can see the dignitaries of that court today, kneeling as donors or venerating saints in the windows of the cathedral, but, superb as it is — in particular, there is a wild jay blue that gives a shock of delight — it is not the glass that brings you to this cathedral but the chance of seeing one of the world's great pictures, which hangs in its treasury, the triptych of the Madonna and Child by the Maître de Moulins. Nobody knows certainly who he was, any more than anybody knows certainly who painted that anonymous masterpiece, the Avignon Pietá in the Louvre. All that can be stated beyond question is that he was a Frenchman who worked at Moulins at the end of the fifteenth century, and that Pierre II and Anne de Beaujeu commissioned the picture from him, so ensuring their own immortality.

There they are on either hand of the radiant Virgin and Child, resplendent in gold and purple and jewels that belie the meekness of their attitudes but are as necessary to the opulent colour harmony of the whole as St. Peter's brocaded cloak, or the marvellous reds and greens at the right of the picture, where St. Anne is leading forward the Duchess and her daughter. André and Julien did not come here when they passed through Moulins, any more than they gave a glance at the cathedral windows. Did M. Bruno and his contemporaries believe that aesthetic experience had no part in the education of the laborious classes? It seems possible; when the young travellers finally arrive in Paris the Louvre is dealt with in four lines. André points it out to his brother in passing, saying that it is filled with beautiful pictures by great painters of all countries, and that the public are allowed in every day, but there is no suggestion that they are themselves part of the public. For that matter the boys never even went to look at the Jacquemart when they were at Moulins, though there is a lesson in democracy to be drawn from it, for the great belfry where, every hour, the figures of Jacquemart and his wife Jacquette come out to hammer the bell, once symbolised the civic freedoms of the town. I get to the *place* beneath it for five o'clock and am so diverted that I go round the corner to drink hot chocolate on a café terrace to fill in the time before I can see their children, Jacqueline and Jacquelin, come out to strike the quarters.

This propensity for dawdling threatens to be the ruination of a carefully planned tour. I have been bumbling happily about Central France for days, enjoying myself vastly and covering the minimum of ground. Back in the hotel I decide that tomorrow I must make an effort to get to Clermond Ferrand, with a stop at Vichy en route. It takes some moral fibre, for this hotel, in a totally different way, pleases me almost as much as the one at Nevers, though the attachment is less personal — other people would like this place too. True, at forty-five francs for bed without breakfast, it is more than half again as expensive, but the smiling welcome of the *patronne* was reinforced by that of a silky cocker spaniel, the wallpapers are enchanting, the whole place gleams with cleanliness and the bedroom, from the well-appointed shower room to the abundant blankets, which one has not found everywhere on this trip, is a model of comfort. The crunch will come with dinner: there are some hotels in contemporary France whose response to the tourist influx has been to adopt the bad Anglo-Saxon idea of paying more attention to the interior decoration than to the cooking. This one turns out to speak well for the National Hotel School, whose diploma, a prominently displayed notice tells us, is held by the proprietors.

77

The *table-d'hôte* at seventeen francs fifty centimes offers *crudités*, a choice between those classic bourgeois dishes, an *épaule d'agneau* and a *blanquette de veau*, with a superb spinach *velouté*, a cheese board that includes the local St. Nectaire in perfect condition and an admirable apple tart. Others please copy, starting with a rather pretentious establishment in the heart of the vegetable-growing area of Britanny, where I was once served with peas, *haricots verts* and *fonds d'artichaut*, all out of tins.

Vichy in the morning is like the realm of the Sleeping Beauty before the Prince came. Those shuttered palaces that are not dilapidated, simply petrified, that notice of a concert given last year by 'The Musicians of His Sacred Highness the Prince of Conti, in Court Dress', those curly white chairs set out under dripping planes and chestnuts, those startlingly expensive garments in the windows of the arcades of shops; is it possible that anybody has ever stayed in, listened to, sat on or bought them, or ever will again? A man walks a prancing poodle across the Parc des Sources; in the Parc d'Allier, virtually water meadows where the lawns are silver-sheeted with daisies and speedwell, a woman of a certain age, with a brown dog on a string, trudges along a slightly muddy path. As I pass the service door of one of the palaces on my way back into the town I sense a quiver of life inside, as a finger might locate, then lose again, a flickering pulse. We are coming to the end of Holy Week : can it be that Easter will see the whole of this inconceivably elaborate apparatus for medicated merry-making leap into life?

If it does, there will be another relapse before it gets into its regular swing. Vichy's season, when life is one long gala performance, extends from May to October, and if it depended solely on those who come for the cure it would scarcely run so long. Taking the waters is not what it used to be in France, in which it resembles England, where people have lost their taste for spas, rather than Germany or Italy, where the *curistes* each year are reckoned by the million. Precisely, 3,500,000 in the first and 1,300,000 in the second. For France the figure is about 400,000.

The spas do what they can to attract hale pleasure-seekers as well as *curistes*. Vittel, in the Vosges, has recently seen the installation of a Club Méditerranée, which involved a delicate balancing act to ensure that the holiday-makers did not outrage the regulars or the regulars dismay the holiday-makers, but if it were not for the growing vogue for drinking mineral water rather than tap water it is likely that more than one spa would have gone out of business during the past fifteen years, which, to aggravate the situation, have seen the number of foreigners, coming to get their livers decoked, drop by fifty per cent. Nowadays the business done in treatment at French spas amounts to barely one milliard francs a year : that for the sale of bottled water, which is despatched to all parts of the country, comes to twice as much. Even Vichy, which claims that its waters are sovereign for the liver, the gall bladder, the stomach, for migraine, diabetes and nutritional and digestive troubles, so encompassing half humanity, and which the rich and royal have been patronising since Madame de Sévigné brought her rheumatism here — she said the treatment was a good rehearsal for Purgatory — has put the renovation of its bottling factory before that of one of its bathing establishments. True, it was the second-class establishment.

What is hard to credit as one strolls among these Kubla Khanine prospects is that, today, eight per cent of the clientèle of French spas are insurance patients, the cost of whose treatment and sojourn are paid partly by the *Sécurité Sociale*. One reason for the restrained demand is that its administrators, possibly because of a lingering Jansenism which makes them feel that a course of treatment involving two or three weeks' leisure in pleasant places cannot be really *sérieux*, is niggardly with its allowances. Even if they were generous, it could hardly be insurance patients who would patronise the toyshops of Vichy, with their dolls costing 119 francs and animals made, apparently, of real fur — there is a notably bedworthy seal — or the gift shops stacked with objects in semi-precious stones out of the Book of Revelation, ivory and coral and rose quartz, amethyst and amber, lapiz lazuli, sardine and cornaline. The first must be for rich and doting grandparents who come here for old time's sake, the second for the gala audiences or the competitors in the international regattas held on the artificial lake which has been constructed by damming the Allier.

Both, indirectly, do their bit towards keeping Europe's biggest thermal establishment in business, and there is the export trade also. On the way back to the station I notice that, in addition to being sold by the bottle, Vichy can now be obtained in pastille form, the pastilles containing 'the natural salts extracted from the water'. I notice, too, the most revolting advertisement I have ever seen. It shows a life-sized chef pouring Vichy out of a bottle into a grossly bloated snail, the implication presumably being that, if you over-eat to the point of silting up your innards, a swig of the magic water will enable you to over-eat again in record time. This was the Edwardian attitude to spas, and I find it so rebarbative that I get the train for Clermond Ferrand without having any lunch.

The compartment is already occupied by four women engaged in an apparently absorbing conversation which my entrance does not check.

'And I tell you that it did not always mean that you had spoiled your chances for the rest of your life,' says one of them. 'There was this girl I knew, during the Occupation she was engaged to a Fritz. But when the war was over she married, and married well.'

The others cluck in a manner that suggests resignation rather than outrage, an acceptance that the girl was no doubt very young, and that you can't keep getting wrought up about history for ever.

Clermond, when we get there, is a welcome antidote to Vichy, which has left a cloying taste in my mouth, even without that snail. It is a stern, vigorous town, the perfect capital for its tough, thrifty, austerely beautiful province. If the Auvergnats have earned the reputation of being the Aberdonians of France, working twenty-five hours out of the twenty-four, never spending two *sous* where one will do and descending on Paris, typically to open a café, in even greater numbers than the Scots come south of the border, it is because much of the Auvergne is hill country which, until the coming of modern transport, was isolated and shut in on itself. Today's Auvergnat is more likely to be working for Michelin than growing rye above 1,500 feet, unless he is cultivating one of the phenomenal pockets of fertility in certain valleys, which is the legacy of volcanic action, as is the fantastic lunar landscape of the Puys, but he keeps the stamp of ancestors whose money was too painfully earned to be thrown about.

Clermont itself is the result of volcanic action. The houses of the old town are built of lava, and there is no playful exaggeration about its title of *'la ville noire'*. The low hill which is its centre was once a spouting cone, and the Gothic cathedral crowning it can be thought of as an emanation : it, too, is built of lava. The effect is less gloomy than one might imagine for, besides being irradiated by glorious windows, the interior has an architectural lightness made possible by the immense toughness of the stone.

But, unique in France though it is, one does not come to the Auvergne to see Gothic churches, which they do better in the Ile de France, but Romanesque, a style whose power and inevitability suits both the landscape and the people. The mother of them all, the basilica of Notre Dame du Port, is lower down the hill. I have never yet been to Clermont, either for business or pleasure, without finding a moment to marvel afresh at its East End, where the chapels of the apse buttress the height of the choir and that thrusts up to the massive octagon of the central tower, the whole looking as though it has grown rather than been built, and this is not the time to depart from that custom. The inside is dark and holy, though with the prayerful accretions of the past thousand years or so rather than with the devotions of the present congregation. Clermont Ferrand is getting on for the Midi, and, in the Midi of France today, speaking broadly, people do not go to church, just as in Britanny and Alsace they do. It is almost a fact of geography. So Notre Dame du Port is barely half full for this Maundy Thursday liturgy. No feet washing, but a bishop in cope and mitre drives home verbally the lesson of that ceremony. 'Do not think of a priest in terms of power and dignity and respectability, though it is well that he should be dignified and respectable, but in terms of service.' All irreproachably contemporary, but the architecture exacts its due during the procession to the Altar of Repose, when the *Tantum Ergo* comes rolling out in Gregorian and sonorous Latin. Anything less would wither under those arches.

By the end of the service the windows have dimmed from translucent mosaic to sombrely glowing tapestry, but it is still light outside, so I set off in search of the curiosity of Clermont Ferrand which I have never seen, the petrifying fountains of Saint-Alyre. Like Vichy in this, though otherwise so unlike, Clermont also has its mineral springs, as have so many towns in this area, which contains one-third of all those in France, but they are used mainly for making Seltzer and table water and lemonade. All but the five in the St. Alyre *quartier*, which are used for turning objects into stone. Not your enemies, as in a fairy-tale, but things like carvings, or medals, or a banana, or a bird's nest that you leave in soak and retrieve two months later, rigid and ghastly white and glittering with carbonate of chalk. Or so it says in the guide book.

The street map is clear in my mind, though not in my pocket, and I set off confidently in a north-westerly direction, turning aside to study one shop window displaying endearingly archaic little white collars and lengths of lace — a century ago there were 70,000 lacemakers in the Auvergne and the neighbouring Haute-Loire, but the machines had captured much of their market long before unisex came in — and another filled with wedding groups in which all but one of the brides are wearing hats rather than veils, which seems a gratuitous blow to such lacemakers as remain. The bookshops are good enough to remind one that this is a university town, where publishing flourishes; the posters announce that the live entertainment available this week includes *Look Back in Anger*, *Candida* and Ionescu's *Délire a Deux*.

At what point I wander from my north-westerly bearing I shall never know, but there comes a moment when I find myself walking along a strange and semi-deserted boulevard with no petrifying fountains in sight and the dusk thickening. A few hesitant drops of rain settle into a steady drizzle and I realise that the reason why Clermont Ferrand has always reminded me of Blaenau Ffestiniog, in North Wales, is not only because both are built of the rock on which they stand, respectively lava and slate, but because Blaenau is, reputedly, the wettest place in Britain, and I have never been in Clermont Ferrand when it did not rain.

There is neither bus nor taxi in sight, which is doubly bitter in a town which might claim to have been the birthplace of urban public transport. At least, it was the birthplace of Pascal, one of whose ideas was that of *'carosses à cinq sous'*, carriages keeping to a fixed time, route and fare. Paris's omnibuses were a development from them. Also, Clermont Ferrand makes most of the motor tyres in France, and started making them through British intervention. The Michelin empire grew out of a small firm which made agricultural machinery, one of whose founders, Édouard Daubrée, married a niece of the Charles Mackintosh who invented the waterproof. She had learned from him that rubber would dissolve in benzine, and one day she used her knowledge to make a few balls to amuse the children. The toys had such a success that soon the firm began to manufacture them on a commercial scale. It went on to make rubber tubing and bands, but it was not until the third generation that the firm began to produce the tyres on which the prosperity of modern Clermont was founded.

Now not one of them is going my way, and every step seems to be taking me deeper into the unknown, and farther from any prospect of supper and bed. It is a longing at least to break out of the infernal circle of the boulevard, which seems to be bordering on the open country, that makes me take a random left turning. For the first few blocks things are even worse, then suddenly I emerge into a wide open space which is vaguely

83

familiar, and, more importantly, is peopled. There is a clue in the Catalpas rocking in the rainy gusts: I know that they are planted here because they are said to be the only trees that will survive the danger of petrifaction.

Certain identification comes with the first glimpse of a huge equestrian statue to the left. There is Auvergne's favourite son, raring to take on the whole power of Rome, so this, unmistakably, is the place de Jaude. It is like getting back to a known trade route. The statue, by Bartholdi, gives the illusion that not one of the horse's hooves is touching gross earth, but there must surely be some contact. Suspended in space or not, never did I believe I should be so glad to see Vercingétorix.

8　　IT IS ABSURD to be suffused with happiness
on a wet Good Friday morning in the later twentieth century
because, several hundred years ago, an unknown Japanese embroidered a panel of birds and blossom, but the fact is uncontest-
able. Here, in the almost deserted Musée Historique des Tissus
at Lyon, before a piece which would not even be counted among
the most remarkable in this collection of textiles and tapestries
and embroideries from sixteen centuries, one feels a sudden stab
of ecstasy.

Partly it is cumulative. It is not the birds alone but the coming upon them, simple and joyful, after seeing the hall hung with
Persian rugs, crimson, blue and silver and as supple as silk, and
the scrap of third-century Coptic tapestry, and the cashmere
horseman's cloak from fourteenth-century Iran, and the black
and silver dais used in the procession of the Penitents of Avignon,
and the juxtaposition of gold and ivory, yellow and pale rose
on a deep blue shawl with a rainbow fringe. Partly it is the
exhilaration that comes from the knowledge that this moment

is one of the entirely disparate delights of a day that began in Auvergne early this morning and will end in Provence some time this evening. Already, between the Michelin tyres of Clermond and this showcase for a city which ranks as one of the world's greatest silk markets, I have seen laid out a section of the industrial history of the past 400 years; this afternoon, going down the Rhône Valley, I shall be moving between antiquity and the atomic age.

Last night there was a difficult choice to be made between the two possible routes to Lyon, both taking in St. Étienne. It was tempting to head south for Le Puy, which I do not know, and spend a couple of hours there before going on to Lyon. The decision made itself once I began to think realistically, not optimistically. If I was to be in Arles for Easter, which was the main object of this part of the journey, it was essential that I got as far as Avignon by the end of today's travelling, so there could not be too much lingering on the way. To suppose that, if I got out of a train at Le Puy, I would get into another a couple of hours later was simply moonshine. Besides its setting in a landscape as fantastic as Colorado, Le Puy's attractions range from, at one extreme, a neo-Byzantine cathedral, one of the stages for pilgrims on the road to Compostella, at the other the higher *kitsch* of the gigantic statue of Notre-Dame-de-France, crowning the Rocher Corneille. It was made from 213 cannon taken at the fall of Sebastopol, and tourists so inclined can climb up inside it as far as the Virgin's crown. Even without doing that, it was obvious that I should stay at Le Puy for two days rather than two hours, so, before putting out the light, I decided to take the northward route across the black earth of the Limagne, which is even more fertile than the Fens.

Comparisons between nations are almost always futile because they are based on the generally erroneous idea that difference implies better or worse. Just occasionally it does, as when one sets the limpness of early morning England against the vivacity of early morning France. At seven ten a.m. the café-bar of my hotel, whose breakfast I had decided would be a speedier affair than breakfast served in my room, is brilliantly awake and bustling, the zinc of the counter shining like the glasses on it, the middle-aged waiter swooping between the tables as on roller skates, with his jugs of coffee and hot milk.

'Coffee for Monseigneur!' The customer so addressed does not look even mildly episcopal, and it is a long time since the title was given to eminent laymen.

'Madame! Coffee? How much milk? A croissant — they are hot!' When I leave he rushes the length of the room to open the door.

'*Vous êtes aimable, Monsieur.*'

'I was born like that — *J'ai éte né comme ça!*'

Across the *place* hordes of students are surging out of the station subway on their way to lectures that, in this country, are well under way while scholars in England are still abed. In the train people are reading the regional daily, *la Montagne*, rather than this morning's *Figaro* or last night *Monde* : there is a feeling that life centres on Clermond Ferrand. The nearest seats in the Pullman-type car are occupied by four of those adolescents bigger than either of their parents who are a post-war phenomenon in most of the developed European countries. They are in fact girls, though their outfit of velveteen trousers fitting snugly round the bottom, with a tight, too-short jersey that rides up with every movement to reveal a segment of back or diaphragm, is standard French unisex, and they are schoolgirls rather than students. Probably, at that, pupils of a CES, the *Collèges d'Enseignement Secondaire,* which educate boys and girls from eleven to sixteen years old, not of a lycée; in spite of their size they are still puppyish.

We run out of Clermont between trim little red-roofed houses with gardens; the earth is black, then, briefly, red, then black again. At Thiers, the Sheffield of France, there are houses climbing up the sides of what is a ravine rather than a valley, and a ten-storey concrete block looming over the pretty little station. They have been making knives here since the fifteenth century; by the sixteenth Thiers, whose population even today is less than

18,000, was exporting blades to Spain and Italy, with the current of the Durolle to drive its grindstones. When André and Julien passed through, and spent thirty-five francs on cheap cutlery, which they sold at a profit in the market of Lyon, the bellows that made the flames of the forges leap were powered by a dog toiling in a treadmill. At least the illustration, which shows two other dogs taking their ease, suggests that they worked shifts. Today Thiers makes motor parts and surgical instruments as well as cutlery, but there is a legacy from the medieval craftsmen in the fact that it still has between 600 and 700 manufacturers, small and skilled like the 'little masters' who make machine tools in the Birmingham area.

One of the girls produces a pack of cards and the four begin to play *belote*. This surprises me even more than the recent appearance of toplessness at St. Tropez. French women do not play cards in public places any more than they play *boules*, though now I recall having once seen a woman among the Saturday *boules* regulars in the Luxembourg gardens in Paris. Doing quite well, too. The girls tire of their *belote* rather quickly and begin to talk.

'Who're you like in your family?'

'Nobody. They've all got curly hair except me.' (This wistfully.)

'My Dad's curly. He's dead good-looking, with a quiff in front. He works for Renault.'

One of the four fishes a packet of chewing gum from her pocket and hands it round to the others, hesitates, then offers the packet to me, smiling shyly. This is elegant, because there is only one tablet left. I hope my refusal is as nicely done.

The four begin to collect their possessions preparatory to getting out at St. Étienne. So far we have been running through an area where small manufacturers are pretty well absorbed into the landscape. Noirétable makes knives, like Thiers, though it is only a fraction of the size, and has timberworks, besides the esoteric cottage industry of military embroidery in gold thread (the women who do it are known as *grenadières*, from the badges,

88

or *grenades* which they work) but the impression it leaves is one of new red roofs among trees, and intensely blue hills glimpsed through mist. Now there are spoil heaps, and gas works, and filthy plumes of smoke trailing from works chimneys : this is a coalfield that has been worked since the end of the thirteenth century, though at first in a rudimentary fashion, from quarries rather than mines, and purely for household use.

St. Étienne was a new town a century ago : in many ways it still is. André and Julien were invited to marvel at a place whose population, over the past hundred years, had grown from 6,000 to 146,000, and where, at every visit, a traveller would find that new streets had sprung up. Today's population is 225,000, model suburbs extend in ever-widening circles from the black core of the old town and the amenities include a theatre company of some distinction and one of the most formidable soccer teams in France. Coal alone is not enough to account for growth on this scale; equally important has been the enterprise and inventiveness of the *Stéphanois*, as the inhabitants are known. At a time when the coal industry has run down, probably beyond hope of resurrection, St. Étienne has made the kind of switch, into electronics, machine tools, glass and plastics, which is typical of its long history as a manufacturing centre. Beginning as a steel town it was quick to anticipate the trend and turn from making swords and daggers to making firearms. Under the Revolution it made so many weapons for the new Republic that it got the name of Armeville, but it had also established the manufacture of ribbons and it still supplies eighty per cent of all the ties, scarves and ribbons produced in France, so escaping the ills inherent in being dependent upon a single industry. In 1827 it possessed the first railway in France. Those twenty-one kilometres of track along which wagons of coal were drawn by horses have a naïvely comic sound to us, but three years later the *chaudière tubulaire* developed by Marc Seguin of St. Étienne enabled Stephenson's Rocket to attain the speed of sixty kilometres per hour. Later still in the nineteenth century, the discovery here of the process of de-phosphorising iron ore made possible the development of the iron industry in Lorraine. St. Étienne itself, in the meantime, was already specialising in quality steel and manufactured goods ranging from bicycles to shotguns.

Guidebooks tend to omit the more absorbing half of the story, which is that of the development of the working population along with that of the industry in which it has been engaged for generations. The character as well as the history of a working class élite can be read in what it regards as its battle honours. St. Étienne was to the fore in the strikes which broke out in France during 1917, after three years of unity in the war effort which had maintained industrial peace. They were the civilian counterparts of the mutinies in the Army in May of the same year, after the butchery of the troops who were thrown into an ill-conceived offensive against the Hindenburg Line. There was, traditionally, an element of pacifist internationalism in the French Left : before the outbreak of war it was expressed succinctly by the Socialist spokesman, Gustave Hervé, when he said : 'Our country is our class.'

After three years of all-out production, the workers of 'Armeville', like their comrades in other industrial centres, began to feel that a negotiated peace was preferable to continued killing and downed tools. They were proud of having done so and when, in October 1933, it was announced that the President of the Republic, Albert Lebrun, was to visit St. Étienne to unveil a war memorial they regarded it as provocation and staged a demonstration, in fact two demonstrations, one on the eve, the other on the day, of the President's visit. These followed the standard model of banner-waving parades, fervid oratory and the singing of the 'Internationale'; they would have been no more than a chapter in local history had it not been that St. Étienne, at that time, was entertaining an angel unawares.

From 1931 to 1934 Simone Weil, intellectual, apostle of social justice, perhaps saint, was teaching philosophy at *lycées*, first at Le Puy, later at Roanne, and devoting her leisure to working with and for the trade unionists of St. Étienne. She supervised study groups for them and spent the bonus which was added to her salary because she was an *agrégée* (the approximate British equivalent would be a salary loading for having a First) on buying books for them. On the day of President Lebrun's visit she marched at the head of the miners' parade, carrying a red flag, and was hauled up on to a window sill to expound the functions of the President of the Republic. She went down a pit because she wished 'to penetrate to the heart of the proletariat', she was dismissed from the *lycée* at Le Puy for making herself conspicuous as a militant.

In all this she was, no doubt, frequently ludicrous — only somebody totally lacking in self-consciousness could, for instance, have crowned her earnest, intelligent horse face with a red paper forage cap as she once did at a trade union party at St. Étienne — and her short sight and extreme physical ineptitude made her as great a liability in any demonstration which might end in a quick getaway from the police as she must have been in Spain, when she went there to help the Republicans. There is evidence that few of the workers of St. Étienne understood her. Probably even fewer read the articles she contributed to various journals, in one of which, as early as 1932, she foresaw the rise of Hitler — unlike the majority of Left intellectuals she condemned Stalinism also — and her remarkable books were still to come, but they understood total devotion to a cause, and they could respect, even if they thought the gesture mad, a member of the bourgeoisie who lived on five francs a day, the unemployment pay of the period, and gave the balance of her salary to trade union funds. Uncomprehending, they loved her, and, ten years later, were genuinely moved when they heard that she had died. 'She couldn't have lived,' said one of them. 'She had too much book-learning and she didn't eat.' Her death in England in 1943, at the age of thirty-four, was indeed largely due to the privations which she imposed on herself in an effort to identify with the victims of the concentration camps and other sufferers in Occupied countries.

After St. Étienne it is old industrial mess all the way through

St. Chamond and Gisvors to the flaming chimneys and glittering tower blocks that mark the beginning of Lyon, a beaten-up landscape of terrace houses and scrapyards and works sports grounds that is at once execrable and poignant. The poignancy lies in the small, indomitable gardens, the green still new enough to be sharp viridian against the framing grime. France has nine million gardeners who, between them, work 500,000 hectares. Well over half the country's households have some kind of garden, and, between the leek and potato patch and the rabbit hutch, they produce nearly ten per cent of what they consume, but these vivid particles in the surrounding waste seem to belong to folk art rather than domestic economy, to be the equivalent of those pot and plaster figures that spawn in the neutral and neuter suburbs of French as of other cities. The *Délégation à la Récherche Scientifique* is financing an enquiry into these last; the professor at the École des Beaux Arts who is conducting it has made clear that he is not concerned with aesthetic judgments but with noting the means by which householders try to modify their environment. It is in that way, rather than in terms of leek soup, that I see these cherished gardens.

The taxi-driver at Lyon has never heard of the Musée Historique des Tissus and is more interested in talking about the Presidential election than in listening to my rather tentative directions. He intends to vote for the Gaulliste, Chaban Delmas. Giscard d'Éstaing, he says, is 'not sincere'. Mitterand, the Socialist leader, he finds 'repugnant — oily'. No word of party or policy, any more than there was from a woman in Britanny who told a reporter that she intended to vote for Giscard because, though Chaban was charming, he was 'more like a lover than a husband'. In the interests of getting to the museum with some time left to look at it, I refrain from quoting that to my driver, just as I refrain from questioning his description of M. Mitterand, who may be smooth but is not a trace oily, and finally we locate the turning off the quai Gailleton and he leaves me to the Persian carpets.

I am the only person I know who is romantic about Lyon.

People think of it as the gastronomic capital of France and as a centre for trade fairs. It is true that, in recent years, it has had as many three-star restaurants as Paris, which is nine times as big, and that the one hamburger bar ever opened there lasted only two months, Gresham's Law, for once, going into reverse and good beef driving out bad. My own first visit to Lyon actually was during a trade fair, but even then, for me, the past over-shadowed the present, and I saw the fair as a minor episode in the history of commerce in this city, a history that began not in the early fifteenth century, when the future Charles VII, then Dauphin, instituted the first fairs at Lyon, but 3,500 years earlier, when already the Rhône Valley was the link between the Mediterranean and the north. Tin and amber came up it during the Bronze Age; the Greeks had planted vines on its slopes before Caesar made Lyon his base for the conquest of Gaul; Christianity was introduced from Asia Minor and, towards the end of the second century AD, France's first martyr was slaughtered in the amphitheatre at Lyon; in the eighth century the Arab invaders came up the river valley. In the twentieth they have come again; more than ten per cent of the population of Lyon and its suburbs, and fully seventeen per cent of the working population of the Rhône Alps region, is immigrant, and half of them are from North Africa. Lyon, which can show a parochialism surprising in a town which has, for 3,000 years, been a centre of inter-national trade, has had its quota of attacks on North Africans by gangs of young louts, some spontaneous, some possibly inspired by Right Wing extremist organisations; it has some segregation, moral and material; it has a great deal of the kind of indifference which it is difficult to distinguish from heartlessness.

On another plane it has what seems likely to be the only official public letter-writer in Western Europe, since France's admirable *assistantes sociales* do not qualify for the title, often as they do the job for their elderly fellow countrymen who are defeated by official forms. She is Madame Bernadette Pourtier, who shared one of the awards offered by the *Prix de l'Initiative Féminine* to women who are concerned 'to break down this isolation in which our society is all too liable to imprison us'. Madame Pourtier tried to combat it by opening in the heart of the old city a small office where, every morning, she receives up to a dozen clients, whose problems range from making sense of official documents to getting a letter to the family in far Algeria or remotest Portugal, when one happens to be illiterate. Her fees range from nothing to thirty francs according to what the customer can afford. Her prize brought her 20,000 francs so perhaps she has been able to fulfil her wish of going to Constantinople to see the street of the letter-writers.

All that flickers through my mind like a film as the train passes through the intense concentration of industry south of Lyon, to gather speed down the Rhône Valley where, nowadays, pipelines and gazoducts as well as a motorway carry the riches of the Mediterranean to the north, while, in the autumn, the clustered grapes weigh down the vines on the hill slopes and, in spring, the orchards in the valley bottom, peach and pear and cherry and apricot, foam with blossom. Nowadays, for the greater part of its course from Lyon to the sea, the 'great, wild river' that Châteaubriand knew has been tamed and harnessed in a series of dams and lateral canals which serve for irrigation and navigation as well as generating power. A 'superb canal' filling the two former functions was already promised a century ago, but it was to be sixty years before the promise was entirely fulfilled.

The compartment is packed and heated to suffocation point, but a youth sitting opposite, who is wearing a thick jersey over a shirt open to reveal a solid vest, does not so much as loosen a toggle of the duffle coat that is buttoned over the lot. Across the gangway a baby in a carry-cot is yelling in crimson outrage, as though it is about to explode, while its parents, a pale girl and a young man in jeans and tee-shirt, clearly a student, who has been working on a mathematical problem, set about preparing its feed from a highly evolved vacuum flask, with a bottom as well as a top that unscrews. I think back a long time, to a journey from Paris to Britanny on seats of slatted wood, and

94

another baby asleep in a hammock slung between the luggage racks, whose plump young mother took it down three times before we reached Quimper to give it a breast as pearly as an Etty painting, with the father acting as impresario and the rest of us lost in admiration. Perhaps not all progress is forwards, but at least the leatherette seats are easier on the stern, and the baby takes the bottle like a fix and stops yelling.

I begin to peel an orange, wondering as I do so when last I ate one in a public place, and watch the name of factories alternate with those of noble vintages, nuclear stations with ruined castles perched on heights as romantic as Waverley. When André and Julien made their way down here, on foot, by charabanc and by train, with the mistral at their backs, there were mulberry trees stripped of their leaves on either side of the road, and all through the Rhône Valley and the Dauphine, and even in the Languedoc, you could hear the silkworms champing, provided your mind's ear was sufficiently fanciful as well as sufficiently delicately attuned. They were reared on virtually every farm as a supplementary source of income. Looking after the *magnans*, or worms, like looking after the poultry yard, was a job for farmers' wives and daughters, who are said to have hatched the eggs in their bosoms. Now the *magnans* are in full retreat before the advance of man-made fibres; like the small silkworks, they have a place only at the top end of the trade, where cost is largely irrelevant. Much of the kind of skill in design and colour that one can study in the Musée des Tissus goes today into the production of nylon and its variants.

Around Vienne I become conscious of a gentle cooing. Instinctively I look at the baby, who is deeply, celestially asleep, a starfish hand thrust outside its shawl like that of one of Luini's infants, its face, once so crimson and crumpled, now pink and flawless. But it turns out to be a pigeon which somebody farther down the coach has in a basket under the seat. At Valence a rugger team comes aboard and the pigeon gives up trying to compete, though the baby does not wake. Montélimar, where they make half the nougat of Europe, is grey and sultry;

95

Donzère's station has a fortuitous still life of a clump of white iris against a silver globe marked '*Air Liquide*', which, unforgivably, takes my mind off the gigantic hydro-electric works and the uranium plant at Pierrelatte, which they supply with energy. Then the valley broadens, and the landscape changes to low, parched hills, grazed by sheep and the occasional goats, which seem better suited to them.

I have just come to the conclusion that, as far as I can remember, I never before have eaten an orange in a public place, because when I wanted to they wouldn't let me, and by the time there was nobody to stop me I had grown a full set of inhibitions about things like that, but now I do not give a single damn, when the train slides into Avignon. I wrap up the orange peel neatly in a piece of tissue and drop it into the waste bin before stepping out on to the platform. Liberation is glorious, whether it comes soon or late, but there is no call to be wanton.

9

PROVENCE IS A harlot, a bawd, a bitch, a whore, a drab, a strumpet, a slut, a jade, a Jezebel.

Over Avignon the rain falls like a drop curtain, the rain of the Midi that is so much worse than Lakeland downpours because it is always resented instead of being accepted as a fact of life. Under it the tourists splash to and fro in search of the pleasure which they know, for have they not been told so repeatedly for weeks past, is the reward of taking your car and getting away from home on public holidays. Behind the windows of the cafés along the main street, those who have arrived earlier look out over their drinks with an expression in which there is a touch of bewilderment as well as frustration. They would recognise as brothers those who are conned by the commercial build-up to a secular British Christmas, then suddenly find that The Day is here, that this is all and that it is not enough, that, in truth, it is nothing.

There are no vacancies at the first, the second, the third hotel. The fourth, a not quite dingy two-star, offers an infinitely

97

depressing room which, I feel, has become available only because the client who had booked it dropped dead as he crossed the threshold. The body was bundled down the back stairs ten minutes ago, and now I am being popped into his sheets. There is no food at the bar where I try to get a bite to tide me over until dinner. Every kind of alcoholic beverage known to Western man, also Espresso coffee, but not as much as a hard-boiled egg or a potato crisp. Then, incredibly, the waiter says, 'Only toast', and it comes, with lavish butter and jam and a pot of strong tea.

Restored, I battle up the hill, wind and tide against me, to the Pope's Palace. The guided visits are over for the day, so I cannot refresh my memories of the interior, but there is nothing inside to surpass the exterior, which impresses above all by the sheer mass of the walls and towers, some of which touch 150 feet. They seem even higher and more massive than I remembered, as the façade of the seventeenth-century palace opposite, now the Conservatoire de Musique, seems even more lavishly decorated. The rain is lashing still, but in the gardens on the crest of the Rocher des Doms, where snowy Aylesbury ducks are circling in the little pool, it is more tolerable than when it is bouncing off the pavements of the lower town, and, though the valley below is as soggy as a sponge, nothing can ruin the view of the smooth curve of the river and the four arches of the old bridge of St. Benezet, the *pont d'Avignon* of the song, which juts out of the walls to span it, then breaks off in mid-stream.

If there had been no Revolution, would the spot where I am now standing be French territory? The Avignon Papacy lasted only from 1309 to 1378, but, during that period, Clement VI bought the city from Jeanne I, Countess of Provence and Queen of Naples. To the price of 8,000 ducats, the pope added absolution for the queen's alleged part in the murder of her husband. Avignon remained the property of the Church until 1791, though Provence had been re-united with France 300 years earlier. It is an academic question, and by the time I have trudged down the hill again, and penetrated the wall of rain beyond the ramparts to eat an omelette at the station buffet, I feel that the Papacy was welcome to have kept the place. The buffet is packed with sodden customers who, if they are not getting dejectedly drunk, seem to be in a collective coma. It is proper to this sinister day that the light in my hotel room is so placed and powered that it is impossible to read oneself out of the encircling gloom. I try to think of how much worse things were for the young Châteaubriand, condemned to sleep in that Stygian room in the deserted donjon of the Château of Combray, in the spirit that made me, when I had to go to the dentist in childhood, try to keep my mind on Nelson having his arm amputated without anaesthetic, but it does no good. Nelson and Châteaubriand have both been dead a long time, and this is now.

Afterwards, the night falls into place as the ideal, the antipodean prelude to what was to come, the taste of aloes that sweetens the honey, the dark against which was to be projected the dazzling set-piece of Arles. Wedged in the corridor of the train in the morning, watching the sky clear and the sun come through, it is impossible to believe in that absolute of misery. Euphoria sets in the moment I have dumped my bags in a locker and started up the normally rather dreary avenue Talabat leading from the station. It is not yet eleven o'clock, but the three-day Easter Feria starts almost with the light on Holy Saturday, and already the town is reeling with noise and crammed with young people as though for a pop festival. The *abrivado* or running of the bulls through the streets, is only just over; the protective barriers are still up along the pavement edges and the crowds have not all dispersed, but already the focus has shifted temporarily from the bulls to the *penas* which are an equally essential part of the fête. Perhaps their nearest British equivalents are the bazooka bands that proliferated in the thirties. True, the brass and percussion of the *penas,* which seem to play almost continuously for the seventy-two hours of the Feria, produce vastly more sophisticated music, but there is a similar emphasis on costumes and parading. The four here are in boaters and sombreros and peaked scarlet caps, in orange jackets, and black flowered shirts, and jerseys as brilliant as racing silks. The group in strict brown blazers has a leader in a topper and a flaunting velvet cloak. They march and counter-march; they erupt into bars and cafés; they animate the dances that start up in the squares; at intervals a few of their members break into a fandango.

I stroll on through the town centre, mildly exercised about finding a bed for the next three nights, but determined to stay until Tuesday morning even if it means sleeping in the lee of a tomb in the Alyscamps, the surviving fragment of what must have been the most idyllic of necropolises. Blanks at the two first hotels I try, at the third the offer of a ground-floor room with windows opening on to the street. Perhaps not for a fête which promises to become as orgiastic as Killorglin Puck Fair . . . Irresponsible rather than desperate I try the four-star Jules César in the Lices, and, while doing so, am reminded of the social changes which have overtaken France during the past ten or fifteen years. It is full of people looking as unstudied as to dress as I do myself. Before the era of dressing down for leisure they would have been defeatingly elegant, and the management, most probably, nothing like so sincerely *désolé* at not having a corner for me. Finally I run down a large, light double room in a friendly little hotel near the place du Forum, which delights me because it is at the seething centre of events, and go back to the station to collect my bags. Astonishingly, there is a waiting taxi, whose driver, as we move off, says to a hairy brown dog who is loitering in the *place* 'I'll be back soon, *mon vieux*. It's chicken today.'

'Yours?' I ask.

'He belongs to all us *chauffeurs*,' says the driver. 'He was abandoned. When we adopted him he was so thin he could hardly stay on his legs. Look at him now! He sleeps in the telephone kiosk and barks when it rings to let us know there's a customer.'

By now the pavements are dry and the weather obviously at *beau fixe*, but when I decide to risk a table on the first-floor balcony of a restaurant on the boulevard des Lices so as to be able to watch the fun below over lunch, the mistral drives me indoors before the first course has arrived. The service has an oriental timelessness, but it is the soul of amiability and the food is delectable — a fish soup, not a *bouillabaisse* but a *bourride*, with a spoonful of *rouille* stirred into it, and *moules farcies* odorous with garlic, a roast saddle of young hare, with a very English baked potato, and an orange to finish. Afterwards there is all the long, bright afternoon to drift about the streets, rudderless as plankton in the crowd that is now even thicker than it was this morning. At every other corner there are sausages grilling over charcoal fires; the smell of frying mingles with that of burnt sugar from the toffee apple sellers; the streets round the Arena have been transformed into a cross between a bazaar and a caravanserai, the self-generated habitat of that nomadic population which, directed by some inner rhythm, moves between Amsterdam and the Ile de la Cité, Glastonbury and Katmandu, Piccadilly and the Spanish Steps and the place de la Grenette at Grenoble.

To step out of the babel into the Cloister of St. Trophime is to be lapped in peace; the quiet is like well water in the heat of midday. Two sides of the cloister are twelfth-century Romanesque, one is of thirteenth- and one of fourteenth-century Gothic, with endlessly varied carvings on the pillars and capitals. The whole is roofed by a delicately blue sky, with the tower of the church thrusting up against it at one corner. St. Trophime itself, high and grey and stern, has a twelfth-century portal of the Last Judgment facing on to the place de la République, which is one of the most remarkable things in Arles. Once, exploring the church, I went down alone into the crypt, which is infinitely ancient, and shadowy, and so convoluted that, after a twist or two, it is easy to imagine that you have lost your direction and will never find your way out. Only afterwards did I realise that, despite a dislike of the dark in enclosed spaces, I had not had a moment's unease. Perhaps that, rather than the smell of hassocks and the end papers of morocco prayer books, is what they mean by the odour of sanctity.

One would have thought that St. Trophime must be the inevitable church for tonight's Easter Vigil, but it turns out to be in the heart of pagan Arles, at Notre-Dame de la Majeur, the church on the high ground overlooking the Arena. The priest kindles the new fire to light the Easter candle with pieces of orange box that flare uncertainly in an enamel washing-up bowl, with a smell like the cooking fires below. At the head of the steps leading down from the terrace before the West Door an elderly Arab in dark robes sits impassive as an image. The sky is drenched with stars and when the rather sparse congregation emerge their breath goes before them in white puffs of vapour. The whole town is as high as a kite, with gaiety as much as with wine, and the circulating police, rather untypically, are caught up in the carnival, seeming to be about equally concerned with avoiding having to make any arrests and with ensuring that none of those who are already ecstatically incapable come to any harm. I fall asleep to the moan and scream and shudder of sax and trumpet and drums in the band at the ball in the place du Forum, just outside my window, and wake to hear the *penas* at it again. Has the noise ever stopped, one wonders, as everybody crowds down once more to the boulevard des Lices, where another *abrivado* is scheduled. In the event we get no bulls, only the ride past of the *gardians,* or cowboys of the Camargue, who, after a long wait, clatter by in a huddled bunch on their unexpectedly small horses, riding with the unstylish ease that marks those whose working lives are spent in the saddle. There is one young woman in the group. Sister, daughter, sweetheart, or can she be a *gardianne*? There seems to be nothing exceptional about the sight as she provokes no cat-calls or wolf whistles.

In the afternoon I go up to the ramparts, from which you look down on the tiled rooftops of Arles that are every colour from pale straw to rusty crimson, like a bed of nasturtiums. Beyond them, looking south, a waste of grey-green lit by the mercury gleam of its lakes, is the Camargue, that delta of salt marsh and lagoons clipped by the arms of the Rhône, where the bulls are bred, and the white horses roam in half-wild herds, and the rose flamingoes are only one among more than 300 species or sub-species of birds that have been recorded in the botanical and zoological reserve that takes up almost one-third of the total area of 72,000 hectares. At closer range one would see that the grey-green is not uniform : it is relieved by the jade of the occasional patches of young corn, and, more often, by the sharp green of the rice fields — rice was introduced midway through the Second World War, and now ninety per cent of France's domestic consumption is grown down there — where, every year, young partridges are drowned because they seem unable to believe that so vivid a surface is not solid. Unhappily, one would see also some regrettable building development, and the white horses meekly saddled to take tourists for promenades, and the tide of candy-floss, actual and metaphorical, that laps at the walls of the twelfth-century fortress church of Saintes-Maries-de-la-Mer, the centre of the gypsies' twice-yearly pilgrimage.

Neither can you see from here the detail of Fos-sur-Mer, France's bid for a place in the industrial sun of the twenty-first century, which, by the time the year 2000 comes, will quite probably have destroyed the Camargue, and a good deal of Provence with it. 'Making a Ruhr in the Mediterranean' was the declared aim of the planners who, in 1966, started work on the largest industrial building site in Europe, thirty miles west of Marseille. Fos, connected by a canal with the *Étang de Berre* which already had four oil refineries on its shores, was conceived as a man-made deep-sea port, capable of taking the one million ton tankers of the future. It was to serve as a vast new industrial complex whose centre would be a steel works built by the old-established, family-owned firm, Wendel-Sidelor of Lorraine, whose chief rivals, Usinor, were already doing well with a new seaside works at Dunkirk. Fos was to be its southern counterpart, and, more importantly, the Mediterranean end of the famous 'Rhône-Rhine axis', which, once the canal system linking the two rivers has been completed, will enormously extend the Mediterranean's markets in the continent of Europe.

The gap between intention and execution being what it often is, perhaps the most remarkable feature of so gigantic a project was that the first stage of the work should have been completed more or less on time. That the cost of setting up the steel works should have so greatly exceeded the first estimate that finally the two rivals, Wendel-Sidelor and Usinor, found themselves, like the lion and the lamb, lying down together at Fos (and even then the great German steel firm, Thyssen, had to be invited to take a share before the financial requirements could be met) was a commonplace of ambitious development schemes. That the horde of building workers, seventy per cent of them immigrants, legal or illegal, Algerians, Portuguese, Spanish, Turkish, who did the preliminary construction, should for the most part have been housed in what was described as Europe's biggest *bidonville*, or shanty town, was a situation for which there is ample precedent. Europe's post-war Industrial Revolution is largely the work of its itinerant army of immigrant workers, the majority unskilled and as expendable and exploitable, though better paid, than their ancestors who built the Pyramids.

The permanent consequences will outlast the *bidonvilles*. Originally the small town of Fos had a population of 3,000: the expectation for the end of the century is that 200,000 jobs will have been created in the new industrial zone and that the region of the *Étang de Berre* will have a population of 500,000 to 600,000. Where, today, there are about 160,000 people scattered in small Provençal villages, tomorrow there will be a million in what is described as 'a very loose urban network', which will join Arles to Marseille. Arles itself will be in commuter country, a Meridional Surrey township, with all that implies.

The Camargue is fifteen miles from Fos as pollution drifts, and cheek by jowl with the new tourist development at Port Camargue and La Grande Motte, as the blocks of holiday flats rise. The industrialists involved in Fos have set up an association to study pollution, the steel works, Solmar, has devoted 530 million of a total investment of 7.4 thousand million francs to preventing it. Meanwhile ecologists claim that already shellfish are dying in the *Étang de Berre*. It has been established that the south-east wind carries spray from Fos up the Rhône Valley as far as Montélimar, and, however excellent the intentions of the current Minister for the Environment, one would have to be naïve indeed to suppose that, in France any more than elsewhere, he would be allowed to stand in the way of 'profitable' development.

I give it up and turn my eyes from the distance to the great elipse of the Arena close by. The Romans thought spaciously; it was built to seat more than 20,000. Round its top storey today there is a frieze of figures outlined against the sky. As I look, the amphitheatre suddenly roars like an angry beast, savage and threatening. The second of the afternoons of bullfighting that are part of the Feria is warming up. There is a widely prevalent Anglo-Saxon fiction that the kind of bullfighting met with in France is not the *mise à mort* but a harmless affair of snatching a cockade from the brow of the bull while avoiding its horns. True, Provençal bullfighting is bloodless, and the black bulls of the Camargue are not bred to be killed but to provide the sport in the so-called *courses à la cocarde*, when local amateurs enter the ring to match their agility against that of the bull and, since the game is not as amateur as all that, to compete for money prizes offered to the man who first snatches the ribbon. But in Arles, Nîmes and other cities of Provence, as of the Basque country, there are every season *mise à mort corridas*, for which the bulls, and most of the *toreros* also, are imported from Spain. Patrons are not lacking, and the style and skill of the toreros are treated to the kind of academic criticism that might be accorded to a performance of the last Beethoven quartets, not in local newspapers only but occasionally in the nationals. I learn later that six bulls were killed this afternoon.

Even in the Provençal fights, do the bulls have as much fun

as the *razeteurs*, the young men who get their name from the *razet*, or running half circle, which they describe in their efforts to snatch the *cocarde*? I remember that question posing itself acutely one night at Guéthary, on the Atlantic coast, when we sat out under flowered skies to watch an otherwise fairly inoffensive display in a floodlit arena. The final item was the releases into the ring of a terrified cow with a cracker tied to its tail. We are spared that in this evening's *course* on the place de la Croisière down in the town, where, to even things up, a number of the *razeteurs* are well pummelled if not gored and some of the bulls leap the barriers into the crowd and have to be lassoed by *gardians*. I missed that by having gone to a *flamenco* spectacle at the Municipal Theatre. I knew I had guessed wrong at first sight of the size of the audience. Most of Arles, quite rightly, had decided that there was more fun to be had in the streets, for no entry fees. The *flamenco* was less than electrifying and the most engaging part of the evening was the sight of small gypsy children in the most resplendent of best clothes watching their kinsmen performing on stage.

10

IN THE MORNING the rain is pelting, but what decides me to spend the day out of town is not the weather but the knowledge that a third successive instalment of total Feria is more than I can take. Normally Marseille on a public holiday is no more a place you would choose for retreat than is Naples, to which, in spirit, it is so close, but all things are relative. With no bands playing and no sausages frying, only ice-cream kiosks and the exotic bouquets of shellfish, including the curious clusters of *violettes*, laid out on stalls in the side turnings of the Canebière, which, cutting straight through the town to the Vieux Port, still its heart though no longer its commercial centre, is the most stimulating main street in Europe, Marseille seems as calm as a cloister.

Already the sky is washed clean : the first thing I see against it down on the quai des Belges is a clump of balloons, scarlet, orange, blue and lemon yellow, with one sharp green and one Pompadour pink, tugging like trout at the string held by a woman seller who looks as though she may take off at any moment. Nearer the ground a little girl is trying to catch the bubbles she is blowing through a small wire frame dipped in suds, ecstasy dawning, and dying, and being born again on her face as the iridescent globes float and vanish between her fingers, then swell to drift again.

On either side of the plaque set in the paving that commemorates the founding of this city 600 years before Christ, by Greek colonists from Phocea, in Ionia, who made it a thriving trading post, their spiritual descendants are doing business, peanut sellers, and Africans kneeling behind their displays of beads and carvings, old men holding out whirring bunches of plastic windmills. This is not France, it is the archetypal seaport, which means that it is a racial *entrepôt*. If you drew a chalk circle with a radius of fifty metres from this spot you would enclose a dozen nationalities, and only the Japanese would seem foreign. Logically this should be the last city in Christendom to encourage any kind of racial consciousness, let alone prejudice, but race riots have flared here during the past few years. Perhaps the attitudes conducive to them were imposed early upon a society which should have fostered tolerance. When André and Julien came here, and had the good luck to be shown over a packet boat, they noticed that most of the menial jobs on board were done by yellow or black men, and the 'instructive print' in M. Bruno's book, depicting a white man in Sunday blacks, with collar and tie, a red man wearing beads and a feather, a yellow man with a pigtail and drooping moustaches and a wide-eyed black man dressed in what looks like a short-sleeved cotta, is still included in an impression dated 1972, complete with a caption beginning: 'The white race, the most perfect of the human races . . .'

In 1870 the packet boat which the brothers visited might have been in the *Vieux Port* itself. Nowadays there are only yachts and fishing boats, bouncing in a fair lop, to watch from the terrace of a restaurant where citizens making the most of the holiday are eating enormous slabs of beef cut off the bone, with the marrow quivering on top. There must be nearly a pound for each person. Not normally over-puritanical, I am oppressed by the excess, wondering who will get the meaty bones, while the Third World, and wartime ration cards, and all the poor little children who would have been glad of it from one's earliest years pass through my mind in an accusatory pageant. The fact that I am not myself eating steak makes things no better.

The lunchers are still there, comatose over their *pousse café*, the cognac that sends what has gone before on its way, and looking safe to stay where they are until at least four o'clock, when I set off to walk up the hill to Notre Dame de la Garde, the basilica that marks the southern arm of the bay. Not for the church itself; it is nineteenth-century Byzantine-Romanesque and the aesthetic equivalent of a good deal of Victorian Gothic, though my own lurking taste for tinsel is pleased by the silver glitter of mosaic inside, but because the limestone peak on which it stands is the most remarkable watchtower on this part of the coast. In the Middle Ages it was a signal hill from which, when a doubtful vessel was sighted, warning was given with fire by night, smoke by day. It remains a landmark for sailors, but best of all it is a superb vantage point from which to survey the coast. Tomorrow I must leave Provence for Languedoc, but, perversely, I long to turn eastward along the coast to Bandol, with its domestic set-piece of church, and vegetable market and small, purling fountain, and St. Clair, beyond Le Lavandou, where you swim in deep water off hard sand, with the red hills of the Maures behind, and come up out of the sea to eat *salade niçoise* whose components have been grown in the garden behind the small restaurant, with a *loup* caught that morning in the sea in front of it and grilled with fennel over a wood fire. This is mere idleness of spirit, of the kind that made Julien want to go sightseeing in Bourges when the good Jurassian pedlar with whom the boys were travelling was heading for the Allier. Anyway, the tomatoes wouldn't yet be ripe for a *niçoise*. I pull myself together and head downhill to have a final stroll through the seething centre of Marseille before catching my train.

Legend says it was Lazarus who converted this city to Christianity, and it seems likely enough. Only somebody who had risen from the dead would have had the audacity to attempt such a task.

I get a corner for the journey back to Arles and am able to read in comfort the *Midi Libre*'s account of the happenings at Castelnau-de-Guers, near Pezénas, on Good Friday, when, at the mass of the Pre-Sanctified in the evening, the *curé* and his congregation saw the face of Christ outlined on the ciborium which had been placed on the altar of repose. Well, strictly, the *curé* saw it first and cried: 'Look!'; and, upon looking, quite a number of his congregation saw it too. Now one or two of the older and simpler residents of Castelnau are reported to be wondering if the vision heralded the end of the world. The *curé*, who is an *intégriste*, one of the hard-liners who stand fast against the present movement for liturgical reform, thinks the vision was a warning against the 'continuing desacralisation of the Catholic Church by questioning not only the rite but certain immutable dogmas', and even the local *gendarmes*, a secular body if ever there was one, who have conducted their own un-official but thorough investigation, because nothing that takes place at Castelnau is outside their province, seem convinced that 'something extraordinary really happened'. Only the diocesan authorities are showing that slightly uncomfortable reserve that is the Church's standard initial reaction to anything like a miracle. Meantime, on Easter Sunday, Castelnau had such a congregation as it has not known in years.

Back in Arles the Feria is still raging, but there are signs that, at last, the batteries are running down. It is drizzling and some of the bars are running out of food, though not drink. By morning the delirium has passed leaving not a wrack behind. Only six huge young Germans and me, all hollow-eyed after seventy-two hours of carnival, remain to sit late over breakfast. The Germans manage to spread apricot jam on their *croissants* in mid-air because, as is common in small hotels, we have no plates, without dribbling it on to the cloth. I chicken and take my cup out of the saucer, using that as a plate. Outside, the sunshine is laced with steel: the taxi-driver says it is the mistral out of season, then adds that, since 1965, there have not really been any seasons, just weather. He does not explain why 1965 was the turning point: if this was Paris one would have expected him to date the change from 1968, the year of *'les événements'*, as the citizens, on the analogy of 'the Troubles' in Ireland, decided to call the students' rebellion which turned their world upside down, however briefly. Seasonal or not, it is so cold that I am glad to be getting out of the Rhône Valley, which serves as a funnel for that cruel wind, strong enough here to rough up the river into whitecaps. At Sète, where I mean to spend the night, it will be less concentrated even if the uplands of the garrigues behind are not high enough to be an entirely effective windbreak.

The garrigues make up that strip of limestone plateaux, bare and bright and arid and spiced with aromatic shrubs, that divide the Languedoc into two countries. To the north are the mountains of the Cévennes, their slopes mantled with chestnuts up to nearly 2,000 feet, to the south the coastal plain where the green sea of vines meets the chain of salt lagoons that border the blue sea of the Mediterranean. Their vegetation, thyme and lavender, broom and thistle and stunted trees, ilex and olive and stone pine, is that of the Corsican *maquis*, but the latter growth, based on silicate rock, is a matted carpet; here the vegetation thrives only in the occasional pockets of soil. The rest is a radiant wilderness, where you half expect to meet a Desert Father, though sheep are more likely.

To speak of the Languedoc, still more of Occitania, is to raise the question whether, today, it has any real continuing existence. On the map, certainly, there is an area known as the Languedoc-Roussillon, a coastal strip stretching from the Rhône to the Pyrénées and extending inland to the Department of the Lozère, which represents less an organic unity than the result of a mixed marriage arranged by the government in the cause of drawing the boundaries of France's new regions. When historians speak of the Languedoc they are not referring to this administrative area but to the feudal territories of the Midi, consisting largely of the possessions of the Counts of Toulouse, which were not united to the Crown of France until 1271. Since the division was a language line based on a variant of the Gallo-Roman dialects from which French has developed — in the north the word for 'yes' was 'oïl', in the south it was 'oc' — it could not have the precision of a political frontier. Approximately, the boundary started at the Gironde estuary and curved north through Angoulême, Guéret and Vichy before dropping south to reach the Italian frontier by way of St. Étienne and Valence. When local patriots today speak of Occitania they mean all areas where there is some knowledge of one of the many dialects of the old language which survive as *patois*, and the central authorities suspect nervously that they imply a concept which can be the inspiration of a separatist movement and an excuse for militancy. They may not be so wide of the mark : I learn later that, while I was on the coastal plain of the Bas Languedoc, a disused viaduct near Millau, in the Aveyron, was damaged by a charge of dynamite, and that the sabotage was claimed by a hitherto unknown group calling themselves the 'Red Brigade of Occitania', who were protesting against the proposed extension of the Army camp on the plateau of Larzac. Without dynamite, other 'Occitanians' had already taken part in the considerable opposition to the extension, which would mean the expropriation of farmland. The 'Red Brigade' claimed that, if the proposal were carried out, the viaduct would be put into service again.

One does not need to have a phobia about Reds to be aware that *gauchiste*s who know their job — and in France the signs are that most of them do — will be quick to capitalise any local grievance, whether it is unemployment in Britanny or the animosity of the have-nots against the haves stirred up by a sordid murder in the mining belt of the *Nord*, but, even without political stimulation from outside, the Languedoc, beautiful, tragic, passionate, with a past at once golden and blood-soaked, is a country which seems as much predestined for martyrdom and dreams of nationalism as Ireland, and more so than Wales or Scotland.

There was a civilisation here when the north was a rabble of warring barbarians; it survived the Dark Ages and the successive waves of invasion by Vandals, and Visigoths and Saracens. West of the Rhône, Gaul was profoundly Romanised, at a domestic as well as an administrative and religious level. Pensioned off legionaries in large numbers, when they hung up their shields, settled on farms in the wine plains. The Midi led France when she emerged from the Dark Ages in the eleventh century; in the twelfth, the Court of Toulouse, the capital of the Languedoc, was one of the most magnificent as well as one of the most brilliant of Europe, and was reflected in the courts of lesser feudal princes in the south. The destruction of that civilisation at its peak had the inevitability of classical tragedy. While the troubadours were hymning courtly love, the religion of the Cathars was introduced into the Languedoc from the Balkans, and a sophisticated culture embraced its harsh asceticism eagerly. A Church which had waxed fat with power and wealth reacted first with a species of counter-Reformation, led by St. Dominic. His preaching inspired the converted, but the heresy continued to flourish. Pope Innocent III went further by launching a crusade for the extirpation of Cathar heretics who were 'worse than pagans'. The crusaders, Germans, Flemings, Northern French, hot for loot and salvation, swarmed down from the north like a new wave of barbarians. In the Midi, after seven and a half centuries, they have left a record of a series of sickening massacres and a folk memory like that of the Black and Tans in Ireland.

The crusade ended in 1229, with the Treaty of Paris, which united the Languedoc to France. The massacres were continued by the Inquisition which followed, which went on with its hideous work until the end of the century. It destroyed the Cathars. Who shall say how much it did also to prepare the Languedoc to receive the doctrine of the Protestants when the Reformation swept it in the sixteenth century.

That is the lurid backdrop to what critics of the Occitanian movement are fond of calling the 'folklore' of Languedoc. The language can hardly be treated so dismissively. How many of the twelve million inhabitants of the old Languedoc speak it today is not easy to determine, since estimates vary with the sympathies of the assessor, but probably less than two million have it as a first language, though far more will have some knowledge of one of its dialects. Against that, Toulouse, since 1945, has had an Institute of Occitanian Studies, and, since 1970, the *langue d'Oc* has been an option for the *baccalauréat* and can be taught in *lycées* where ten pupils ask for it. Echo of Bishop Morgan's translation of the Bible, which saved the Welsh language from degenerating into a babble of impoverished dialects, an oecumenical translation of the Scriptures in the *langue d'Oc* is in progress, an event which is likely to have more influence today, when the Catholic Church is preaching the value of Bible reading, than it would have had twenty-five years ago. Meanwhile, militants combating capitalism as well as those opposing the intense centralisation of French administration, which can make the remoter regions indeed feel that they are being colonised from Paris, are quick to seize it as a weapon. Less consciously, as is happening with other minority languages, in France and elsewhere, there seems to be among young people — perhaps one should qualify that by saying more or less intellectual young people — signs of a revived interest in the tongue which was the first if not the only language of their grandparents, and which, only a few years ago, they would have despised as an uneducated *patois*. Is this a phenomenon like that nostalgia for the cosiness of working class culture that Richard Hoggart noted nearly twenty years ago, or is it, more fundamentally, part of an urgent search for identity in a society which its members feel to be unstructured and out of control? One leans to the second idea; language, and, almost as vitally, landscape, urban or rural, is an essential factor for the nurture of identity.

The landscape through which the train for Sète passes once it has left behind Nîmes, where the view from the window is not of the Roman arena, more perfect than that of Arles, if less large, or the miniature temple, Greek in feeling though Roman in execution, known as the *Maison Carrée* which stands in the centre of the town, but high, narrow apartment blocks, and the scrubby hills around Montpellier, is the featureless steppe of the vineyards. A glitter of light to the south indicates the lagoons. The railway here follows the road by which Hercules walked west to find the apples of the Hesperides. After him Hannibal and his elephants came east along it, and after him the legions, measuring off the leagues as they marched to the next billet along what was then the Via Domita. For generations the area, suffering most of the disabilities which result from being tied virtually to a single industry, has been known as a region that exported coarse wine and minor civil servants. All through the present century the growers have revolted intermittently against falling prices and unfair competition, sensationally in 1907, when Clemenceau sent in the Army to quell them, and the men, mostly young conscripts from the region, refused to fire on their relatives. Falling prices and unfair competition are still the causes of unrest; a recent demonstration was provoked by the import of Italian wine. Basically the trouble is over-production, but how can the growers be expected to go for quality when the price structure makes it more profitable to produce an ocean of plonk.

For the past fifteen years or so there has been an attempt at diversification by the development of the coast for the tourist trade. First the mosquitoes were liquidated, then modern holiday resorts were built from scratch on these lost, sun-soaked beaches, which, not so long since, were visited only by the enterprising and discerning. Now the August crowds are thronging.

Will the transformation be of lasting benefit to the Languedoc or will its people feel only the more colonised when they learn, for instance, that, at one of the new resorts, the casino is owned and run by Japanese, who see a promising investment in the leisure industry?

11   Sète praise be, has escaped all that by
having been planned and exploited 300 years earlier. It can only
be a question of time before the syllabus for environmental studies
in one or more of the new university centres includes in its obligatory fieldwork an examination of the comparative results of development when the developers were mandarins providing for an
age of leisure, with the help of property tycoons, and when they
were Colbert and Louis XIV, working for a utilitarian end, with
the help of an engineer of genius like Paul Riquet.

Henry IV had the idea, never fulfilled, of linking the Atlantic
to the Mediterranean by a canal, and he envisaged that its south-
eastern outlet would be at Sète which, at that time, was no more
than a fishing village on an island in the lagoon of Thau. The
Romans had thought of it before him, but it was not until 1666
that the idea was acted on by Colbert, who, according to my
private heresy, was the best thing that ever happened to France,
as Napoleon was the worst. The job was entrusted to Riquet,
born at Béziers, where he had been ruminating over the problem

116

for the previous eighteen years. It took another fourteen to complete the work, which involved raising the canal over the 194-metre watershed of Naurouze, near Castelnaudary. Riquet died bankrupt six months before the canal was opened : he had put into the enterprise the 3,000 *livres* which he possessed and another 2,000 which he did not. It was only in 1725, forty-five years later, that his descendants finished paying off the deficit and began to profit from his achievement. The glory remains, even though, as a waterway, the Canal du Midi is inadequate for today's traffic.

Things went better with the town of Sète. While Riquet was driving a canal from the Thau basin to the sea, and constructing jetties to protect the outer harbour, Louis XIV encouraged the growth of the town by exempting from toll all persons who built houses and 'sold and retailed all kinds of merchandise'. The place got off on the right foot as an organic community, where trade and commerce and pleasant living all had their rights, and throughout its steady growth it has kept that character. There are not so many towns where you come out of the railway station to see an ocean-going ship discharging at the bottom of the road, and, beyond, narrower canals crammed with smaller craft, their hulls painted in Bakst blues and emeralds, with one crashing sunflower yellow, in an ecstatic dissonance of colour. Modest their scale may be if your standards are set by Venice or Amsterdam, but this waterborne town has a feature that either might envy. At its western side it rises out of the coastal plain to climb the flank of the 175-metre Mont St. Clair, a limestone crag that provides a corniche walk as well as an ethereal panorama.

Between the visual euphoria and the sudden warmth of the sun, I turn into the first hotel on the right in the happy certainty that 'all manner of thing shall be well' and indeed, not only is it remarkably cheap as well as clean and calm and abundantly roomy, but there is also an uncovenanted blessing in a notice in the foyer which reads, 'Travellers will found by employes the best welcome we prayed them to ask all they could desire and it will be done the best to please them'. If the syntax is shaky, the heart is true. The dining room also, it later turns out.

I was right about the mistral, but if one gets under the lee of something solid it is warm enough to sit and read in the sun on the sands below Mont St. Clair, though two little German girls who have been splashing bravely in the diamond-faceted sea admit through bluish lips that it is *'ein bischen kalt'*. They are part of the advance guard of holidaymakers who are sprinkled surprisingly thickly along the promenade when I have a lazy lunch on the terrace of a restaurant. Northerners all, only the Germans, and the British, and the Dutch and the Scandinavians would treat this April glitter like summer, exposing unaccustomed necks and arms to be turned puce as much by wind as sun, parading the kind of floral dresses which suggest that the women who choose them are their own worst enemies. It would be so much better, for instance, if that amply-fashioned woman of a certain age who is passing at the moment had not decided to go bare-legged. But better for who — whom? She is manifestly happy, with a touching middle-aged innocence, in the feel of sun and breeze on her rather doughy calves, and if one is dealing in aesthetic absolutes one might equally well say that it would be better if I was not wearing, or rather, toting around, a venerable anorak, its dark blue exterior and crimson interior alike stained and faded with the sun and snow and salt and showers of mountain and seaside holidays unnumbered, but it is the most useful garment I own, serving as rug and cushion and, by virtue of its large zipped pocket, wallet and lunch bag as well as windbreaker.

The middle-aged woman is German. For the moment the only English in sight are a party established at a table against the wall, the not very young parents of two small children, one a toddler in a folding high chair which they have brought with them, the other perhaps three or four years old. The voices are what used to be called upper class but the menu appears to be causing them as much dismay as that experienced by an Eastern peasant faced for the first time with a cereal other than rice. It is a question of finding something that the children can/will eat. One would hardly have thought it could be so difficult : the choice includes a plain roast, and grilled fish, and omelettes and an abundance of fresh vegetables, and even pasta. Something for everybody who has started on solids, you would think, but here you would think wrong.

Finally the problem is solved. The little ones will have cold ham and chips. The waiter is *désolé*, but *frites* are served only with certain dishes on the *prix fixe* menu. Ham goes with salad. From the way he says it, you sense that principle is involved, not mere pedantry. In just the same tone the proprietor of a bar in my Paris *quartier* refused me when, exceptionally, I asked for a black coffee instead of a glass of Sauvignon or Médoc with my sandwich of country bread and goat cheese. Wine went with sandwiches : coffee was for the chocolate biscuit or the slice of cake which one might quite properly order afterwards.

The Anglo-Saxon pair are outraged. They gather up the children, and the folding high chair, and a beach bag and three jerseys into an amorphous bundle and flounce out, in so far as it is possible to flounce in trousers, which she as well as he is wearing. I cringe for my kith, or what the world might take to be such. Thanks be, my Welsh forebears enable me to deny kinship. Is the cringing part of the 'I travel, you have Continental holidays, he is a package tourist' syndrome, or are the English really more awful than most other peoples when they are abroad? Recalling a couple seated in the midst of the congregation for ten o'clock mass at the church of the Annunziata in Florence, who flourished a Baedeker throughout the service and made audible comments about Ciro Ferri's ceiling at the moment of the elevation, I am tempted to say yes. Also, like the waiter, though for different reasons, I am outraged. If, these days, people are weaning their young from breast milk to chips, the Dark Ages are come again, and all hopes for standards of public eating are ended. Can there be a link between this addiction to *frites* and the steadily growing number of the Anglo-Saxon young, pretty evenly distributed through the income groups, who eat like wart hogs? I do not like all French children all of the

119

time, and I have seen a few whom I did not like even some of the time, but one virtue which seems almost universal among them is that they manage a knife and fork competently from an early age. Probably, of course, all this indignation is rooted in the most tedious form of snobbery.

If so, I am unrepentant. Chips at eighteen months! Snorting, if not flouncing, I leave the restaurant and head for the corniche road and the first stage of a pilgrimage which is not scheduled for this tour but is an entirely personal affair. The graveyard perched high on Mont St. Clair is the *'Cimetière Marin'* of Valéry's poem. The poet, who was buried there in 1945, was born at Sète and once said — true, it was in a letter of thanks to the municipality which had congratulated him on his election to the *Académie française* — that he felt all his work to have been affected by his origins. Certainly, 'The Graveyard by the Sea' is *cinéma vérité* at the same time as being a poem about the destiny of man. From the height where, now, there is a Valéry Museum, housed in a long, low building that marries more happily with its surroundings than one might have dared to hope, you can check off, text in hand, one detail after another, the sombre pines, the white tombs, quiet like sheep grazing, and the sails flitting like doves over the sea below which, seen over the trees, gives the illusion of being a sky above. It is pellucid and pale, the colour of forget-me-not and harebell rather than the gentian blue of high summer, not yet brushed with the gold of sunset and lyrically calm. Faced with such a vision of peace and purity it is all but impossible to believe what one knows as hard fact, that it is a sewer. Perhaps in 1922, when Valéry wrote of the Mediterranean, his 'sea ever renewed' was as unsullied as it now looks. More likely since, being tideless and virtually land-locked, it never is renewed, it has been more or less polluted since the Phoenicians threw their rubbish overboard. Now, as the speed of the build-up increases, the pollution is nearing the point of being irreversible. What would Valéry find to say about the destiny of man today if he contemplated what may soon be literally a dead sea? Possibly he would find the truth as hard to realise as I still do myself when I look down at the town mapped out below, and the docks neat and bright as a child's model, with busy steamers going in and out on strings and the whole exquisitely pointed by a single heap of sulphur that makes a perfect cone of primrose yellow on one jetty. Sète's port has fallen away a little from its nineteenth-century prosperity, but it still ranks seventh in France. These days the tankers taking wine out pass the tankers bringing crude oil in to the refineries at Frontignan, to the east, but down on the waterfront of the *Vieux Port*, when the fishing fleet is coming in, you could still be in an ageless Mediterranean harbour, with a jetty rugged with drying nets and idlers gathering to gaze at the squirming life in the bottom of small boats. Behind, though the season has not really started, long rows of stalls devoted to the pleasures of eating *fruits de mer* have composed their still lives of oysters and mussels and urchins and other such, and a few early visitors are attacking them with the serious enjoyment that is the hallmark of the French attitude to food. I begin myself to have a hankering, soon to become a craving, for *moules farcies*, which, in passing, shows that, even now, against all the facts, I am not emotionally convinced of the state of the Mediterranean, since, of all the molluscs, mussels are the most liable to pick up infection, but, before gratifying it, I stroll up to the station to work out tomorrow's logistics. On the way I am pleasantly distracted by the gift shops that succeed the *fruits de mer* pavilions. All have followed the recent fashion of offering for sale as souvenirs not more or less repulsive shell objects, but shells themselves, unornamented, beautiful and beautifully useless. There are bags of small ones, like durable Dolly Mixture, for children, and large ones whose names, *casque rouge* and *rose de sable*, *lambris* and *bénitier* and *haliotique verte*, are as exotic as their colours and shapes, scallops and fans and conches, stained with pink and purple and lustrous with mother of pearl.

The station is distracting too; it is the only one I have seen that adorns its hall with an exhibition of railway uniform caps of many nations. The two most splendid are those of an SNCF

— the French State Railway — *chef de gare*, who has a white-topped cap with gold stars like an American admiral, and a Soviet driver, who wears his gold badge on a fur toque, which no doubt he needs on the trans-Siberian run. It is a little wounding that the display does not include the silk hat in which the stationmaster at Euston greets royalty, but possibly it is regarded as a quasi-sacred object and does not come on the market. For compensation there is a model of Stephenson's Rocket.

The logistics concern the next stage of the journey. From Sète André and Julien went to Bordeaux by way of the Canal du Midi. The voyage took them a month, which is about the time it takes a barge to get from the Mediterranean to the Garonne today, and M. Bruno gives his readers little idea of how his young heroes spent all that time. I have no intention of travelling by barge, but the mere idea of having a month in hand is an invitation to divagate from the straight line of the canal, and the place to which I want to stray is Albi, which, because it is not on the way to anywhere, has eluded me during the whole of eight years spent in France. Now I establish that, if I get the morning train to Toulouse I can catch a connection which arrives at Albi in the afternoon.

Sète's station platform is as engaging as the entrance hall, having beds of geranium and a goldfish pool with a fountain. The only other waiting travellers are an elderly couple, she carrying a country bunch of lilac and snapdragon wrapped up in the local evening paper, whose manners and bearing are noticeably more expensive than their clothes. They are more forthcoming than the French norm, even for these parts, and when I sniff the lilac, and have regretfully refused a gift of half the bunch because I am travelling, we become engrossed in conversation. They are Spanish, but settled in France since the Civil War or its aftermath. Whether they were part of that dreadful exodus of defeated soldiers and uprooted civilians who poured over the frontier from Spanish Catalonia in February 1939, to fare as ill as most refugees, whatever their host nation, or came earlier or later does not emerge. There are questions which one does not ask, however immediate and instinctive the sympathy between acquaintances. When they hear that I have been in Spain within the past three months they are eager for reports. Having spent only fifteen days there I am able to pronounce with confidence — there is no truer cliché than that, to present a portrait of a country, one should stay there a fortnight, or else twenty years — that historic necessity, accelerated by the impatience of modern businessmen, in Barcelona and Bilbao particularly, is causing Spain to move out of feudalism, but that the American money on which the country's industrial development largely depends will ensure that she does not move any dramatic distance Left of Centre. The man nods with something between relief and surprise. 'I had had an idea that there was a retrograde frame of mind in Spain at the moment.' He and his wife will never go back, any more than the rest of their countrymen who came over at that time, unlike today's immigrant workers, the most competent of whom calculate their term of exile with some care. Like the woman I met at the *Préfecture* in Paris when we were both renewing our *Cartes de Séjour*, who had every intention of returning but, like St. Augustine and heaven, not yet. Every summer, when she went home on holiday, she noticed the progress that Spain was making, but she felt she would do better in France for a while again. She was thinking purely in terms of earnings : as these things go she was getting quite a decent wage. My two Spanish friends would be more likely to think of the chalked slogans I noticed near the station at Sète. One read : ' "No" to the suppression of the Communist League', the other : 'Beware of the police'. Both would be subscribed to by a fair number of people in Sète, which, its placid aspect notwithstanding, is one of the reddest patches of the Midi *rouge*. The probably young militants who inscribed the slogans could hardly be expected to understand, still less to agree, that the possibility of writing such things on walls is in itself proof that they live in a democracy, or, at worst, that they do not live in a police state.

carriage into which I settle for the journey to Toulouse. Only a businessman in a corner seat, who makes it clear that he is slumming, is slightly alien. He is wearing a good dark suit and carrying a morocco *serviette* full of documents which he leaves to mark his seat when he goes down to the dining car at lunch time. The rest of us, two women with shopping bags, a good looking dark boy in a short-sleeved check shirt, and two old gentlemen, of whom one carries his ticket and his money in a fold-over purse like a pre-war schoolboy, the other wears a pale beige cap and borrows my newspaper, produce huge rolls stuffed with ham and garlic sausage, or, in my case, a regrettably flimsy cheese pastry and a *croissant*, and drink beer out of bottles. There is a last glimpse of the lagoon, azure freaked with green, soil that is first sandy pink, then a deeper red, rocky hills round Narbonne, before the train swings away from the coast into the valley of the Aude. Somewhere past the majestic set-piece of Carcassonne — restoration it may be, but the distant view of its towers and battlements printed on the sky is justification enough for Viollet-Le-Duc — I wonder for a moment at the brilliance and solidity of the cumulus clouds floating high in the southern sky before realising that I am looking at the snow-clad summits of the Pyrénées, which, around here, rise to 2,785 metres in Mont Canigou and 3,400 metres in the Pic d'Aneto farther west.

The next white to catch my eye is dingier as well as duller. It is that of the high-rise blocks of the new town of Le Mirail, which has been built to the south-west of Toulouse, whose population threatened to explode through its encircling boulevards. Le Mirail is a showpiece in which the architects of other new towns in France, Échirolles, near Grenoble, among them, have found inspiration. Whether it and the rose-red city itself can ever become visually and aesthetically complementary, is a question which the scramble for the Albi connection does not leave me time to brood over.

12   RED BRICK AND grey stone, which, being translated, implies not simply the new and the old, but the crude and the classic, the aspiring and the established, the third-rate and the first: somebody must have coined that prejorative comparison, but by now it is as anonymous as a proverb. Standing on the old bridge over the Tarn, looking up at the towering mass of the Cathedral of Albi and the Palais de la Berbie, once the residence of the Archbishop, with that lurch of the heart that you experience before master works like the great brick church of the *Frari*, in Venice, or the castle and the bridge over the Adige in Verona, I think again that whoever perpetrated it must have been an untravelled visual illiterate, and muddle-headed with it. Because mean terrace houses in industrial towns and ill-conditioned villas in seaside resorts are often built of red brick, therefore red brick is an ignoble building material, runs the reasoning. Its refutation soars overhead, walls and towers and buttresses in this evening light, purple like Ronsard's rose, as, in the full sun of midday, they will have opulent undertones of gold.

Albi was built of brick, as Cotswold cottages were built of amber stone, because brick was what was there, which is one of the basic rules for perfection. It was built austere and impregnable as a fortress because, in the thirteenth century, the Church in this part of South-West France was militant indeed. We are back with the blood-drenched history of the Languedoc. Albi was the heart of the Cathar country — it was from the city where they found refuge that the Cathars got their alternative name of Albigensians — and its bishops, who were feudal lords as much as, if not more than princes of the Church, were to the fore in their persecution. Bernard de Castanet, who built the cathedral, was Grand Inquisitor for the region during the heresy hunt which followed the crusade. The atrocities committed by both crusaders and inquisitors were so hideous that they tend to obscure the fact that Catharism was itself a dreadful doctrine, denying the humanity of Christ, holding that the world, being the creation of Satan rather than God, was fundamentally evil, and imposing a system of spiritual elitism upon its followers. They were divided into a small group of the 'Perfect', the extreme asceticism of whose lives made a lurid contrast with that of many priests and bishops of the period, and the mass of the laity, from whom little was demanded, but whose hopes of Paradise depended upon their receiving the sacrament of the 'Consolamentum' from one of the 'Perfect' on their deathbeds.

A cathedral built at that period was required to symbolise the temporal power of the Church, and so Albi was conceived as a strong point, with windows high and narrow, massive towers embedded in the walls and a West tower like a keep. Against it the flamboyant south porch of grey stone, which was added in the early sixteenth century, though exquisite, is as incongruous as a lace ruffle on a suit of mail.

The interior gives you a physical shock. Where you are prepared for austerity to match those implacable ramparts, there is a rood screen and choir in which Gothic sculpture reaches its height of luxuriance, and frescoes whose blue ground adorned with gold transport one to Renaissance Italy. They were indeed

Italian artists, imported from Bologna, who painted the whole of the roof of the nave with figures and scenes from the Old and New Testament. The enormous Last Judgment on the West Wall is the work of French artists. Late in the seventeenth century an act of vandalism as idiotic as it was brutal robbed the fresco of the central figure of Christ, the *raison d'être* of the composition, in order to pierce a window in the Chapel of St. Clair. The whole is a wonder, inexhaustible in its detail and stunning in its total impact. I leave it only when the sacristan begins to jingle his keys, at once humbled and exalted, and already looking forward to returning the next day to see it all again in the light of morning.

The road back to the hotel passes the statue of one of Albi's more renowned native sons, the eighteenth-century navigator, La Pérouse. The legend on the plinth tells us that he 'destroyed the English establishments at Hudson Bay' but omits the grisly speculations concerning his end during the course of a round-the-world voyage commissioned by Louis XVI, who hoped that, through his admiral, 'people whose existence is still unknown to us' would learn to respect and, above all, would learn to love France. For three years, from 1785 to 1788, news of La Pérouse's progress was relayed to France as regularly as communications allowed. Then silence, and searches revealed no trace of the admiral and his ship, *l'Astrolabe*. It was not until forty years later that the Norman navigator, Dumont d'Urville, found the wreckage of *l'Astrolabe* off the Island of Vanikoro in the New Hebrides. The thesis that all the ship's company had gone down in her had to be abandoned when some of their possessions, including La Pérouse's watch, were found in the hands of the natives, and d'Urville's enquiries gave some credence to the idea that the admiral had been eaten.

Will there before long be a new statue at Albi, to commemorate the President of the Republic, dead since last week, who spent part of his school career at its *lycée*? There does not appear to be one to a greater Frenchman who, in an earlier generation, was on the staff of that same *lycée*. Jean Jaurés, who was to the French Socialist Party what Keir Hardie was to the British Labour Party (the total dissimilarity of the two men conveys something of the difference between the two parties), who was born at nearby Castres, was a professor of philosophy at the Albi *lycée*. He has, though, a living memorial here in the thriving glassworks, the Verrerie Ouvrière, which supplies bottles for half the south-west's production of wine and brandy. It was Jaurés who, in 1896, encouraged the striking workers of the several glassworks at Carmaux to set up their own factory at Albi.

Now that the sun has gone it is deadly cold, and the dark grey concrete exterior of my hotel does not promise an excess of comfort. Inside, on a material level, it provides the same kind of experience as the cathedral. At one end of the long dining room there is an immense wood fire with, roasting over it, a succession of *gigots* from sheep grazed on the hill pastures of the Causses. Not underdone, either, and faintly, perfectly pointed with garlic. It is preceded by a fully ripe grapefruit, accompanied by a green salad and followed by what deserves to be ranked as the definitive apple tart. All for seventeen francs and fifteen centimes. At what point does simple human well-being become happiness? I eat, and think back to the cathedral, and expand in the warmth, while experiencing what the psychiatrists call 'an elevation of mood', in which the mutton figures on equal terms with the frescos. After dinner I had planned to read guide books and write up my notes, but such is my state of idiot contentment that I get no farther than the bar, where I drink coffee and watch the whole of an equally idiot Western on the telly. In the morning the cathedral, inside and out, has a clarity that puts it into a different hemisphere from last night. You would need to watch it the clock round, like Monet painting Rouen Cathedral, before even beginning to know it, and this morning I have to leave it too soon if I am to visit the old Bishop's Palace. Since 1922 it has been the Toulouse-Lautrec museum, but even without its contents the palace would demand to be seen. One bishop, Bernard de Combret, built it, another,

Bernard de Castanet, who started the construction of the cathedral, converted it into a fortress which gives the illusion that it would be impregnable even against modern armaments. From the top floor there is a stupendous view over the hills to the north : from the battlements it seems that you could dive straight into the Tarn, running green and swift and snarled under its three bridges, blossoming into foam over a shallow fall. Actually you would smash like an egg on the dirt road below, so better turn from the vertiginous side to the sunken garden within the *enceinte*, where the first red roses are breaking out of their furled buds.

The museum contains the most complete Toulouse-Lautrec collection in existence : the pictures which were left to the municipality of Albi by the painter's mother and his friend, Maurice Joyant, give visitors a rare opportunity of comparing those which everybody knows, the portraits of Paris music-hall stars of the Belle Époque, with those which relatively few people know, the paintings of horses and dogs and landscape, besides what may be called private portraits. The earliest of them dates from 1880, when the artist was sixteen : it is a 'Gunner Saddling his Horse', a very predictable subject for a son of the Count Alphonse de Toulouse-Lautrec. During the two previous years he had suffered two successive accidents which had condemned him to face adult life as a cripple as well as a dwarf, a full-grown man on stunted legs. Without them, would he have continued to find his subjects in the Languedoc rather than Montmartre, and, if he had done so, how far beyond it would he have been known today? There is no answer to that kind of speculation; you can say only that, wherever or whatever he had painted, Toulouse-Lautrec's draughtsmanship would have been a constant, and that alone would have brought him recognition, if not the kind of fame he earned with his portraits of Yvette Guilbert, Jeanne Avril and the rest.

Meanwhile I am involved in a parallel speculation. If I catch the midday train to Toulouse, will there be a connection that will get me to Lourdes by a reasonable time this evening, and, if there is, do I really want to go to Lourdes? By mid-afternoon, the first question settled for me, I am unpacking in a hotel bedroom where the wardrobe contains nineteen wooden, five plastic and three wire coathangers but the bed has only one blanket under its emaciated eiderdown. On the back of the door, along with advertisements for hairdressers, dry cleaners and the like there is one announcing that the Le Vega Club is *plus chic*, without indicating the standard of comparison and another saying just: '*Club Privé — Travestis.*' '*Travestis*' may or may not mean transvestite. More probably just fancy dress, but even that seems a trifle odd unless this splendidly Mediterranean city is trying to meet what it imagines to be the tastes of tired business men from the north.

From the north or elsewhere, the business men are coming in steadily increasing numbers. When André and Julien were here Toulouse was already 'a great commercial city'. The population was 150,000 and it was a centre for flour-milling. One can still find that Toulouse down by the Garonne, flowing broad and strong between its quays. Modern Toulouse, with a population above 330,000, is still a market for the surrounding agricultural region, but, pre-eminently, it is occupied with chemicals and aeronautics. These past few years, for many of the British who, previously, had scarcely heard of the place, Toulouse has meant the Concorde, and I am prepared to find that all the model aircraft in the toyshops have gone supersonic. Far otherwise; I cannot spot one in the window of a well-stocked shop which chances to be virtually next door to a notice announcing a lecture by Captain Turcat, Concorde's test pilot.

So perhaps we are not yet in at the birth of a legend that will overlay if not efface the old one, which, it so happens, is being commemorated this week. Two streets in Toulouse are being named respectively after Didier Daurat and Pierre-Georges Latécoère. The former was the administrator of the first regular airline to operate from France, the second the constructor of the aircraft which flew on it. Flying was still in the heroic age: the first airmail service between France and Morocco was inaugurated in September 1919, with aircraft which were hardly different from those which, twelve months earlier, had been flying over the Western Front. By June 1925, the line had been pushed as far as Dakar. Five years later came the first commercial crossing of the South Atlantic, which was the beginning of a regular air service between France and South America. It was an epic, and it had its poet. The *corps d'élite* of pilots included Antoine de Saint-Exupéry, who chronicled the adventure, and who, when he flew to his death on war service in 1944 — his aircraft vanished without trace over the Mediterranean — had conveyed the rapture and terror of flying as has no other writer I know, in poetry or in prose. Against all that, Concorde, earthbound by problems of pollution and cost benefit return, does not really measure, potent as it may have been in establishing the contemporary image of Toulouse beyond the borders of France.

What I have never been able to understand is why its image as a tourist centre is not more compelling. It is proper to declare an interest here because, since my first visit years ago, Toulouse has been one of my favourite French towns, one of a group as disparate as Bordeaux and Quimper and Marseille. But, personal leanings apart, it has so much to offer, from the terra cotta glow of its buildings to its richness in art and architecture, which includes what is probably France's finest sculptural museum, that it is astonishing to be able to spend a whole day in its streets without hearing any language other than French, except, possibly, Spanish. Left to itself, this part of France would vote overwhelmingly for admitting Spain to the EEC. Principles about democratic government are fine for Brussels, but business is business, and when you are close to a frontier you naturally hope that trade across it will be made as easy as possible.

This time I quell my instinct to visit first the Basilica of St. Sernin, whose five-storey, octagonal bell-tower beckons above the rooftops, and which has relics of 128 saints, including six apostles, stacked in its two crypts. It is not that one could ever tire of the blend of elegance and majesty of its pale stone and brick, or fail to be moved by its interior, vast, as befits a pilgrimage church — St. Sernin was one of the last stages on the road to Compostella — but I am guiltily conscious that this is at least my sixth visit to Toulouse and I have not yet seen the Capitole, the town hall after which the crack train which is the town's link with Paris was named. It took its own name from the 'capitouls', the consuls, varying in number from four to twelve, who governed the city during the period from the ninth to the thirteenth century, when Toulouse was the seat of the brilliantly civilised Counts Raymond, and kept most of their functions after the territory was annexed to France.

The immense arcaded *place* before the eighteenth-century palace which succeeded an earlier building is a natural gathering place, with that air of being in an open-air drawing room which you sense in Italian *piazze*. The shop windows around it are a reminder that the third speciality of Toulouse, along with chemicals and aeronautics, is violets, indeed the first if you judge from the displays in the gift shops. Violets in this region are cultivated even more for processing than for sale by the bunch. Crystallised, they are piled in every confectioner's window; violets are painted or embroidered on a wide range of knick-knackery; ceramic violets are used impartially for earrings or for wreaths in the windows of *pompes funèbres*, for decorating bits of pottery or the necks of wicker-covered flasks of scent. The scent has a dual function. The best quality is still affected by the older generation of Frenchwomen; Colette's mother always used to lay in a supply during her rare visits to Paris. The *ordinaire*, the plonk of perfume, is sprayed lavishly over the baskets of violets which, in early spring, send out their drenching sweetness from every city street corner.

The *place* has its social, early evening air, with half the town sipping coffee and apéritifs at café tables or shop-gazing beneath the arcades. Behind the bland façade of the Capitole is an older inner court, where the statue of Henri IV, after whom it was named, looks out from above a Renaissance doorway, and behind that again, surrounded by green lawns where fountains play, is the donjon which is all that remains of the old sixteenth-century Capitole. Now it houses the *Syndicat d'Initiative*.

All this might be another city from the area around St. Sernin. Threading my way back towards supper — so strong is the sense of territory as defined by the *quartier* in any French town that, even when you visit a strange place, you have a powerful instinct to eat as near as possible to where you sleep — taking the long way through the peaceful boulevards bordering the Canal du Midi, I am aware of being in yet another. One of Toulouse's most appealing characteristics is that, more than almost any other French town, I know, it is not an amorphous urban sprawl but a cluster of linked communities, each small enough for intimacy.

The bistro, fifty yards down the road from my hotel, where I finally decide to have supper, is snug like the inside of a cigar box, and patronised by a clientèle of which a good half come there every evening. I am reading of the stirring scenes which marked the four hundredth, and last, performance of *Hullo Dolly!* at Toulouse when there is an explosion of voices and laughter in the front part of the bistro, where there has been an irruption of pleasantly hearty young women who are shouting : 'We won ! We won !'

They turn out to be the basketball team of the University of Toulouse, who have knocked Lyon into the middle of next week. Just like home, one thinks, as rather often in the south-west, though even oftener in and around Bordeaux than here in the shadow of the Pyrénées. Perhaps those three centuries of British domination, followed by later centuries of British participation in the wine and brandy trade, have inculcated a predisposition for games-playing in the region, where you find not only basketball, but hockey here and there, and rugger — though not yet for women — absolutely everywhere. It is the one part of France where Miss Joan Hunter-Dunn would acclimatise quickly and painlessly.

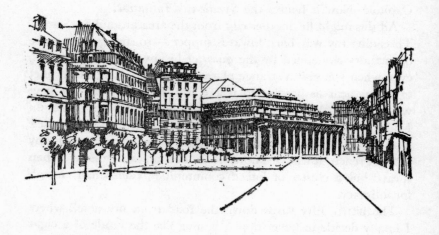

13

                 'Allons!' SAYS THE head of the rather attractive family whose table I am sharing at breakfast. 'Let's go!' He rises and begins to gather together various items of luggage.

On the chair beside him his small son puts carefully into the pocket of his anorak the toy spaceman whom he has been supporting in a tipsy tightrope walk round the rim of his empty cup before sliding to the ground. His wife, on my right, picks up the Siamese cat whose delicate moleskin paws have been advancing gradually farther on to the table, stuffs it into what looks like a knitting bag and pulls the zip fastener up to its chin. The cat screams ritually as the party makes for the door, gazing out at the world with eyes like lanterns. They are the same lambent blue as the little boy's; perhaps that is why his parents chose a Siamese when they wanted a family pet.

I reach for another *croissant* while, with an eyebrow, signalling to the waiter to come and refill my coffee cup. At the moment when the cat was being folded into its carry-cot I realised, rather than decided, that I was not going to Lourdes, so, while I consider what I will do instead, I might as well start another round of breakfast. I tell myself that my reason for not going is that I do not want to have my memory of little Bernadette, calm behind the ceramic roses of her casket at Nevers, overlaid with impressions of a town where she is, among other things, big business, but I know this for a rationalisation. What I am really doing is indulging to the full the sensation of having got off the hook of a daily, weekly, yearly programme which was of necessity closely structured, governed by clock and calendar and involving constant decision-making. Now I can let myself drift and eddy with the current, rejoicing in trains missed through pleasant idleness, routes whose details evolve organically rather than being planned. Since I am not going to Lourdes I will go to Bordeaux, have a couple of hours there, then, rather than pressing on northward, spend the weekend by the sea at Arcachon. There is no train for Bordeaux for an hour and a half, but the station restaurant is a pleasant enough place, the *croissants* are warm and crackling and the *Dépêche*, the radical daily paper which, very rightly, is the pride of Toulouse, has a gripping story about an outbreak of violence after a pop concert by an American guitarist, during which fans threw stones at the police, and one young man, presumably in the interests of male liberation, took off his pants in public.

More seriously, I learn that Professor Lafont, of the Arts Faculty at Montpellier, a leader of the Occitan revival, has had his candidature in the presidential elections as the representative of national minorities refused because it would be 'an attack on the integrity of the national territory'. Can the authorities really believe that the Republic is threatened by a centrifugal force which will cause one region after another to fly off until the government is left embattled in the Ile de France? More probably it is the automatic reaction of centralised bureaucracy to anything that has a whiff of power-sharing, but considering the dottiness of some of the fringe candidates in both presidential and legislative elections, it seems hard on Professor Lafont.

The Bordeaux train runs down the Valley of the Garonne, with views of the lateral canal as well as the river; for a brief stretch near Agen it passes between the two. This part of the south-west is essentially agricultural. In spite of the discovery of a large deposit of natural gas at Lacq, many people still think of it first in terms of tomatoes, which are grown in vast quantities around Marmande, the prunes of Agen, which are halfway to Elvas plums, and tobacco, a crop that might have been made to measure for small farmers, since its cultivation, which involves an unusually large number of rather fiddly operations before the picking, leaf by leaf, and hanging to dry, employs every member of the family, from small children to great-grandparents.

If this were a first visit, two hours, which, in the event, turn out to be two and a half, in Bordeaux would be a tantalising experience, and when Michelin's normally reliable Green Guide says that the town can be dealt with in three it must have in mind those demon sightseers who look up from their street maps only in order to tick off another item on their itinerary. Since I know Bordeaux rather well I am absolved from sightseeing, and I am in no doubt about what I want to do, which is to take a bus from the station to the place de la Comédie, then settle in the sun on the *terrasse* of the Café de Bordeaux, lunching off a glass of Médoc and a *baguette* stuffed with Gruyère and contemplating one of the most civilised prospects in France, the façade of the Grand Theatre opposite.

It is one of the relatively small number of theatres which are equally successful within and without. The dome and the double staircase inspired Garnier when he planned the Paris Opera; the colonnaded front, with statues of the nine muses and the three graces posed above it, has a gaiety and richness which sets it apart from the grave elegance of the rest of the city's eighteenth-century set pieces, like the magnificent Bourse, or the Hotel de Ville, which was once the palace of the Archbishop, Cardinal Rohan. This is an eighteenth-century town, even though the cathedral and one or two of the churches were already standing when England ruled over Aquitaine and the

Black Prince had his headquarters here. It was the *Intendants*, the great provincial administrators first appointed by Cardinal Richelieu, who laid out the town we know, after bitter clashes with the burgesses, who were all against such innovations. A couple of centuries later, though the protagonists may not have realised it at the time, the situation was to be reproduced when a dynamic young mayor with an impressive Resistance record came to a town whose image, up to the Second World War, was more gracious than progressive. M. Jacques Chaban Delmas galvanised his city in ways as diverse as causing two new bridges to be built over the Garonne and establishing a May Festival of art, music and drama in which contemporary work has a large place, and generally dragged it into the twentieth century. Whether, even when he became Prime Minister, he was completely accepted by the *'aristocratie du bouchon'*, the local families who, for generations, have owned the great vineyards, is a moot point. There are aspects of Bordeaux, even today, which recall Boston, Massachusetts, in the era when the Lowells talked to the Cabots and the Cabots talked only to God. It may be relevant that the April attractions at the theatre opposite include *The Tales of Hoffmann* and *The Desert Song*, possibly by way of a prophylactic against the disturbing experiences which the May Festival is likely to bring.

Arcachon is the playground of the *Bordelais*, both the patricians who have boats and weekend houses there and the plebs who go down on Saturdays and Sundays, as is evident from the station, where there is a rather complicated ticket machine to obviate queuing at the booking office. After a good deal of mental stress I think I have mastered it, only to realise too late that I have taken a cheap concessionary ticket to which I have no possible right. When I explain the situation to the ticket collector at the other end he says only : 'These things happen', and waves away my proferred francs.

The train runs through a landscape of pine forests and cultivated clearings, with occasional sinister areas of scorched earth — all through the dry season fire is a constant menace here — which is so apparently autochthonous that only with an effort can one keep in mind that it is not only man-made, as are three parts of the landscape of any developed country, but fairly recently made. Until the eighteenth century the Landes, the tract of coast between the Gironde and the Adur, was an unbroken sandy beach backed by dunes which the Atlantic rollers piled to steadily increasing heights. The dune of Pyla, near Arcachon, at 114 metres, is the highest in Europe. Inland was an area of marsh where shepherds really did get about on stilts as they do now only in folkloristic parades. Towards the end of the century, an engineer, Thomas Brémontier, who came from Normandy, and so presumably did not share the local attitude that drifting sand was one more Act of God which had to be endured, began to put into effect an idea which had been accepted since the Middle Ages, that the sandhills could be stabilised by sowing reeds and marram grass whose roots would form a close network, then planting maritime pines further inland. The work went on through most of the nineteenth century and was accompanied by the draining of the marsh. Now the economy of the Landes is closely bound up with its pine forests, which provide ever more sophisticated derivatives of wood, as well as timber of various grades. The small earthenware pots fastened to trunks here and there may suggest that the trees are being milked for ouzo, as a complementary export to the more orthodox wine trade. Actually they mark the first stage in the process of collecting resin, from which turpentine is distilled.

Arcachon, set beside a lagoon the size of an inland sea, is two-faced, like so many seaside towns, both British and French, of any age. Age as holiday places, that is, not as working harbours. By that standard Arcachon certainly qualifies; it is a railway resort which grew up with the coming of the train service from Bordeaux to the coast.

'Bournemouth,' I murmur at first sight of the bosky avenues where magnates' mansions, confident, ostentations, fantastic, nestle among semi-tropical shrubs, and 'Bournemouth' again at the feel of the private hotel which, by an imperative instinct, I have chosen here instead of the one-star pub whose life is concentrated in the bar which is my more usual habitat. Nearer the sea there is a newer stratum of social geology in the anonymous rectangular buildings which are the contemporary equivalents of all those turrets and pinnacles, as their owners, some of whom are already baring torsos and trying out new bikinis on their balconies, are the equivalent of the generations of pleasure seekers, from the Second Empire to the *Belle Époque*, who took the sea air here protected by layer upon layer of silk and cambric and flannel and whalebone.

Nobody is swimming yet, but off the shore skin divers are going in rather splashily, while, as if in a patient demonstration, from which they are clearly incapable of profiting, a razorbill keeps vanishing without a ripple, to surface each time a surprising distance from the spot where it disappeared. Further out, sails drift like gulls across the baby blue of the lagoon. It is the popular magazines' concept of a civilisation of leisure, so smooth and seductively coloured that the row of citizens fishing off the jetty introduces a slightly disorderly note. This is fishing almost on the industrial scale, consisting of lowering a basket net, baited with fish heads and entrails or, in one instance, the bright yellow feet of a chicken into the water and, in due course, hauling it up, half filled with a tangle of crabs, among which small fish and shrimps or prawns writhe and flicker.

By the end of the afternoon the sense of having got into a holiday brochure becomes slightly oppressive, so I break out of the picture by walking to the harbour, where there are working craft as well as sailing boats, to eat oysters for supper. If I do not eat them here I never shall. Rabelais appreciated the oysters of Arcachon, and they have been bred here on the commercial scale since the mid-nineteenth century. Now the beds in the lagoon are among the largest in Europe. It means that half a dozen turn up as starters to the most modest meal, whether they are the delicately flavoured 'flats' or the plumper but more commonplace Portuguese, which, introduced accidentally during the nineteenth century, now dominate the native breed, like the grey squirrel the red. The boulevard de la Plage, which leads to the harbour, is, in fact, divided from the beach by a row of large houses set well back from the road, not holiday villas, but the permanent dwellings of solid bourgeois families. Their gardens are tranced with summer, though it is still only April, with roses climbing above hedges and curtains of wisteria dropping over walls. One gate swings half open to frame a picture clear as a cameo. There is a shaded, intensely green lawn, a hammock slung between two trees, and a young girl lying back in it, swinging so languidly that the movement is only just perceptible. Facing her, a boy in a white shirt, with brows startlingly dark in a pale face, is leaning forward in a cane chair, talking vehemently. No matter that they are probably discussing the coming *bachot*, or lamenting that it is going to be yet another *blanquette de veau* for dinner. They are enclosed, enchanted, trapped for eternity in a prism, like the wedding feast in *Le Grand Meaulnes*, or the doomed, landlocked tennis parties in the garden of the Finzi-Continis.

Even round the port new, white buildings are spawning, but there are still houses with steps going down to the water and a cluttered working jetty, though, at a guess, there are twenty playboats for every one that earns its living. At the tip of the outer arm of the harbour the memorial to drowned sailors, the veiled figure of a woman bowed against a great anchor of granite, is a reminder that the lagoon is not devoted wholly to pleasure sailing.

There is a spectacular sunset, deployed over illimitable distances, with the sky eastward and overhead still the colour of a periwinkle, the west stained green and yellow, then faint lilac, then a fiery pink, while the sea changes from a fresh young blue to turquoise before taking on a translucence in which light and air and water mingle. I wait till dusk before tracking down my oysters in a little restaurant where, at the few other tables which are occupied, diners are sitting before platters of *fruits de mer* abundant and intricate as a Flemish still life. It is a rare experience to feel virtuously frugal through eating oysters. They taste of oceans, and the contrast between the nacreous gleam of the inside of the empty shells and the glitter of the crushed ice on the seaweed-fringed tray holding those still to be eaten is a subsidiary pleasure.

In the morning, the quality of the bread and the quantity of butter on my breakfast tray is a reminder that, appearances notwithstanding, this is not Bournemouth. Enough breeze has got up to raise tiny frills of foam in the lagoon, and harden the sails that are leaning away from it. The boat trips taking tourists to Cap Ferret, where they can see the oysters at home, have not yet got into their stride, so, instead, I walk far along the shore to the muddy shallows where rows of rather sinister stakes mark the area in which mussels are cultivated. They cluster like grapes on the poles, swelling to that stage of plump succulence when the *'boucholeurs'*, so called because the French word for the stakes is *bouchots*, come to harvest them, again rather like grapes. I am lucky enough to see one of them propelling himself across the mudflats on what looks more like a shallow box than a punt, one of the *'accons'* which are used at low water.

By the time I have walked back to Arcachon, an idyllic week-end lethargy has set in, and I join the sprinkling of French visitors who are heading for restaurants where they will sit over lunch for much of the afternoon. The one I choose, chiefly because it has a sunny *terrasse*, offers for fifteen francs a menu that begins with half a dozen oysters and goes on through a couple of dabs to plaice with a green salad, finishing with an orange.

In the evening I realise how many of those visitors were day trippers. They have caught their trains back to Bordeaux; the more prosperous, who have second homes here, have their feet under their own tables, and suddenly the sea front is empty. A few of us gather in the corner café where the TV is showing a party political broadcast. This evening the speaker is the one woman candidate for the Presidency, Arlette Largillière, who speaks rather impressively out of passionate commitment to a creed which is far to the Left of the Communist Party.

'*Dingue!*' is the consensus when she has finished, from one young and three middle-aged men, and one woman other than myself. '*Dingue!*' — bonkers.

14

LEAVING ARCACHON IN the morning costs
a pang. It is the beginning of another flawless day; the sea-front
tamarisks stir in a whisper of breeze; an eight and two coxed
pairs are setting out across the limpid surface of the lagoon;
this evening, without a doubt, there will be another phenomenal
sunset. Unfortunately, the only bus to *Pointe de Grave*, the spit
of sand forming the western bank of the mouth of the Gironde,
that arrives early enough to let me go on farther if I cannot
find a bed for the night there, leaves Bordeaux around noon,
which means catching a relatively early train from Arcachon.

The bus, which is three parts empty, is self-determining in the
way of country buses everywhere, making unscheduled and
indefinite stops and acting as carrier and news agency as well
as means of transport. Soon after we are clear of Bordeaux it
pulls up at a bungalow draped with wisteria from which a young
couple rush out to embrace the driver and engage him in an
animated conversation before entrusting to his care a small boy
named Stéphan, who is going to spend the day with auntie

farther along the line. He sits up in front and is treated to a running commentary on the passing scene, accompanied by sweeping gestures.

The road runs north through the blank, Sunday morning landscape of deserted village streets, gardens with roses and lilac and the arum lilies that reek of mortal flesh all blooming at once, a line of weekend washing here as a reminder that about one-third of Frenchwomen spend the week working outside the home and a notice saying : *Syndicat de Chasse* there to mark off a shoot. Rugby football is not the only sport of the south-west. We are between two worlds. On the right is the oyster-grey water of the Gironde Estuary, where, these days, fishing and the oil industry struggle to resolve their mutual incompatibility; on the left, as far as eye can see, the vineyards of the Haut-Médoc, with its *châteaux* — the buildings, not the vintages — rising from the invading tide of low-trimmed vines.

The oil industry centres on the towns along the estuary which are outposts of Bordeaux, Blaye, Pauillac and Bec d'Ambès. The fishing is of the slightly esoteric sort. At this time of year eels and lampreys, smelt and shad come up the river to spawn. Allegedly there are sturgeon, too, the source of that *caviare de Gironde* of which I can speak only from hearsay, since I have never seen, let alone tasted, a grain of it. The fine-mesh, hammock-shaped nets hung over the surface of the water from a pulley are for the elvers, which appear on the fishmonger's slab as a squirming, gelatinous mass. The nets, called *carrelets*, are no more than an improved version of the wicker baskets which I saw lowered off the jetty at Arcachon.

The vineyards are a delicate subject for more than one reason. Since the recent scandals involving the doctoring by certain wine merchants of what England knows as claret and France as Bordeaux *rouge*, formerly trusting, if not always perhaps highly discriminating consumers have become convinced that nothing is what it seems. In particular, they regard a Bordeaux label as virtually a guarantee that the contents are not what they purport to be. At the price the consumer paid, they probably never were, or have not been for years past, but to conclude from that that all Bordeaux is suspect is to travesty the situation. As the owner of one of the Big Five *Premier Cru châteaux* said soon after the trial of those involved in the scandal : 'Only one major firm was concerned. The rest were crooks, and known to be crooks.'

When prices have rocketed as they have been doing recently, the wonder is that there has not been an even greater proliferation of crooks. Over the past few years the trend of drinking in France has been away from the cheap and coarse *gros rouge*, the litre bottle which, with a long loaf hot from the baker, still constitutes the midday dinner of many Algerian and Portuguese workers in Paris and other big cities, to something better. At the same time, the world beyond Europe began to drink wine. The result is that, while the growers of the Midi are blocking the roads with their tractors in protest against imports of Italian wine that further depress an already stagnant market, growers elsewhere, whose product is of higher quality, are at their wits end to fulfil their orders.

The shortage is particularly acute in the Médoc, which, traditionally, has exported its wine northwards by sea, to Belgium, Sweden and Britain. England remained faithful to claret during the period before the war when Burgundy was in more general demand. Now, not only Americans, and Americans other than the tiny minority who have long had it, but the Japanese are developing a taste for claret. There are sceptics who doubt this latter, believing that what Japan, a nation of businessmen, has developed is an awareness of the possibilities of claret as an investment of the same order as Old Masters or Persian rugs, but, either way, at least one vineyard in the region is Japanese owned.

Eighty to ninety per cent of the great wines of Bordeaux are exported, and their price has gone through the ceiling. Among the more modest, a bottle of St. Émilion, not one of the aristocrats of the Médoc but a good red wine produced on the other side of the Gironde, about forty kilometres east of

Bordeaux, which, in 1968, cost two francs a bottle from the grower, cost eight francs in 1972. What it would cost on the restaurant table would be, according to the classic formula, what the market would bear. At the other end of the scale, what it would bear in a fashionable restaurant for a bottle from one of the world famous *châteaux* might be 400 francs. I have heard of a Mouton-Rothschild marked at 1,300 francs a bottle, but, supposing this to be true, and supposing that there was a real bottle and not a myth behind the item that was the glory of that particular wine list — after all, before the boom, I never saw anybody drinking the Romanée-Conti, at something above 200 francs, listed by a Paris restaurant famed as a Burgundy house — I am convinced that it would have been the proprietor's fetish and that he would have refused to open it. As the wine correspondent of a British daily newspaper was to write some years later, who but Greek shipowners could have bid for the few cases of 1945 Château Lafite which made £600 for twelve bottles.

When demand outstrips supply to that extent, it is inevitable that there should be merchants ready to capitalise the situation by importing cheap wine in bulk from Algeria or the Languedoc, treating it chemically to soften the worst of its asperities, then bottling it under an impressive label. The only surprise about the Bordeaux business was that an old-established firm of merchants with an honourable reputation should have lent themselves to the practice.

The vineyards through which the bus is now passing are 'château bottled' territory. Château Mouton-Rothschild, Château Lafite and Château Latour are all at, or near, Pauillac, within sight of the oil port and the Shell-Berre refinery. They say in Bordeaux virtually all the great vineyards have a sea view, though the oil installations are not obligatory. The Big Five are completed by Château Margaux, which is about twenty kilometres farther up the estuary, and Château Haut-Brion, not a Médoc at all, but a Graves, which, with that disregard for logic when it is convenient of which only a people as rational as the French are capable, was included in the original *Premier Crus*, or first growths, in the classification of the wines of the Médoc made for the 1855 International Exhibition in Paris.

The term *cru classé*, which can be used only in conjunction with the year of classification, is, to quote a producer, 'neither a brand nor an appellation, it is an honour — a title of nobility', and, incidentally, a gold mine in the auction room. Like the lordship of a manor in Britain, it is attached, not to an individual or a group, but to a property, whose owner has the usufruct, not the possession of the title.

The classification of 1855, which established only four *Premier Crus*, was to remain unchallenged in law until 1973, though in practice, for about fifty years, the world had recognised that there were five. In 1855 Mouton-Rothschild was classed first of the *Deuxième Crus*. The property had been bought only two years earlier by Baron Nathaniel de Rothschild, great-grand-father of the present owner, Baron Philippe de Rothschild. 'He was English as well as a newcomer,' says the latter today. 'Can you imagine French judges, in 1855, putting a British neophyte in the first class?'

Baron Philippe took over control of Mouton in 1922. In the following year, at the age of twenty-one, he proposed an innovation which revolutionised the marketing of the *Premier Crus*, a rule that the entire crop, every year and without exception was to be château bottled — no more bulk deliveries to merchants to do with the product what they would. Château Margaux supported the scheme, and its co-proprietor, M. Pierre Moreau, converted Count René de Beaumont, for Château Latour. These two were the first of the present Big Five to apply the rule from 1923 : ironically, Mouton had to wait until the vintage of 1924 because it had no accommodation for bottling.

Since that year, Mouton, which, in 1973, after protracted legal proceedings, was granted officially what it had enjoyed in fact for half a century, the status of *Premier Cru Classé*, has had a *chai*, or wine-making plant, which has made the château a place of pilgrimage in the Médoc. Which brings us to the second reason why the wine of Bordeaux, and specifically the products of the Big Five, can be a delicate subject today. Partly, one would like to think, as a reaction against all the bad prose that has been written about good wine, but partly also from hostility to the concept of élitisme, there has grown up an inverted snobbery which holds that wine is plonk, is pleasant, is plonk, is for drinking, is plonk, is plonk, is plonk, and that any other view is pretentious.

Plonk is indeed pleasant, or can be — it comes in a surprising number of variations, from the agreeable to the horrendous — and makes cheerful enough drinking when one cannot get anything better, which, at current prices, increasingly one cannot. Its main drawback is that, as it does not merit being lingered over, the only thing to do is to drink rather a lot of it, and a surfeit of plonk has effects far more deleterious than a surfeit of a *Premier Cru Classée*, 1855 or 1973, or even a surfeit of a *Deuxième Cru*.

Unrepentant reactionaries will greatly enjoy a visit to one of the world famous châteaux to see how a great wine is made. Ask if such a wine can survive industrial methods and you will cause surprise and be told that there is no reason to change the classic method. Until 1963, Château-Mouton still used horses and oxen to harvest its grapes. Since then it has converted to tractors; also it uses pesticides in the vineyards, and, in the vat room, the clusters of grapes are stripped from the stem by machines. Otherwise the method remains that of 1853. The grapes spend one month fermenting in huge, wooden vats, with no addition of any kind. They are then poured into 225-litre hogsheads, which are renewed every year, at a cost of around £16,000. Most of the oak comes from the forests of the Limousin, some from the USA, some from Yugoslavia.

'There's nothing like wood,' says the *maître de chai*, who started work at the *château* forty-eight years ago, when he was thirteen, and grew up to follow his father as overseer of wine-making. 'It lets the wine breathe, and when it breathes it lives.' The wine is left in the hogsheads for three years before bottling, still with no addition, unless one counts as an addition the white of egg used for clarification, which is always tested by candlelight because electricity gives a false brilliance.

In the enormous cellars the bottles, whose labels, since 1945, have been designed by artists of the calibre of Cocteau, Braque, Dali and Henry Moore, lie quiet as chrysalids against the day when they will unfold the glory of their wings. The wait may be reckoned in decades rather than years. Château-Mouton still has eight bottles from the first vintage of 1853, which will never be opened. In 1959, the centenary of France's victory over the Austrians at Solferino and Magenta, Baron Philippe sent some bottles of the 1859 vintage to General de Gaulle, who visited the battlefields with the Italian President to open them on the spot. The General's verdict on the quality of the wine was not forthcoming, but, after that length of time, what you uncork may be nectar or a sad ghost. According to the *maître de chai*, you cannot know what will come out, but you know what is going in. He says confidently that the vintages of 1947, 1957 and 1961 will last a hundred years and that 1945 was 'the year of the century'.

What makes Château Mouton stand apart from its peers is the museum, converted from former cellars to make a rarely beautiful setting for a collection of works of art in any medium which are related to wine. There are moments when the connection may strike the visitor as tenuous, whether he is looking at a white jade teapot from eighteenth-century Agra or a pair of miniatures of Italian clowns in gold, pearl and precious stones, German goldsmith's work of the second half of the seventeenth century, which once belonged to Catherine the Great : the variety of the pieces is as staggering as their quality. Tapestries from fifteenth century Strasbourg showing scenes from the *vendange*, Roman glass and a tortoiseshell cup with a profile of Charles I at the bottom, a tiny Silenus of 300 BC from Boetia and pictures by Picasso and Giacometti, each is excellent of its kind. The unifying factor over and above the theme, and one which adds to the charm of the museum, is that it is an entirely personal collection, built up over nearly twenty years by Baron Philippe and his gifted American wife. A rich man's toy, as they say: if only all rich men played in such a fashion.

The memory of all that casts such a glowing mist over the last few kilomètres of the bus journey that I get out at *Pointe de Grave* without really having noticed the oil tanks at Soulac. In 1917 the Americans landed among these dunes, and built a seventy-five-metre pyramid to commemorate the event. Twenty-five years later the Germans knocked it down. The replacement is less overweening. Here the sea comes up the strand with all the weight of the Atlantic behind it, each wave rising clear as glass to curve and hang for an instant before breaking to be stained and scattered on the sand. *Pointe de Grave* itself is hamlet rather than village, with a pilot station and a nice messy little harbour. There is almost a crowd of Sunday motorists, some long settled for such eating and drinking as is possible at the one rather simple café-restaurant, others taking off shoes, and even shirts, to sit in the bountiful sun. But the café-restaurant has no beds, and the onward way is by the ferry boat which links *Pointe de Grave* with Royan, the model seaside resort on the other side of the water. It crosses the mouth of the Gironde Estuary, which must mean a rough ride at times, but today we glide over a sea that is all satin and diamanté, with the buildings of Royan, growing ever larger as we near the opposite side, as white as the gulls which wheel and bank overhead before swooping to wrangle, raucous as fishwives, for scraps tossed over the side.

15

'SHE DIDN'T DIE of decapitation,' says the voice. 'They cut off her head after her death.'

Without swivelling right round in my chair I cannot be certain which of the three men sitting at the table behind me is the speaker, but it sounds like the one with pince-nez and a neat beard. Whether the setting for the atrocity was Chile, or the USSR, or just the pages of *France Dimanche*, the macabre sentence accords with the cheerless dining room of this seafront hotel at Royan, which itself accords with the dispiriting menu. It is a little disappointing to discover, as the conversation goes on, that the victim was Madame de Lamballe, faithful friend to Marie Antoinette, who perished in the massacre of September 1792.

When I go upstairs after a fairly dire meal I find that the bedroom hot tap runs cold. On my only previous visit to this town there was monsoon weather and I missed a train. It is enough to explain at least partly my lack of enthusiasm for the place, but I recognise that the chief reason is my nostalgia for the

Royan of yesterday, which is only keener because I never knew it. That town was a ripely perfect example of the Victorian and *Belle Époque* resort, from the luxury of its villas to the architectural higher camp of its hotels. It was flattened in the autumn of 1944, when, during the Liberation, Royan was one of the pockets on the west coast where the last, desperate handfuls of German soldiers held out. After the war it was rebuilt as an equally perfect example of a modern seaside resort. The site, with its miles of sand, and its coastline where dunes alternate with cliffs indented by small, sheltered bays, keeps its charm: the town which now occupies it gives me the feeling of being still fresh from the drawing board, with too much windy open space, too many angles — I lose myself unfailingly in streets laid out on a grid pattern, while those which have grown up organically usually have a logic that leads the visitor unerringly to the town hall, or the church, or the market square — worst of all, too much concrete.

The concrete reaches its peak, sixty-five metres to the top of the tower, in the contemporary church of Notre-Dame, set on a high point of the town, whose narrow verticals give the impression of a great ship moving into harbour. At my first sight of it I was excited by the lordly silhouette and revolted by the ignobility of the material. This time the stern, almost windowless walls, the tower like a prow, awaken a recent memory. Give or take a turret or two, this is Albi, and the poverty of the reinforced concrete compared with the red brick is enough to set one keening. What will happen when it weathers does not bear thinking of. Perhaps, like other concrete buildings at various times and in sundry places, it will fall down first. I am so enraptured by that idea that I all but walk under the wheels of an Alfa-Romeo coming at speed round a bend in the promenade. The driver's enraged cry: 'You want to die, eh?' rings in my ears all the way to the station.

The train loiters through a landscape of marsh and reeds, sprigged with little white houses, until it gets to Saintes, where there is a connection for La Rochelle. Now I remember, there is a connection also with last night's conversation in the hotel dining room, for Saintes was the birthplace of Dr. Joseph-Ignace Guillotin, who introduced into France the instrument which bears his name. Far from being a monster, he saw himself as a public benefactor. A Professor of Anatomy at the Faculty of Medicine in Paris, as well as a member of the Constituent Assembly of 1789, he believed that the chopping machine already used in Italy would provide a more humane — I seem to remember, though I cannot verify it, that the actual word was 'philanthropic' — end than the axe for victims of the Revolution. It went into operation in April 1792, so was thoroughly run in by the time of the Terror, which opened in June 1793. It would have been poetically apposite and, in the climate of the times, it was almost an even chance, if Dr. Guillotin had benefited by his own innovation some time between that date and June–July 1794, the last frenzied months of Robespierre's power, which saw 1,400 executions, but he died in his bed in 1814.

There is half an hour to wait for my train, so I settle to yet another lunch *sur le pouce*. No, says the young waiter in the buffet, there are no cheese sandwiches, only ham, but leave it to him, he will do something special. He returns with a section of *baguette* filled with Bonbel fore and Camembert aft, but cannot rise to such heights over the accompanying glass of wine. There is only *rouge supérieure*, then with a radiant smile : 'Well, not very.'

La Rochelle is two towns. The first and most generally known comes into sight as the train draws in at the station, with the bay opening out on the left, muddy grey inshore, deepening to the Atlantic blue-green, and the sentinel forts at the entry to the old harbour, the Tower of St. Nicolas and the Chain Tower, both dating from the fourteenth century. Once there was a real chain — it can still be seen in the garden of the d'Orbigny Museum — which, at nightfall, was strung between the towers, barring the harbour for the night as a cathedral close is locked up at curfew.

This is the La Rochelle which one met first in the pages of

Dumas, when Richelieu was laying siege to it in 1627–8. It fell, not because the Cardinal and the Royal Army were too much for the *Rochelais* and their British allies, who had invaded the Ile de Ré, but because Richelieu employed an architect of genius, Clement Métezeau, who achieved the apparently impossible task of building a mole across the bay, and so blockading the town. Its foundations can still be seen at low tide. The twin towers, also the Lantern Tower, are open to visitors, who can recreate the past while enjoying panoramic views of the present, with the *Vieux Port*, choc-a-bloc with fishing boats and small sailing craft, as their centre. The big ships go to La Pallice, round the headland. Everyone has painted it, from Corot to Marquet. In recent years, during which La Rochelle has profited from the enormously increased popularity of sailing — every second year the competitors in the deep-sea race from Plymouth arrive in its harbour — there has been a blossoming along the waterfront of trendy boutiques, and the kind of small, conscientiously picturesque restaurants whose décor calls for more attention than the menu.

The other La Rochelle lies behind the gate in the old city wall that is crowned by the *Grosse Horloge*, a restored Gothic clock tower. Here are narrow, arcaded streets with no hint of a seaport, here are houses, timber-fronted or patterned with bands of slate, where the fifteenth century nudges the eighteenth, here, most notably, is Protestantism. Those who think of France as a Catholic country overlook, or are unaware of both the unchurched masses of the industrial areas and the minority of Protestants, chiefly Calvinists, whose influence, like that of the Quakers in Britain, is greater than their numbers, less than 800,000, would suggest. French Protestants also are often found in banking; their traditional characteristics of energy, austerity and rectitude were exemplified by M. Maurice Couve de Murville, who, for ten years, was General de Gaulle's Minister for Foreign Affairs. Their society used to be so self-contained that, according to a friend, not until the present day was there any interchange between Catholic and Protestant *salons* in Paris. They are numerically strong in France's eastern border, as might be expected, but also in parts of the south and south-west. La Rochelle is a Calvinist high place which is known, more or less seriously, as 'the French Geneva'. In 1571 a synod was held there to draw up a statement of faith known as the Creed of La Rochelle, which was intended to replace the Nicene Creed.

The Protestantism whose imprint lingers today dates from the eighteenth century, La Rochelle's second period of prosperity, when trade with the West Indies throve and the town's merchants grew rich on their dealings in cocoa and spices, sugar and slaves. Their aristocracy lived on the west side of the town, in the area of the *Bourse* and the *Palais de Justice*. These big, grave houses, shut off from the world behind a high, balustraded wall and a courtyard, illustrate very well what is meant by an enclosed society. Though the architecture is dissimilar and the scale grander, the affinity is with Edinburgh, the New Town rather than the Royal Mile. It is no ambience for the *arriviste* or even for the extrovert and bonhomous.

A little crushed in spirit by so much restraint and nobility, I stray briefly into more democratic quarters, where there are distractions like crabs and sardines on a barrow, and the window of a confectioner's shop is almost filled by a chocolate egg weighing seven and a half kilos, 'entirely executed and decorated by the firm's chef'. I used to wonder what happened to works of art like that when Easter was past, but only yesterday I discovered the answer. A local paper, picked up at Royan, reported that the children of the *maternelle*, or infants' school, in a neighbouring small town, in the course of studying the world about them, had visited a *pâtisserie* to see how Easter fish and eggs and chicks were made, and that, before they left, the proprietor had given them the set-piece, a chocolate hare weighing five kilos sixty-five grammes. The visit and the gift were both typical happenings in the life of a *maternelle*. For my money they are by some way the most effective, as well as much the happiest section of the French educational scene. It is admitted that, for a number of children, the transfer to the bleaker world of the *école primaire*, where competition begins, and it is every child for him or herself, can be traumatic. The nature of the change was conveyed by a small girl I heard of, who had recently made it, and was being asked by a rather unimaginative adult why she seemed to be reluctant to set off for her new school every morning, when she had been so happy at the *maternelle*.

'*Mais, là, ils s'occupaient de moi*,' said the child. 'They paid attention to me there.'

There is another antidote to the *gravitas* of that mercantile West End in the cathedral of St. Louis on its northern border, at the corner of the place de Verdun. Not in the building itself, for here the wires have got crossed and the cathedral is at least as austere as the great houses, while the Protestant Temple has a decorated classical façade of outstanding charm. The fact that it was originally built, in 1708, as a chapel for the Récollets, a reformed Franciscan order, probably accounts for the fact.

For me, the main attraction of the cathedral is the collection of *ex votos*, at once spirited and naïve, which have been assembled in a chapel in its north aisle. Only two are ship models, and, for once, they are the least interesting. The rest are paintings from the seventeenth and eighteenth centuries, depicting ships and smacks and brigs and schooners rolling broadside on, leaning over at a terrifying angle, the cargo having shifted, or foundering in a smother of foam. In no case does it seem conceivable that the situation can be retrieved, and there is no hint of a lifeboat, or similar, but, usually top left, the threatening skies are rent to show a vision of Our Lady. The *ex voto* is evidence that deliverance came, but anybody with the slightest interest in ships and seafaring must long for some indication of how, to take only one example, the *Stella Maris*, dismasted and going down by the head in frightful seas in 1696, came safe to shore. In each instance the name of the master is given with the utmost formality, but there are alternative formulae. Sometimes it is *Commandeur* — Mr (presumably denoting Monsieur) Thomas Bertrand, sometimes Capt. Beauregarde, never the name with no prefix. There is one interloper in the collection, a painting, dated 1741, of a young woman who had fallen into a well and got out without human help through the intercession of Our Lady. A captain's daughter, no doubt. She is shown halfway down, or up, according to how you look at it.

There are cafés under the arcades along the east side of the *place*, but this is where one pays the penalty of having left the bustling waterfront, where café proprietors work around seventeen hours a day. Here they keep provincial hours, and I can only peer through the fast-closed door at the splendours of what seems the most inviting of them, an interior all glittering mirrors and tarnished gilding, untouched since it was done up in the most modish way in the nineties, timeless as much in its appearance as in the hours for which regulars would certainly be able to linger there for very modest outlays. Such places now are rare enough to be almost museum pieces, like the old *céramique* restaurants and cafés of Paris, almost all of which have changed their decorated tiles for something more commonplace.

Here there is an unexpected compensation in the form of an equally authentic interior in another genre which I discover behind the plain, flat front of a hotel diagonally across the *place*, which, on sight, seems to be the French equivalent of the establishment in an English market town which still does a good farmers' ordinary. The dining room is low and spacious, adorned with aspidistras and coloured that mélange of beige-to-brown-Windsor which is the background to so much good, simple eating in France. Here it is lightened by a great deal of crackling white linen, in tablecloths and napkins and the ample aprons of the waitresses, all women of a certain age, all deft and swift-footed, and deeply involved in the preferences of each customer. The *patron*, patrolling his dining room like the deck of a ship, antennae sensitive to what is going on behind the serving hatch while he gives a word to every diner, is of more than a certain age. There is no sign of a *patronne*, still less of a young master, which gives one cause to fear that when Monsieur gives up, and though that is unlikely to be before he dies, all flesh is grass and he must be at least seventy, we shall very probably not see the like of this place again. The phenomenon has been too often repeated in recent years to justify much optimism. So, for posterity, let us put on record what Monsieur offered his customers on this out-of-season mid-week night. First a platter of *hors d'oeuvre* on which, set out like a still life for the contemplation of each diner, were prawns, shrimps, a small crab, three kinds of sausage, *carotte rapée*, tomato salad, *céléri rémoulade*, red cabbage, a quarter artichoke and very young broad beans in the pod. Then a meltingly perfect gigot, with flageolets of velvety softness. Then a crême caramel or fresh fruit. A quarter of very respectable red wine was thrown in, and the price of the lot was twenty francs.

16

I WANT TO go home.

Standing on the station platform at La Rochelle, at nine o'clock in the morning, I experience a sudden empathy with Julien. He is not my favourite child, but I feel retrospectively ashamed of my impatience with him when he started whimpering about being tired of always having to move on before he and his brother had got clear of Valence, which is no distance at all from Phalsbourg. Now I, too, am not far from whimpering at the thought of at least another fortnight of one-night stands, with the filling in of a different hotel registration card every evening and the check every morning to make sure that I have not left my toothbrush in the *cabinet de toilette*. I want to go home.

Home has nothing to do with England, and is more specific than just Paris. As for so many of the French, it means a *quartier*, which is something far more restricted than the *arrondissement*, being a clearly defined, though often irregular area within which one is a known member of a known community, where life proceeds on familiar tracks, where *on a ses habitudes*. For me, its core is the narrow canyon of the rue du Dragon in the sixth *arrondissement*. It contains the little bar where I sometimes have breakfast on Saturdays, and the lady in the wine shop who tells me about her rheumatism, and the small family restaurant where I have watched the son of the house, the third generation, grow from a little boy who went to bed early into a tall lad capable of giving a hand in the enterprise, and M. Guy who does my hair and is good for a loan *in extremis,* and the shoemaker and his wife who were among my earliest friends and counsellors. There are extensions. On the one side they reach down into the boulevard, with the Flore and the Deux Magots and Lipp, but not the drugstore, and the bookshop that stays open until eleven p.m. and the *place*, with the church, and the rue de l'Abbaye as far as the place Furstenburg. On the other they go along rue Cherche Midi as far as the wonderful baker whose wood-fired oven lies under the street, along rue du Vieux Colombier, where there is the pâtisserie that makes the best *tarte au citron* in Paris, to the place St. Sulpice, for the sake of the fountain and the shops that sell crib figures at Christmas, and, beyond that, the Marché St. Germain where, daily, the country comes into Paris. That is it, and within those few acres, with a dispensation to go up to the Luxembourg Gardens or down to the *quais* for exercise, any reasonable person can lead a full life.

Like the Hebridean exile, I behold it in dreams, and all that is needed to make them reality is the resolution to take the nine eighteen train to Paris instead of the nine thirteen to Nantes. It is the second occasion for decision that has arisen over this stage of the tour, which is scheduled to take me into Britanny, with Quimper as my first night's halt there. Nantes is the inescapable point of entry: the choice I pondered last night was whether to go directly there or to make an inland detour through a region which, since first I knew it, I have thought of as the heart of France, the *pays de la Loire*, which takes in a broader area than the Loire Valley.

Traditionally it has been known as the garden of France; these days, in a modest fashion, it has become a small part of the workshop also. It has seen almost as much history as the Ile de France : over the centuries everyone seems to have been here, whether you think of Alcuin teaching at Tours after Charlemagne had fetched him from Rome, and Leonardo, who was invited by Francois I, and died at Amboise, or the native born, like Clouet, who painted the royal house of France, Rabelais, who used the settings of his native province in his work, Ronsard and Du Bellay who hymned its sweet air and mild skies, Balzac, who kept returning here from Paris, which was the other half of his life. From Charles VII to Henry III the Kings of France held court in the *châteaux* of the Loire : twice, during the war of 1870 and that of 1939–45, Tours, briefly, has been the seat of a French government which had withdrawn from Paris and was about to fall back on Bordeaux. In 1429 Joan of Arc bundled the English out of Orleans and, in the confusion and demoralisation of 1940, when a defeated army was retreating southwards, the officers and cadets of the cavalry school at Saumur, with a handful of North African troops and totally inadequate equipment, fought in the same spirit when they held up for two days, on a front of twenty kilometres, a German army more than ten times their strength. Was it reasonable to subject the town of Saumur to heavy bombardment and give orders amounting to : 'Die where you stand' to those young men for what was no more than a point of honour, since the announcement that Pétain had asked for an armistice had already been made? The question was asked even at the time, but there are moments when a nation needs a legend more than it needs reason, and 1940 was one of them.

All that I could take in by travelling from La Rochelle to Poitiers, then going down the Loire to Saumur. From Saumur, a local train, or, more probably, a complex of local trains would take me to Sablé, to hear the monks of the Benedictine Abbey of Solesmes singing the plainsong, 'grave and passionless and undulating', which is the music of eternity. History is repeating itself, for, as the Benedictines preserved civilisation during the Dark Ages, so Solesmes is the custodian of Gregorian, which, over the centuries, has been part of the very fabric of the Church's worship, at a time when the movement for liturgical reform is filling French churches with the kind of jiggy little tunes which, as the late James Agate said in a quite different context, you remember the moment you hear them and forget the moment they stop.

What makes me resist the temptation is the realisation that, once I let myself stray from the appointed route, there will be no end to it. Albi was an exception, but the point about exceptions is that they are isolated. What makes me get on the nine thirteen when it draws up at the platform is sheer moral fibre. I sit next to an elderly man who is reading a cinema magazine with a picture of a naked girl on the cover and the caption : 'Eroticism or pornography?' Whichever it is, he shows no more sign of emotion than if he were reading *Tante Marie* on the best way to produce a *petit salé aux lentilles*. The country is kempt and green and uneventful, then all the roofs are slate instead of red tile; there is mistletoe in apple trees; we are in Britanny. Or are we?

It was in 1956 that a re-drawing of boundaries detached the *Loire-Atlantique* from Britanny to make it part of the *pays de la Loire*, but in their hearts many Bretons are still not reconciled to the loss of the city which was the ancient capital of the Duchy of Britanny and the seat of its Parliament. True, with the Loire serving as a highway into what, in Britanny, one tends to think of as 'mainland France', it has never been so purely Celtic as the embattled granite townships further west, but for that very reason it would find its place in modern Britanny. The separatists who would claim it as part of the province stress its Breton traditions, but they are conscious, too, of the value of a major port and industrial city to any project for autonomy. Also, since separatism is more and more tangled with party politics, and the parties are of the Left, they would welcome the recruitment to their cause of the trade unionists of St.

Nazaire, the outport of Nantes, whose militant solidarity is a byword in France. The days when Britanny was a stronghold of Royalists and Gaullistes have passed. If it remains one of the most Catholic regions of France, it is increasingly often a New Wave Catholicism in which the clergy are at the side of, and occasionally at the head of, the militants. Even when it is not contesting, the Church in Britanny is showing signs of questioning some of the more 'picturesque' aspects of the faith.

So far as I know, nobody so far has spoken against the Pardons, the annual pilgrimages to the churches and shrines of saints, notably in Finistère, in which religious processions are accompanied by folk festivals, but, early in 1974, the diocesan review of Vannes published an article representing the views of port chaplains in Britanny who had reservations about the advisability of blessing ships at their launching, as well as the significance of a religious ceremony on such occasions. They thought that to conduct such ceremonies was to discharge very lightly the task of the evangelisation of a *milieu* which was known to be one of the most de-Christianised — many of the sailors would see no more than invoking good luck in the blessing of a ship.

Some observers hold that militancy is part of the Breton temperament : certainly '*têtu comme un Breton*', pigheaded as a Breton, is a phrase that has passed into the language. What gives it its distinctive character today is that many workers are a first industrial generation who have come off the land into factories, and have not yet cut away from their roots. Employers who saw in this the advantage that they would not be steeped in union wiles and well-versed in their rights discovered — the phenomenon is not confined to Britanny — that there were accompanying disadvantages. They were not well versed in the imperatives of industrial discipline either; used to working intensively when the situation demanded it, as when the cows needed milking or when, at last, the weather let up and it was possible to get on the land for drilling, they found it hard to accept clocking in and the assembly line, and might come out on strike without benefit of shop steward, let alone a directive from party headquarters.

Once they were out, they could count on the support of the hinterland, otherwise the peasant population from which they sprang. That happened during the '*événements*' of 1968, when, for a time, the most hair-raising rumours circulated in Paris about goings-on in Nantes, where the 'insurgents' were credited with having taken possession of the town hall and establishing their own Commune. What certainly did happen was that the factory workers got supplies from the country. It happened again in 1972, when the striking workers of the *Joint français* factory at Saint-Brieuc were able to hold out for eight weeks and gain their claims because the farmers kept their larders filled. In return, when, in the same year, the Breton farmers, protesting about prices, staged a ten-day strike, during which churns full of milk were poured away instead of being sold, they had the population of the towns largely behind them.

Ironically, the militancy has increased when, at last, economic development in Britanny has become a reality. There are few regions which, in recent years, have done so well in government grants, and, if there is still no motorway, there are other elements of the kind of infrastructure that attracts industry to an area. Emigration is at last dwindling, after generations during which Britanny knew depopulation in spite of a high birthrate because the young people had to leave home to find work, usually in Paris. There has even been some immigration. At Rennes there are, or, until recently, were, a large enough number of Portuguese to make the university set up a course in the language for French adults who came into contact with immigrants through their work.

The development is still too recent to have changed long-term trends. Average life spans are short; suicide rates are high; on the shaded maps indicating the level of alcoholism in various areas of France, Britanny is shaded black. Also, not all development is welcomed by everybody. The French government's plan to build a complex of four 1,000 megawatt nuclear reactors on the rocky coast of the Quiberon Peninsula, in South Britanny, moved the 1,800 strong population of the neighbouring village of Erdeven to form a committee dedicated to resisting the project. Some of their propaganda suggesting the possible effects of radio-activity may have been more lurid than accurate, but it stirred up the population to the point where the mayor and councillors, who had been eager to see the reactors built in the commune because the rent paid for the use of the sites would transform their budget, were obliged to vote against letting them. Useless to argue that the reactors, far from being part of a deliberate policy of victimising an already unprivileged area, represented only a tiny part of the government's plan to set up 200 nuclear power stations along its coast, and on the banks of the major rivers, the Loire, Rhône and Rhine. The wisdom of such a plan, with its commitment to the American enriched uranium technology, which some experts consider to be unsafe, is another question. If you are a true Breton, you are automatically against any government that is based in Paris.

All that seems far removed from Nantes at the moment, where my arrival platform is decked with pots of hydrangeas and the black and white ermine banner of the Duchy, with, dead-centre, a red-carpeted dais with mikes in position. The most retiring of us have our moments of Walter Mitty high fantasy, but the splendour turns out to be not recognition at last for a Celtic cousin, but preparation for the baptism of a new turbo-train, to be named the *Ville de Nantes,* which will give the city a hot line to Paris. Its godmother, who will perform the naming ceremony, is the wife of the mayor, who is also a Senator. I do not stay to see whether champagne is involved, as at the launching of a ship, because I am lured into the *Jardin des Plantes* opposite the station. Here is an aspect of Britanny overlooked by those who picture it as a grey, storm-swept peninsula, half hidden in mist and spray. The Atlantic gales are real enough, but the obverse of the medal is the mildness of an oceanic climate. It is still only April, but the intensely green lawns are enamelled with the pucey pink of rhododendrons, waxy camellias, rose and white and near-crimson, and magnolias, each an annunciation of blossom. All the colours are so vivid that you experience them in the pit of the stomach rather than on the retina.

Afterwards I walk along the *cours* John Kennedy to the Duchess Anne's *château*, which keeps its grim exterior though now the protective moats have been laid out as gardens, and the mallard and their broods glide over the surface of the water while the fish flicker through its depths. The contrast with the inner courtyard repeats that of the twin aspects of the Breton climate : where you expect a keep there is a Renaissance palace. When Duke Francois II, the Duchess Anne's father, held court here, there were seventeen *chambellans* and four *maîtres d'hotel* at the head of a cohort of servants which makes one think of Versailles. What people call 'the way of life' at that court recalls nothing so much as an Edwardian house party at the period when practical jokes were fashionable, though, in place of apple-pie beds, there was a gay trick of tossing people into the moat if they failed to get up at the appointed time. The study of history gives one a great feeling of continuity. We may no longer behave like the Edwardians, but nowadays the Americans seem to take delight in pushing people into swimming pools. Blinking in the blessed sunshine I give thanks very smugly that I am not an Edwardian, or an American, or, indeed, a member of Francois II's court, before opening the current issue of *Ouest France* at the serial-story page. Yesterday Deborah, the heroine, had sunk up to her waist in a quicksand before Percival, the hero, got her out by lassooing her and then putting his horse into reverse. You know it was going to be all right in the end, although both were engaged to somebody else, because his kiss 'tasted of lavender, honey and fruits', but one likes to be quite sure.

17

FINISTÈRE. BRITANNY, TOO, has its Land's
End, and anyone who has the misfortune to choose August for a
visit to the *Pointe du Raz*, the headland where France thrusts out
farthest into the Atlantic, will recognise a kinship with the
Cornish equivalent in the commemorative gewgaws as in the
threadbare turf on the cliff top. The Breton name is *Penn ar
Bed*, which means equally the end, or edge of the world, and,
in the winter gales, when the Atlantic rears up to explode against
the land, the edge of the world is what this terrible and beautiful
coast feels like.

The terror is hard to envisage on this spring afternoon at
Quimper where, under the lee of the old ramparts beside the
cathedral, the sunshine is honeyed with wallflowers and, on the
stone benches, a thoughtful municipality has laid planks to
protect the shrunken hams of the elderly who chiefly frequent
them. The stone is granite, like that of the ramparts. Taken with
the camellias and the coral azaleas that are in luxuriant bloom
in the gardens behind them, and the old men sunning themselves

in front, it provides an evocative abstract of this *departement*. The whole of Finistère lies within *Basse-Bretagne*, the area west of the language line, where a million people more or less still speak Breton, unlike *Haute Bretagne*, east of it, where French has taken over. This is where one finds the majority of the 80,000 regular followers of the Breton language programmes put out by the ORTF, which were represented as a generous gesture to national feeling. Since they amounted to no more than eighteen minutes a week, or sixteen hours during the year, the gesture was less than excessive, but, whatever the language used, television has transformed life in some of the remoter areas of Finistère. No single action by the Breton Liberation Movement robbed them of as much popular sympathy as their dynamiting of a transmitter which blacked out TV screens for some weeks during the early part of 1974. There were optimists who let themselves dream that the void might encourage a resurrection of traditional culture, with its fireside evenings of song and story on the lines of the Scots *ceilidh* or the Welsh *noson lawen*, but, if it did, they were not publicised. Instead, bookshops reported an increase in sales, first of magazines, then of whodunnits, then, tentatively, of best sellers which had been published in paperback editions. All of which, of course, were fully as alien to the 'Breton way of life' as the programmes on the ORTF's national network, which have contributed as much as tourism, and more than improved transport — the improvement is relative only, as those who try to get about the region without a car soon find — to the 'Frenchification' of Britanny.

Not that it can be blamed for all the changes in and around Quimper since first I knew it, thirty years ago. Then, to travel in a crowded bus was to risk having your neck severed just below the ears by the razor-starched edges of the *collerettes* of women who, as a matter of course, wore their regional costumes to come into market, and, at Concarneau, you were awakened every morning by the clatter of *sabots* on the quay. Now the traditional dress is kept for red letter days, sacred or secular. At Quimper I see only two old ladies wearing bunchy skirts and the tall, stove-pipe *coiffe* of Pont l'Abbé — each district of Finistère and the neighbouring Morbihan has a distinctive style for its *coiffe* and *collerette* — and a single pair of modified *sabots*, which have felt uppers attached to wooden soles. On the market stalls the new potatoes are offered scraped and scrubbed, ready for the pot, instead of smelling of the fresh earth, and the occasional slab of cowslip yellow farm butter stands out among the wrapped packets. Up a cobbled lane I find not a *crêperie* but a *pizzeria*, with Chianti flasks and bunches of plastic grapes hung up outside. A notice in a shop window announces that, tomorrow evening, somebody is giving a lecture on 'Magicians and Lamas of the Himalaya : Astrology, Gurus, Shamans, Exorcists'. This is even more disconcerting than the *discothèque* in the austere fishing port of Douarnenez, where I spend the afternoon, and the chichi *brocante*, or junk shop, on the roadside near Quimper.

It takes the *gemütlichkeit* of an evening entertainment, where two children's choirs sing acceptably but not remarkably, and a group plays the *biniou*, or Breton bagpipes, to an audience of unashamedly partisan parents, the whole as cosy as a parish concert, to reassure me that some things have not changed. Foremost among them is the feeling of having come home that I have never failed to experience in *Basse Bretagne*. It is different from the sense of being on familiar ground which many of the British are aware of in Normandy, and more than Welsh whimsy. The Celtic cousinship is real. To the Romans, Britanny was 'Britannia Minor'. Later, over a couple of centuries, its population was increased by refugees from Britain, who were fleeing from the invading Angles and Saxons. They brought their language and customs with them : ultimately the name of *Armorica* was changed to 'Second Britain', or Britanny. Anyone who shares the language is likely to sense the difference between 'Britain' and 'England' even more clearly than at home.

The next day is one of complicated travel that will take me round the coast to Lamballe, which is well over the line into *Haute Bretagne* and in another world from maritime *Cornouaille* and the *Léonnais*, the vegetable growing area of the north, with its fields of cauliflower and artichokes and onions. Roscoff, its port, has been the point of departure for generations of the Breton onion sellers who pedal round the streets of British towns, their bicycles festooned with strings of their wares. During the bus journey to Brest, which is the first part of it, I amuse myself by imagining the hopeful young farmers and their wives who would seem to be the most likely occupants of the dozens of small white houses, trim as daisies, that we pass on the way. The truth is far otherwise; mostly they are the fulfilment of the returned American's — there are more Bretons in New York than in Britanny — or sometimes the returned Parisian's dream. Emigrants who have made their modest fortunes come home to build their modest houses and contribute to the imbalance of the region's age structure.

Brest is an exultant town, in atmosphere as well as in situation, rising easily above an English guide book's debatable statement that it is 'of no great interest to the ordinary traveller' and its better-founded one that it is the rainiest of French towns. Rain it does, but, where there is so much air and space and light, the intermittent downpours are no more noxious than a series of Ireland's 'a soft day, thank God'. From the terrace of the *château*, a fortified place since the days of the Romans, you look down on what is perhaps the most magnificent natural harbour in Europe, big enough to offer a haven to all the navies of Europe together. Beyond it the vastness of eternity opens out; once you have passed between the lights on the *Pointe de Penhir to* starboard and the *Pointe de St. Mathieu* to port, the first landfall is America. Trading and fishing off that fanged coast is an incomparable school of seamanship, and Britanny, traditionally, provides the heart of the French Navy as well as an impressive proportion of its complement. There is a superb poignancy about the choice of the extremity of the *Pointe de St. Mathieu* as a site for a memorial column to French sailors killed during the war of 1914–18, but the Second World War was to provide one even more stirring.

The tiny Ile de Sein, five miles off the *Pointe du Raz*, a treeless, windswept square mile of land surrounded by murderous rocks, is in itself a memorial to one of the most inspiring episodes in the records of the Free French. When, in 1940, news of the fall of France reached the island, every active man in a population of fishermen in which boys virtually stepped from the cradle into a boat sailed to join de Gaulle in England. They numbered 140, of whom twenty-seven were to be killed in action. I first heard the story from a friend who was a young girl on the island at the time. She could never tell it, or I hear it, without tears. Officially the age limits of manhood were set between sixteen and sixty. Actually, the oldest of the party, the *patron* of a fishing vessel, who had not dreamed of retirement, was sixty-six. The youngest was his grandson, a boy of fourteen, who, as a member of the ship's company, claimed the right to sail in her.

For the next four years daily life on Sein was carried on by women who had only boys and old men to help them. They were well equipped to grapple with its rigours. It was always the women who had tilled the fields, and not so many years earlier they had carried up from the harbour on their heads the stones used to build the modern church. In 1946 de Gaulle visited the island to present in person the Cross of Liberation awarded for its gallantry. It is probably the only place in France where he was received not as the reincarnation of Vercingétorix, St. Louis and Joan of Arc all rolled into one, but as *primus inter pares*. The fishermen of Sein, devoted as they were to the cause of Free France, regarded the General with the healthy but un-awed respect which those who had done what they saw as their duty felt for another who had done the same. One can be fairly sure that de Gaulle understood and reciprocated this attitude.

Brest itself, devastated by bombing during the war years, when the arsenal and the dockyard were occupied by the Germans, for whom the port was a naval base, has been rebuilt, largely in the native granite, which gives vigour and substance where new towns too often seem raw and flimsy. It is possible to sympathise with the resentment felt here when the deep-sea oil port for which the town had hoped went instead to Le Havre while at the same time feeling that that kind of development was not in Britanny's destiny. The university centre, established since the war, is more in the native tradition. Like other Celtic countries where living standards are generally modest and local employment possibilities limited, Britanny has a high proportion of young people going on to the university, and, again as in Wales or Scotland, higher education is not socially elitist. Thirty per cent of Brest's students come from working-class homes, the highest proportion in the country, and the establishment of the university centre has had a noticeable effect on the town's intellectual climate. All the same, Brest still belongs to the French Navy as intimately as do Portsmouth and Plymouth to the British.

Sailors carrying pusser weekend cases of metal covered with leatherette make up half the passengers on the train for St. Brieuc : a group of them form in the corridor round one of their number with a beard and a guitar, and most of the journey is accompanied by Radio Luxembourg's current hits in close harmony. We pass through Landernau, with its three-tier church spire like a Victorian whatnot, but, unfortunately, the railway passes well south of St. Pol-de-Léon, whose fantastic belfry, the Kreisker, seventy-seven metres of granite, has four elaborate turrets supporting an airy spire which Vauban, speaking as a professional, admired as 'a marvel of balance and daring'. To make up for it we pass over the stunning two-tier viaduct at Morlaix, which carries travellers lifted like gods above the town in the valley of the Dosson, fifty-eight metres below.

St. Brieuc, since I last saw it, has expanded into flats and housing estates, again with the granite stiffening the concrete and pebble dash. According to how you look at it, more flats than you would expect in Britanny or more individual houses than you would expect in modern France. The tradition in Britanny, where populations relatively speaking, are low, space is ample and therefore cheap, and characters are fiercely independent, has been for houses. In new towns it has been to some degree modified, but it remains a protection against egg-rack apartments.

By the time the bus from St. Brieuc arrives at Lamballe I am beginning to feel battered with much voyaging, but I am not too far gone to be jerked back to attention by the difference between this town, which is new to me and St. Brieuc, little more than thirty kilometres away. It boils down to a feeling that now I am back in France, whatever the departmental map may say, and indeed, as long ago as the tenth century, this part of the diocese of St. Brieuc, of which Lamballe was the capital, was French rather than Breton-speaking. It is Britanny none the less: Lamballe, like Moncontour to the south-west, was one of the fortified places that protected the Duchy against its French neighbours. The *château* which crowned the hill above the town is long vanished, destroyed by Richelieu in punishment of its owner. César Vendôme, a natural son of Henry IV, for siding against him. One gets some idea of its scale from the collegiate church, itself fortified, which was once the chapel of the *château*. Where the castle stood is a wide promenade that would serve as a look-out platform. Beneath the inscription on the *monument aux morts*: 'Died for France', somebody has scrawled: 'Died for Krupps'. The wind blows cold and the light is fading: the sense of those vanished battalions, whatever or whoever they died for, mingles with the re-awakened memory of that other victim whose gracious head was promenaded through the streets of Paris on a pike after she had died for her loyalty to her queen. In fact, it is unlikely that Madame de Lamballe ever saw this town, which was part of the domaine of her father-in-law, the Duke of Penthièvre.

At my hotel the painters are in upstairs, so Madame has billeted me across the way, with her commercial rival and, apparently, close friend, who has the painters in in the dining room. The crowd eating with us suggests that there is a reciprocal arrangement. The room is full of people working their way through the admirable *table d'hôte* dinner of prawns mayonnaise, followed by skate with black butter, superbly disregarding the TV in the corner, which is blethering out somebody's election address. I note that the *menu régime*, at twenty-five francs, is dearer than the *table d'hôte*, though people who choose it presumably eat less, also that there is an awe-inspiring sixty francs menu which must be lobster all the way.

In the morning last night's unquiet ghosts are laid and Lamballe has once more become a cheerfully bustling little market town, with a famous stud down the road and streets where there is occasional evidence that it is a centre for pig and cattle fairs. Its daily life is laid out in a news sheet: *La Vie Communale de Maroué* (the name of the district) displayed in the window of the *Mairie*, which is open from eight fifteen a.m. to noon except Saturdays. There are instructions for getting on to the electoral roll, an exhortation about the Campaign Against Hunger and a Prefectorial order against thistles, which must surely mean against the people who allow them to grow on their land. The *Amicale des Chasseurs de Maroué* are allowed to use poison against '*nuisibles quadrupeds*' during the fortnight April 5th–May 1st, and somebody has found a purse containing 'a little money, a belt and various gloves'.

Then an item about pullets for sale, just coming into lay. The vendors are a Monsieur and Madame Fou Chou. The world is smaller than you think.

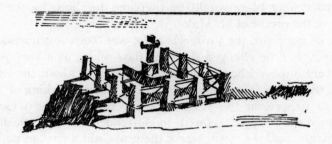

18 IS THERE IN the world another grave where humility rises to such heights of arrogance? Before it only the sea, kingfisher blue today, in winter raving up towards the blunt, granite cross on top of the headland which it has not shaken in 126 years. No word on the stone. Even General de Gaulle conceded a name and a date. Châteaubriand lies on the seaward extremity of the islet of *le Grand Bé*, off the shore of his native St. Malo, in total anonymity.

It is hard to connect the spirit of this superb burial place with the rather complicated manoeuvres which went on to secure it. As a nation the French tend to be more preoccupied about burial places than the English even when their funerary tastes are conventional; it is quite usual to take steps about securing a concession in an agreeable cemetery long before, in the normal course, one would expect to occupy it. Châteaubriand put his unorthodox request to the mayor of St. Malo with the suggestion that it might be granted in recognition of the service he had rendered to the townspeople by helping them to get a wet dock which they wanted to construct. The mayor was willing, but the Army engineers, presumably seeing in the headland a possible site for a gun emplacement, raised difficulties, and it was three years before he was able to let Châteaubriand know that the desired resting place would be prepared for him 'by the filial piety of the people of St. Malo'.

In its externals, the town where he was 'born a gentleman' is surprisingly little changed since the days when, as a very young and very impoverished gentleman, he ran wild about the waterfront with the local urchins, particularly when you think of what was to happen in the years between. In 1944, the Germans occupying St. Malo refused to surrender to the advancing Americans, and the town, where there was still a civilian population, was subjected to a bombardment which, with the fire that followed, destroyed the greater part of it. Miraculously, the ramparts, whose foundations date from the twelfth century, though there were additions and modifications until the seventeenth, survived intact. When it was all over, the town was reconstructed within them, on the old plan, from the immemorial granite. In the circuit of the ramparts which is the standard constitutional for visitors, and which offers the contrasted pleasures of immense prospects over coast and ocean on the one hand and, on the other, involuntary voyeurism as you see into people's windows willy-nilly, the only painful anachronism I notice is a board announcing for sale apartments of *grand standing*, with garage, *cave* and *ascenseur*, and even then the building which contains them is as austere and solidly built as anything that went before. The *grand standing*, though, is proof of a sad adulteration in the spirit of the *Malouins*, who, Châteaubriand tells us, constituted 'a single family' when they were locked into their city at night, and who, during the seventeenth century, declared themselves a republic in order to keep clear of the warring religious factions of the *Ligue*, expressing their independence in their motto : 'Ni Français ni Breton, Malouins sommes.' Individuality would have to approach the pathological if it was to remain uninfluenced by the hordes of visitors, many from beyond Europe, who pour into the town every year. One of them has written: 'Hot dog!' on the plinth of the statues of two of St. Malo's great seamen who are stationed on the ramparts as on a quarter deck. That of Jacques Cartier, who discovered Canada in 1535 and took possession of it in the name of the King of France, though it was not colonised until 1608, was raised in 1905, with the help of Canadian subscriptions. Robert Surcouf had to wait for his statue until 1932, though he was more in the St. Malo tradition, which, basically, was piratical. First slave trader, then corsair, he amassed a fortune so enormous that, at the age of thirty-six, he was able to come ashore and settle to making more money by ship-building. Duguay-Trouin, who preceded him by exactly a century, being born in 1673 to Surcouf's 1773, progressed from being a pirate to being a naval officer, and died a lieutenant-general in the *armées navales*, which were created in the seventeenth and eighteenth centuries for the defence of the colonies. His statue is down in the town, in the square named after him; I never find out if that, too, has been captioned: 'Hot dog!'

My hotel is blissful, with the central heating on and the kind of ample, unfashionable comfort which Britanny at its best does as well as Alsace. On my breakfast tray in the morning, instead of apricot jam or red currant jelly, there is authentic home-made marmalade. When I ask the girl at the reception desk whether Madame has made it she says: 'No — M'sieu. He always does.' Perhaps, these days, *Malouin* individuality comes out in these lesser ways, like the habit of keeping the town's splendid aquarium open until midnight, which is done in no other resort that I know, and was a godsend one wet night when I was waiting for a midnight train back to Paris.

What I need to catch at the moment is a bus which will take me over the border into Normandy for the weekend, though where in Normandy I am not yet quite sure. It is while waiting for it down on the quay that I meet my travelling companion for the day.

The small woman with the day's needs stowed into a sensible white plastic satchel, who wants to get to Mont.-St.-Michel, addresses me in gallant French. Since, as I soon discover, she comes from California, was not educated in Europe and is not an academic, this is in itself surprising. When I learn a little later that she commands even more heroic German it becomes astonishing. More, she is alone, no longer young, totally unpackaged and intending to stay on this side for five and a half weeks, or until the money runs out, taking in during that time Holland, Germany, Italy and Switzerland. It is her fourth trip to Europe.

'My friends say : "Why are you going to Europe again? You've been there," ' she tells me.

This is my mirror image, give or take a white satchel, and I am happy to find that the rapprochement seems to be mutual. By the time we have boarded the bus for Pontorson, which is her jumping-off place for Mont-St.-Michel, and mine for somewhere deeper into Normandy, we are talking like a *kaffe klatsch*. Besides being surprised at her wanting to come to Europe twice, let alone four times, her friends are alarmed at the idea of her travelling alone, but she finds you meet more people that way, and stay in more interesting places. In St. Malo she is in a real Breton house. When she found a bowl laid for her at breakfast she expected groats, but Madame explained that it was for coffee, and now she has learned to drink out of it.

When we arrive at Pontorson we find that there is an hour and a half to wait before the afternoon bus to Mont-St.-Michel, and three before I can get a train going up into the Cotentin, that finger of land sticking up into the Channel, so, with difficulty, I lure her into the *estaminet* opposite the station, feeling an unlettered pedant's pride in knowing that word, which is used only in and around Normandy. Usually, she says, she keeps the *croissant*, which is a part of the standard French breakfast, to eat at lunch time. I should be doing the same myself; economies of that sort are what makes it possible to spin out five and a half weeks into seven, and I feel ashamed of my beer and the accompanying section of *baguette* with a double frill of ham hanging out all round. It looks excessive compared with the cup of chocolate which my new friend allows herself with her *croissant*. While she drinks it she works out for me a tour of the USA which can all be done by Greyhound bus once I have arrived at San Francisco by air, because the west is the side to start from. San Diego, Grand Canyon, two National Parks, Brice and Zion, down to New Orleans, then Arizona, Virginia and Williamsburgh. I am ready to start at the drop of a dollar, feeling, not for the first time, that it is uneducated never to have crossed the Atlantic, and undaunted by my companion's warning that New York and Washington DC are to be avoided because of the violence. If you are there, she says, you have to be in before dark, go to your room, lock the door and stay there till morning. I know somebody who does that at the Regent's Palace Hotel, but at least she has her dinner sent up, whereas in New York you would never dare to open the door to a waiter for fear of what might come in with the Chicken Maryland. Even my intrepid Californian, swanning around Europe un-escorted, says she would be afraid to go to Rome again, because, when she was there before, she had some candles which had been blessed by the Pope taken from her room, and some friends of hers, when they were in Naples, were robbed of their tooth-paste and their car wheels. I am struck once again at how perilous a place Europe seems when you look at it from outside, and I want to know why the Neapolitans, whom circumstances have made Europe's greatest survivors, left the car behind, but I do not like to ask for fear of seeming flippant and unsympathetic.

When she has gone off in the Pontorson bus I set off myself to walk in the same direction along a picture-book French road, straight and white and empty, with the larksong dropping down on it in bright garlands. Three kilometres along the road I see Mont.-St.-Michel, suspended in the clouds like a medieval vision of the New Jerusalem. Impossible that anything so insubstantial is the wonder of architectural engineering one knows it to be. A

triple wonder, in fact, for the airy Gothic of the Abbey crowning
the rock that rises 260 feet above the sands and shallows of the
Bay St. Michel surmounts and encloses two earlier churches, one
Romanesque, one Carolingian, and there was an oratory even
before that. According to legend, in the eighth century the bay
was covered by a forest from which rose the rock which is now
Mont.-St.-Michel and was then known as Mont-Tombe, and,
north of it, the rock called Tombelaine. It was a visitation from
the Archangel Michael which inspired St. Aubert, Bishop of
Avranches, whose diocese included the forest, to build a sanctuary
dedicated to him on the summit of the rock. The archangel had
to repeat the instruction three times before the bishop acted on
it. The third time it was driven home by a sharp rap on the head,
and Aubert's skull, with a cautionary dent in it, can still be seen
in the Treasury of the Basilica of St. Servais at Avranches.

By the time legend has given place to history, the waters have
covered the forest, Aubert's oratory has been succeeded by a
Carolingian church and, the college of twelve canons who were
charged with guarding the relics of the oratory having relapsed
into decadence and worse, they have been turned out by Duke
Richard of Normandy and replaced by thirty Benedictines from
the Abbey of St.-Wandrille. The Carolingian church became the
crypt of a Romanesque basilica built on the summit, and when,
early in the thirteenth century, that was partly destroyed by fire,
work started on the Gothic abbey, 'the Marvel'. Over twelve
centuries the monks built like bees, leaving no trace of the name
of any architect.

The human history is at least as fascinating as the architectural,
tangled as it is, like so many of the chronicles of this coast, with
that of England. Through much of its existence, Mont.-St.-
Michel was a strongpoint as well as a holy place, with successive
French kings sharing the cost of constructing fortifications and
maintaining a garrison. It sent several ships to take part in
William the Conqueror's invasion of England, and, in the next
century, was successively a refuge for Henry I and a setting for
the court of Henry II, in their personae of Dukes of Normandy.

As late as 1203, when they supported King John, whose French possessions were forfeited after he had murdered Little Arthur, the monks remained staunchly pro-English; after Normandy was united to the French crown they were equally staunchly pro-French. Only Mont.-St.-Michel held out for the French king when Henry V was sweeping across Normandy in the campaign which culminated in Agincourt. Before the end of the Hundred Years' War it had withstood three sieges by the English, during the third of which the garrison not only beat off their assailants but captured most of their artillery. Two English bombards, with their cannon balls, may still be seen near the gate of the little town which climbs up to the feet of the abbey.

Aesthetically, the bombards are greatly to be preferred as souvenirs to most of those sold today along the Grande Rue, the narrow street of fifteenth- and sixteenth-century houses more or less — usually more — mutilated by later tinkering. It may be true that hucksters were well-established hangers-on of the medieval pilgrimages to Mont.-St.-Michel, but plastics did not exist in the Middle Ages, and holy medals, and leaden bulbs filled with the presumably sanctified sands of the bay, and even bits of old bones are visually inoffensive enough.

My Californian friend will hate them. I hope that, in compensation, when she gets to the abbey, she finds that the group of Benedictines from the Abbey of Bec-Hellouin, who, for the past few years, have occupied Mont.-St.-Michel in the summer, are already installed. If they are she will hear Gregorian sung once more in a building which, during a great part of the nineteenth century, served as a factory for making straw hats.

That the abbey should be restored permanently to its original purpose can scarcely be hoped for. It is less a question of lack of vocations to the religious life, though, in France as elsewhere, they have been falling off rapidly, than of the virtual impossibility of making the building habitable in winter. Even in summer medieval domestic architecture has its drawbacks.

'It's the stairs,' explained the acting abbot, to coin a non-existent title, of the group from Bec Hellouin, whom I met a few years ago. 'Thank goodness, when we are not in choir, we are usually dressed like this.'

'This' was a dark blue boiler suit, whose wearer had greeted me with a *baise main* of an elegance that would have adorned a diplomatic reception. St. Benedict, most practical of holy men, would have approved, but I hope all the same that the Californian visitor will be spared the culture shock of finding the community dressed like that.

Back in Pontorson I have a mild culture shock myself, but of the agreeable kind given by this morning's home-made marmalade, when the *pâtisserie* provides strong tea in a proper brown pot to go with a chocolate Grand Marnier. At the station it becomes clear that my overnight stop must be Coutances, which is excellent, as its cathedral is one of the few in Northern France which I have never seen. There is a train in half an hour and I wait for it in company with a man who has a serious but friendly dog on a lead. It is a Schnauzer, he says. His brother's dog, but his friend. 'And of an intelligence — but an intelligence !'

19

THEORIES ABOUT THE influence of environment on character are often self-evident. The intemperate suns and vivid landscapes of Latin countries may be expected to stimulate violence, verbal, emotional or physical. The soft climate of the Western Isles can only have a slackening effect on moral fibre. If you live in the Auvergne, or Aberdeen, or Cardigan, where a frugal living has to be scratched from ungrateful soil, it is unlikely that you will grow up to throw money out of the windows.

Then one comes to Normandy. Here is a climate broadly similar to that of the South of England, with, as in the South of England, pockets of extreme mildness where palm trees flourish out of doors. Here is earth so fertile that, says the old joke, if a Normandy farmer thrusts his stick into the ground, he finds it has broken into leaf by the morning, pastures so lush that the cream comes straight from the cow. And here, mystifyingly, are a people for whose traditional character 'near' is a diplomatic description. Reputedly the Normans are both legalistic and litiginous, so reluctant to commit themselves that they find 'maybe' preferable to a straight yes or no, and as tough as they are stolid.

Such a character can hardly be ascribed to their Viking ancestors, who settled on this coast in the tenth century after raiding and pillaging it through most of the ninth. People are not like that in Norway, nor is the re-exported article, which took root in England after the Conqueror's successful invasion, and in Sicily at about the same time. The three brothers of the Hauteville family, Guillaume, Robert Guiscard and Roger, who founded the Kingdom of the Sicilies, came from this very area of Coutances, but though you can still find blue eyes in Sicily, never have I found there anybody remotely like the trio of nobly granitic women who confront me in the bar-cum-reception of this most inviting hotel.

All are handsome in a Rhine maiden sort of way, all are personally immaculate as though scrubbed up for an operating theatre, all have an adamantine quality no more than two centimetres below the perfectly correct and courteous exterior. The type is at its most perfect in *Madame*, who presides over the kitchen — brilliantly, I later discover. Alone, you feel, she could repel an invasion. Her daughter, who rules over the bar, will be a worthy successor, though for the moment a youthful bloom, like sea thrift springing out of rock, rounds the edges of her character. *Madame*'s mother, who is in the *caisse*, and so wears a black apron in contrast to Madame's surgical white and Mademoiselle's neat *chemisier* and skirt, has mellowed a little with age, but the process is relative only. This is a formidable regiment of women in which no member of the triumvirate falls away from the prescribed standard, and their empire reflects it. Dinner is a dream, and my room is admirable, warm, charmingly papered, with blankets and towels in abundance and toothpaste and mending materials provided as well as soap. It is just that I have a lingering feeling that if I were to break a toothmug, or spill something indelible on the cloth, I should have to appear before Madame, cringing and culpable, to give an account of myself.

After dinner, when I go into the bar to have coffee, I see *Grandmère* leaving the *caisse* briefly to carry a tray into an inner room where, through the half-open door, I glimpse a man watching TV. He is smaller than any of the women and there is an air of meekness about him. If this is Monsieur, Madame must, as they say, have 'married out'. I feel sure that his tray is furnished from the *table d'hôte* and does not include any of the starred items on the menu.

In the morning I have to repent, at least in part, of such uncharitable judgments. While I am having breakfast, with a length of *baguette* still warm from the baker at the corner, and about half a pound of deep gold butter set down carelessly on the table, a tiny old man in a suit made for somebody two-and-a-half times his size, which has been cut down so that it will clear the ground, rather than fit, comes in and says. 'Thérèse!' When the daughter at the bar looks up he hands her a shrivelled orange and she pulls him a pint, saying severely: 'One!' Evidently it is a regular Sunday ritual, and I take it as a sign of grace. But will she do as much when she is her mother's age, the blossom fallen and the mellowing process not yet set in?

The answer is *carpe diem*. By the time Mademoiselle is set into inflexible middle-age, the little man will be past the need for beer. For the moment his nose is happily buried in his Sunday morning pint. He is still spinning it out when I set off for the cathedral, so I never know whether, in response to pressure or pleading, one becomes two.

Coutances climbs up the side of a hill to spread out on top of it round a cathedral whose remarkable quality can best be summarised by saying that everything goes up. It is a brutal simplification, but it is, nevertheless, the only way to convey the perfection of that moment when the Gothic style, born in the Ile de France, met and married the powerfully austere Romanesque of the Norman tradition. Coutances was its triumph.

There was a Romanesque cathedral on the site in the

185

thirteenth century, built partly with money which the Hauteville brothers made during their conquest of Sicily. When, like so many medieval churches, it was ravaged by fire during the thirteenth, the new Gothic cathedral was built on and around the surviving frame of the old. Architecturally speaking, the method was either mad or inspired, perhaps the latter, since the result survived the blast of the bombing of 1944, which laid the town around it in ruins. It stands intact today, the two west towers culminating in narrow pinnacles like a sheaf of arrows, from which octagonal spires drive upwards. The central tower, from which, on a clear day, the view extends as far as the Breton coast and the Channel Islands, is topped by an exquisite lantern. Inside, all the lines soar, so that the roof seems even higher than its actual forty-one metres, an effect that is a bonus of the simplicity and purity of the detail.

This morning the light from the windows chalks with blue and rose and gold and purple the albs of the boys and girls of Coutances, who are making their *Communion Solennelle*. Afterwards they mill about the wide *parvis* before the cathedral, for the bombing had one good effect, it made possible a new town planned to show to the best advantage its most superb building. They mingle with the members of the local soccer team and those of Ilkley Rangers, who are playing each other today, and people coming out of *pâtisseries* carrying careful, peaked bundles, containing the dessert that will crown the most elaborate meal of the week, and a scatter of racing cyclists in brilliant *maillots*, all the bustle of a typical French Sunday morning.

I start down the hill for the elaborate meal which, having experienced last night what Madame can do, I am confident awaits me at the hotel. Afterwards I cannot understand how I could have forgotten an aspect of French life of which I am perfectly well aware, that, outside Paris and flighty tourist centres, Sunday belongs to the family, and there is no place for the rootless and unattached, particularly when they are wilfully so. In provincial France the attitude has not changed all that radically during the century since Julien, on his travels, periodically whimpered about the desolation of having no relatives. His pride as well as his delight at being united with his Uncle Franz at Bordeaux — 'Now I, too, have an uncle, a second father. I have a family!' — illustrates perfectly the attitude which sees the lack of the proper complement of relatives not only as unfortunate but as slightly shameful. The family means more than the mere nuclear cell, though that makes claims which are startling by Anglo-Saxon standards. I have known a highly contemporary young woman, self-supporting in a good professional job, defer a much-needed holiday because her sister had a baby on the day she was due to leave. Mother and child both doing well, a case one might think for flowers wired from the airport, showers of postcards from distant places and return in time for the baptism bearing a present from Corsica. In France — and this was Paris, too — it was an occasion for daily visits to the clinic, bearing one's flowers by hand.

Far beyond that nuclear cell extends the clan, whose members assemble, if not, these days, always altogether willingly, at least remarkably faithfully, for Sunday visits to aged aunts, and baptismal luncheons with forty covers, and weddings which can keep a middle-aged couple, both of whom have several brothers and sisters who are themselves parents, posting about France most weekends between July and October. The clans are gathered now, to the last *cousine germaine*, in the hotel dining room, whose uttermost centimetre of table space is occupied by the family parties which are here for the *Communion Solennelle*. Madame bars the door like an angel with a sword; all I can hope for are the broken meats afterwards, and 'afterwards' seems likely to be about five p.m.

Without a word I turn and trudge up the hill again. The streets are empty, the broad *parvis* deserted. All good citizens are united round the family board. I am thankfully astonished at last to find a corner in an agreeable restaurant whose proprietor, a man, and so a softer touch, welcomes me with warmth, not merely professional courtesy, and where my immediate neighbours are a youngish couple whose five-year-old son listens

187

to the menu, as it is read aloud by his parents, with the serious attention of an embryo *bon vivant*. It is a little disappointing that he does not start with oysters, preferring a large mixed *hors d'oeuvre*.

When, later in the afternoon, I am stricken dramatically by what I have long been sufficiently French to describe as a *crise de foie*, though I know well enough that it has nothing to do with my liver, I have no hesitation in ascribing it, not to the oysters which I have myself eaten, but to my earlier experience of rejection by Madame. Not that recognising the cause as psychosomatic is any help in enduring the effects. As they say about sea-sickness, first you're afraid you're going to die and then you're afraid you're not, but, in this instance, there is room for neither fear nor hope. Madame would not countenance dying between the pretty, flowered walls of one of her best rooms : the idea is not to be contemplated.

In the morning, the *crise* having subsided as quickly as it blew up, she serves me another of her faultless breakfasts, then looks at my travellers' cheques, and they French, not English, as if they are slightly malodorous and refuses to cash them, so that I have once more to tramp up the hill and find a bank before I can check out and take a ticket for Cherbourg.

The Cotentin flows past the windows of the train, green like Gauguin and almost oppressively opulent. They were already exporting eggs to Britain from this part of Normandy a hundred years ago, which may be news to the British farmers who reacted so violently against imports of eggs from France not long after their country joined the EEC. The railway line runs well to the east of the Hague peninsula, and, in these lush pastures, it is difficult even to imagine that granite coast, with the current in the race off it making eight knots.

Cherbourg is like a man-made Brest : in the one nature has provided a harbour that will shelter navies, in the other it took three-quarters of a century to construct the present trans-Atlantic port. M. Bruno called it 'the most magnificent military port constructed by the hand of man'. He was born too early to have seen Mulberry Harbour at Arromanches, which, after the Allied landings in Normandy during June 1944, substituted for Cherbourg until that port had once more been put into operation. For a few months the tonnage landed at that tiny holiday village was comparable to the bulk landed at Le Havre, one of France's major ports, before the war.

The building of Cherbourg's harbour began in 1776, and Louis XVI was present to see the sinking of one of the ninety enormous cones, stuffed with rubble and mortar, which were to be the base of the *digue*, two miles off shore and two and a half miles long, which was designed to shelter it. The sea engulfed them ravenously, and more also; it was not to be subdued even by the orders of Napoleon I, who decreed that Cherbourg should be a naval base. This explains what would otherwise be the obscure legend of the plinth of an equestrian statue of the Emperor on the seafront, proclaiming: 'I will re-create at Cherbourg the wonders of Egypt.' In fact, the *digue* was not to be completed until 1853, under Napoleon III, though, by 1840, it was possible to land the Emperor's remains here when they were brought from St. Helena in the frigate *Belle Poule*. I am able to do the statue only rather cursory reverence, since I am bound for the scene of another Emperor's landing, Bayeux, the first French town to be liberated in 1944 and the first to be visited by General de Gaulle when he returned in triumph to French soil on June 14th, 1944. He came ashore on Juno Beach, known in normal times as the tranquil little seaside resort of Courseulles-sur-Mer, renowned for the quality of its oysters. Along the coast of the Cotentin and Calvados the holiday beaches have entered history under new names, Omaha and Utah, Sword and Gold and Juno.

Just as the train is pulling out of Cherbourg, two little French sailors, hung about with luggage that looks a lot more than standard full kit, come aboard, radiant with delight rather than drink. One dives into a vast duffle bag decorated with pin-ups, to produce a *lei* or a mayoral chain, according to which society you move in, of scarlet plush, with an anchor made of two brass fish dangling from it. He puts it on, chucks his cap with its red pom-pom into the air, and shouts: *'Finit le mer!'* It is the end of National Service for him and his mate. They sing: 'John Brown's Body' in duet, with *'Finit le mer!'* between each verse, then buy beer for everybody in their neighbourhood. By the time we are passing through Carentan, which is about level with Utah, their cup has run over, and they are embracing with equal warmth a young French Army officer, who is quiet but friendly, and a group of large, sun-burned, highly extrovert Germans, with string vests showing through very clean white nylon shirts.

20

'HAROLD BROKE HIS promise,' says a woman's voice.

'Like Harold Wilson, then,' comes the reply from her husband.

It seems unkind to both sides. What is culpable in politicians is not that they should occasionally break promises but that they should ever be so silly as to make them, liable as they are to be swept from their chosen course by the current of world events. As for Harold Godwin, if ever a promise was given under duress, it was the vow he made to William, Duke of Normandy that he would recognise the Duke's right to the throne of England. Swear on sacred relics he may have done, but he probably had his fingers crossed while he did so. If blame must be apportioned, one could argue that some of it should rest on Edward the Confessor. Had he announced more firmly and publicly before his death that he wished the crown to go to his cousin, William the Bastard, perhaps there would have been no Battle of Hastings, and so no occasion for producing Queen Matilda's Tapestry, before which the English couple, and a clutch of French visitors and myself are at the moment standing.

Its seventy-five yards, sheltered behind careful glass, are unrolled round the walls of this cool, skilfully lit museum which was once the palace of the Bishop of Bayeux. It is like a *cor anglais* or the Holy Roman Empire in being neither a tapestry — it is embroidery done on heavy linen — nor worked by Queen Matilda, but, under whatever description, it remains the most remarkable strip cartoon or action film we possess, besides being a priceless record of life in the Middle Ages. War horses paw the ground, and charge, and pile up in the ravine at Hastings in extravagant attitudes like Grand National runners coming to grief at Becher's. The foot soldiers die like insects, pricked full of arrows. The goodies may be distinguished from the baddies, the classification varying with the nationality of the beholder, by the fact that the Anglo-Saxons are moustached, the Normans cropped and clean-shaven, in contrast to their horned and hairy ancestors who first landed on this coast two and a half centuries earlier. Both horses and men give an impression of size which is enormously at variance with the thirteenth-century coat of mail, looking like knitted dishcloths, displayed in the entrance hall of the museum, along with slot machines for coffee, ices and soft drinks.

Everything is in these fifty-eight scenes, lavishly captioned in Latin, from the Confessor's promise that William of Normandy should inherit his throne to the flight of the arrow that pierced Harold's eye. It is a marvel, and, when I find myself standing beside a French couple who are admiring it audibly, I surprise myself by saying in a proprietorial fashion that it was made in England. Odo, Bishop of Bayeux and half-brother of William, almost certainly commissioned it from a school of Anglo-Saxon embroiderers. It would probably be wrong to read into the placing of the commission a wish to humiliate further the defeated Saxons. No doubt Odo, who was as much warrior as bishop, wanted to commemorate the Conquest, but he wanted equally to adorn the choir of his new cathedral at Bayeux and went to the best people for the job.

What did Norman and Saxon mean, anyway, in the epoch opened by the Conquest, whose final result, it has been said, was that, rather than the Duke of Normandy's ruling over England, the King of England ruled over Normandy, and, eventually, over a good deal more of France? Even in 1077, when the cathedral was consecrated, the archbishops and bishops present at the ceremony included Lanfranc of Canterbury and Thomas de Bayeux of York. Today's British visitors, who may wonder what a carving of the murder of Thomas à Becket is doing in the thirteenth-century tympanum of the South Porch of Bayeux Cathedral, will cease to be surprised if they learn that, when King Henry II was excommunicated after the murder, it was through the intercession of the Abbot of Mont.-St.-Michel, Robert de Torigni, that he finally obtained absolution, and it was on the steps of the former cathedral at Avranches that the King of England knelt in penitence for his sin.

An even greater marvel than the tapestry itself, is the fact that it should have survived to our day in the condition in which we now see it. An inventory of the cathedral property made in the fifteenth century includes it, but, during the upheaval of the Revolution at the end of the eighteenth, the tapestry narrowly escaped being used as a wagon cover. We owe its existence to one of those intelligent officers who have been responsible for preserving quite a number of works of art during periods when the urge was for destruction. It would be nice to think that he got his reward from Napoleon who, a few years later, sent the tapestry on tour through the principal towns of France to drum up support for his own great invasion of England.

When the cross-Channel invasion did come, it was in reverse. Bayeux was the first town in France to be liberated after the allied landings on June 6th, 1944. It was freed on the following day, without damage, though not without cost. On the outer wall of the Bishop's palace a bronze commemorates 'all ranks of the 50th Northumbrian Division who laid down their lives for justice, freedom and the liberation of France'. Opposite, steps lead down to the cathedral which is unmistakably sister to British churches as diverse as Durham Cathedral and tiny Kilpeck. The Norman builders left their mark unequivocally; here it strikes you first in the diaper work and carving of the massy pillars.

Of the distressingly aberrant bronze cupola known locally as 'the bonnet', which crowns the fifteenth-century central tower, one can only say, like Daisy Ashford of Mr. Salteena's social standing, that, at this stage, it can't be helped. Things might have been even worse. The original addition was a neo-classic cupola, which was popped on to the tower in 1714. When, half-way through the following century, it was found that the weight of the cupola was threatening the foundations, there was a serious proposal to solve the problem not by removing the cupola but by pulling down the whole tower, with most of the transepts. Mercifully, and also a little surprisingly, since good citizens are not always reliable in aesthetic matters, the townspeople objected and, finally, the piers supporting the tower were strengthened and the cupola transformed into the existing 'bonnet'.

Much of Bayeux is built of the dark local stone that gives the cathedral its air of sobriety. According to taste, you like it or you find it gloomy. Personally, I delight in it, and delight still more that the gravely elegant houses have survived intact while so many Norman towns have been devastated, sometimes to be re-planned in ferro-concrete. It is these tranquil, prosperous-looking streets that make me think of Bayeux as a Balzacien town, and Balzac, in fact, knew it well and set three of his novels here. I spend half an hour strolling among them now before walking back along the long boulevard Sadi-Carnot to have dinner at the small but *sympathique* Hotel de la Gare, where I am staying. It is nobody's fault but my own that I have omitted to find out that it does not serve meals other than breakfast, nevertheless, during the equally long walk back, I manage to distribute the blame between Monsieur, Madame and their three pleasant children. I am looking for a hotel which has stayed in my memory from a previous visit, partly because, arriving late in the afternoon without a booking, I was offered a bedroom with private bath which turned out to be a bathroom with private bed, partly because, that evening, the President of the Republic, M. Pompidou, and his Prime Minister, M. Jacques Chaban-Delmas, appeared on TV to announce a devaluation of the franc. The set was in the dining room, which, as it was summer, had a good sprinkling of British visitors. It was interesting to watch those of them who gathered what it was all about striving to compose their features into a suitable expression of sympathy with the host nation while at the same time calculating what the difference would mean to them in terms of an extended holiday, or excursions into the *à la carte* side of the menu.

Either I arrive at a different hotel or the original one, in the interval, has gone up the market so steeply that I am slightly disconcerted by the impressiveness of its exterior, and still more by the prices. Surprisingly, the waiter proves to be a friend and a brother. I tell him about my recent *crise de foie* and he at once assumes responsibility for choosing my dinner, prescribing a grilled sole with a squeeze of lemon rather than a *meunière* with the seriousness of a top gastro-enterologist making a choice among drugs.

The morning is awful, though, thanks no doubt to the grilled sole, my *foie* is fine. There is an early bus to be caught for Caen, and a wait there for the connection which is to take me farther along the coast. I never seem to have any luck with Caen, though I know that its reputation for learning and noble architecture got it the title of the Athens of Normandy, and I can reel off its attractions like a page of Baedeker. The two abbeys founded here by William and his queen, Matilda, the Abbaye aux Dames and the Abbaye aux Hommes, are among the finest in France; the university dates from 1432. In contrast to Bayeux, Caen was badly damaged in 1944, when the centre was virtually wiped out, but here the rebuilding has been done not in ferro-concrete but in the milky 'Caen stone' which, for centuries has been sent to England from this river port to build many of our churches and cathedrals. So much for the image, but it happens that my brief visits have always been spent, as now, waiting for a connection at the bus station or, worse, battling by car through the industrial zone between the Orne and the canal connecting Caen with the sea which is part of the town's remarkable post-war development. When André and Julien, as they sailed along the Normandy coast, were told that Caen did a great trade in horses bred in Normandy, Baron Thyssen's acquisition of mining concessions at Soumont and Perrière, twenty or so kilometres south-east of Caen, was still more than thirty years ahead. Today, their exploitation has given Normandy one of its most important heavy industries and helped to make the first part of my bus journey out of the town a waste of smoke and slag and lowering skies that is the more painful because you enter it fresh from the verdure of the Cotentin.

We are quickly through it, with only the stained clouds as a reminder. Streams bordered with willows, horses grazing with such concentration that they do not raise their heads at the passing of the bus, green corn and apple blossom; then the road crosses the Orne Estuary and we run down towards the coast of Calvados, which, at this end, has some of the clutter of shacks and 'campings' and flimsy bungalows with names like 'The Home' that accumulate round the get-away route from any industrial area.

It ends abruptly, the road turns slightly away from the sea and the bus stops beside an open space with, opposite, a small, bright hotel totally unlike the norm for a fashionable seaside resort. There is something vaguely wrong with Madame's accent, though nothing lacking in her welcome. Then she switches from French to fluent English, but that, too, has a curious flavour. It is the kind of thing that is likely to happen if, being English, you spend thirty years in France, or, of course, the converse. Madame explains that she married a Frenchman in 1945 and, whether or not she is technically naturalised — I did not ask — it is obvious that now she feels herself to be a Frenchwoman. I lunch in a dining room already prinked up for the holidaymakers who have not yet begun to arrive, then start down the avenue de la Mer with a noticeably heightened sense of expectancy. This is Balbec, or, if you insist on fact rather than fiction, Cabourg, and I am in search of *temps perdu*.

21   ON THE SANDS below the promenade
Marcel Proust one white dog and four black and white dogs, a
mother and her sons, it seems, are frolicking in defiance of a
notice that reads: 'Happy holidays and clean holidays! Keep
dogs on leash!' which is displayed near the steps leading down to
the beach. The notice says also 'Do not walk on the lawns',
'Refrain from circulating with vehicles on the *digue* or promenade', 'Use the waste paper baskets', 'Do not eat on the beach or
promenade.'

There is nobody in sight to respond to the admonitions and
prohibitions, or react against them, except two corporation
employees levelling the sand near the sea wall and three adults
of ripe age, with whom the dogs appear to be loosely associated,
who, warmly happed against the wind, are trudging along the
promenade. The very promenade, I tell myself with a painful
effort of the imagination, along which drifted the Princesse de
Luxembourg, inclined over her folded parasol so that the arab-
esque of her figure seemed to undulate like a scarf around a

197

diagonal shaft, invisible and inflexible, that supported it.

The sea is Channel grey with deeps of Prussian blue, far removed from the pigeon's breast pink, the azure, the misty emerald, which brimmed the windows of the Grand Hotel for the young Marcel. The hotel itself presents difficulties. Not that it lacks grandeur, but it has only four floors, and, even allowing for the relative slowness of elevators during the *Belle Époque* — but were they slow, or did they, like yesterday's trains, travel faster and farther and more often? — it is hard to see how there could have been time to knit a relationship with the lift attendant.

On the landward side, where, on Sunday afternoons, the guests gathered to wait for the hired carriages which would take the more distinguished of them to visit the Cambremers, it is easier to project oneself into a vanished epoch. The lawn is of a more than Gallic green, the beds of wallflowers, warmed by the sun, are voluptuously, drunkenly fragrant. I hope for an insight into present life at the Grand Hotel which, after a period of decline, has been modernised and given a face-lift, from a woman who, with her husband, is luxuriating in the scent of the wallflowers while enjoying the sun on a seat on the lawn, but it turns out that they are not staying there, but spending ten days with the woman's sister-in-law.

The season is short, she says, but there are still some old families who have houses here, and the young people come to spend at least part of the season with their parents and grand-parents. It seems an unlikely setting for those almost tribal holidays which have for so long been a part of upper and middle class life in France, and are now threatened by newer fashions, the endless three months, half boring, half idyllic, during which adolescents, supposedly, and often actually exhausted by the strains of the *lycée* recuperate in order to face them again in October. The English tend to be repelled by such a polarisation of work and leisure — why not a shorter holiday and a more humane curriculum? — but, up to now, France has preferred totality.

The houses curve round the green and extend along the promenade, half-timbered, brick faced with stone, red-tiled with stepped Flemish gables. There is one that sparkles with the gold of a Byzantine mosaic. Whatever the age of the families who own them, none of the houses are earlier than the Second Empire, when Cabourg, with its leafy avenues radiating fanwise from the centre formed by the Casino and the Grand Hotel, was built to meet the fashion for sea-bathing, which by then was firmly established, though, it seems, still approached with some caution. The author of *Le Tour de la France* notes that salt water is fortifying 'particularly when one does not stay in more than five minutes'. At the time that he was writing, the City of Paris sent selected pupils from its schools for seaside holidays every year, but prize pupils rather than those whose health might have been expected to benefit.

Apart from those families who are faithful to their old habits, my new acquaintance goes on, it is not *chic* on the beach during the season. Deauville, where there are more attractions, and a train from Paris arrives every evening, has drawn away a large part of the more elegant clientele. Who, then, stays at the Grand Hotel, I ask. It seems that, as in British spa towns, conferences provide a good deal of custom. Also 'there are rich people who are not *chic*, as I am sure you know'.

I am intrigued by a certain detachment in the intimacy with which both the woman and her husband talk about the French : it is explained when she lets drop that they both came to France from Roumania decades ago. When the two take a friendly farewell before starting back for supper with the sister-in-law, I go exploring among the spokes of the fan, where both the architecture and the names of the dwellings tend to the bizarre. A bungalow called The Key of C and a Hôtel Marie-Antoinette with a Coca-Cola sign on it, dispiriting flats in which grey slate is allied to slate grey glass and a startling villa that looks like a yearling *château* prepare one for a miniature golf course whose holes are decked out as the Sphinx, and Westminster Abbey and the Leaning Tower of Pisa. A shop offers *pizze* to take away; amid so much that he would deplore, Proust would surely salute that correct plural. A poster advertises this evening's Karting at the *Cercle Hippique* and another announces that, tomorrow, the Cabourg Association is staging a *Nuit de Muguet* at the Casino, tickets twenty francs. *Muguet*, lily of the valley, is the flower associated with the First of May, when posies of it are presented to friends as a compliment and good luck token, but the implications do not come home to me until I am having dinner at my hotel, where the dining room which, at midday, I shared with a young couple, is now totally deserted, though still having its air of expectancy. In France May Day is a public holiday. It is unthinkable that I should spend it in the pre-season void of Cabourg, whose desolation will be accentuated, eating take-away *pizze* with the shade of the Princesse de Luxembourg. The decision to check out first thing in the morning is made before I have the slightest idea where I will head. That comes only as I am paying my bill. I will take a bus to Honfleur, thirty or so miles along the coast, which, because it has no bathing beach, has never become fashionable, and the only ghost I am likely to meet is that of Boudin. I can spend the day wandering round the little port, and eat fish at one of the waterfront restaurants, and see again the wooden church that is, quite literally, a ship turned upside down. I will stay at the ancient, creaking hotel from whose windows you can spit into the harbour, where, in or out of season, there is always a pleasant bustle.

What I have overlooked is that French *penchant* for totality about which I was thinking only yesterday. May 1st is Labour Day, and so, quite logically, a workers' holiday. There are no buses to anywhere, and even if I go to the station at the neighbouring resort of Dives, on the other side of the river, there is no train from it that will take me to Honfleur. It is with an appalling sense of sin that I decide to travel the thirty-six kilometres by taxi. One legacy of a provincial, if not unduly puritan, upbringing is a feeling that taxis, other than to or from railway stations, are for infirmity or extreme old age. I have long overcome it during working hours, but still not for self-indulgence.

The ride costs sixty-seven francs, and it is not difficult to believe the driver when he says that, unless four or more people can share the cost of the petrol, it is cheaper to travel by train than by car these days, but in this instance it is my sanity that is at stake.

I know I have done the right thing the moment the taxi sets me down at the hotel where, incredibly on this public holiday, there is a vacant room which, by chance, is the same, with the undulating floor and almost a straight drop into the outer harbour, that I had the first time I came here. There is no void at Honfleur, there is no desolation even when a small rain begins to fall before lunch and continues intermittently through the day.

The visitors who throng the streets, peering into the jazzy boutiques round the harbour, crowding into bars to drink *apéritifs* before settling to lunches which will last at least two and a half hours and bring a dangerously heightened flush to those cheeks whose rose is already tinged with purple, are no more able to damage the integrity of these serious, slate-hung houses than are the boutiques themselves, which are as irrelevant as a slash of lipstick on a perfectly sculptured face. These days the basin is given over to pleasure craft, but in the tiny trickle of water between the livid mudbanks of the outer harbour, the fishing boats are waiting for tomorrow's tide.

The Boudin Museum is closed for alteration, which at least delivers me from an occasion of falling into the sin of covetousness. Pictures can be classed on a scale of desirability as well as greatness — there are masterpieces which one could not possibly live with — and Boudin, who was born at Honfleur, where his father was a fisherman, has painted more pictures that I should want to take home than any other artist I can think of except Chardin, and possibly David Cox. I have a private theory that, far from deploring today's industrial development along the Seine Estuary, Boudin, like many of the Impressionists, of whom he was a precursor, would take pleasure in the steely glimmer of the petrol tanks through the early mist. To a painter, an old cylinder and the Empress Eugenie and her ladies scudding, crinolined, along the shore at Deauville are equally artefacts which may be the basis of a composition. Since Boudin has been dead this three-quarters of a century there is not much danger that the theory will be contradicted.

Failing the museum, I fall back on the window of the local photographer, who is showing a gallery of portraits of former Presidents of the Republic, beginning with M. Pompidou, looking out, keen and confident, into the future he was never to enjoy, and working back through recent and more remote history, from Auriol, watching his wife arranging flowers, through Doumer, benign like an intellectual Father Christmas, and Sadi Carnot, handsome in a slightly caddish, black-moustached sort of way, both assassinated, to the great survivor, Adolphe Thiers, who, even if he had not had his phenomenal capacity for bouncing back, would still have been sure of a line in history for saying: 'La République est le Gouvernement qui nous divise le moins.'

After that, the wooden church, the inverted hull that was the finest work of the shipwrights of Honfleur, though they turned out so many fine craft. The story of its building is the most outstanding example of local self-sufficiency that I know. After the end of the Hundred Years' War there was a surge of building in France. Some of it was for restoration, some went into the construction of new churches to commemorate the final departure of the English. The result was that architects and masons were at a premium and Honfleur was faced with a long wait before it could build its own new church. But, as the dictionary reminds us, a nave is a ship, and the craftsmen of Honfleur needed no lessons in shipbuilding. They raised their own church, twin naves with two aisles, all of timber, sound and tight as the hull of a ship. It stands today, beautiful as well as remarkable, and I never enter it without thinking of what the consecration must have been like, with so many members of the congregation having their eyes on the roof beams during much of the ceremony, appraising and approving their own and their mates' handiwork, and at night everybody getting beatifically drunk to the greater glory of God.

Back at my hotel I eat my fish — halibut and very good — and read in the local paper that the commune of Ouistreham on the Calvados coast has had to raise the age limit for its annual old people's dinner to seventy-two, because if they kept it at the present seventy there would be seven hundred and twenty people eligible instead of four hundred and forty. There is a centenarian among them, which does not seem to be all that unusual in Normandy. Perhaps it is the air, perhaps the fish. It has been a splendid day, in spite of the rain, its pleasures heightened by the thought of what it would have been like if I had stayed at Cabourg. I sleep celestially in my irregular little chamber, waking briefly in the small hours to the throb of the fishing boats standing out to sea. And there is still the greater part of the following morning to observe the working face of Honfleur. It offers a sight I had thought extinct years since, a two-wheeled high cart with a hood, whose owner has driven in from the country with produce to sell. There is a certain amount of coming and going at the public wash-place where, though launderettes are now beginning to penetrate the French provinces, there are still women who treat their weekly bundle in the old fashion, with cold water, and *eau de Javel* and impressive muscular power. At Honfleur's wash-place there is a touch of luxury in that each woman, as she bows over her scrubbing board, has a modified *prie dieu* with a cushion on which to kneel. Above that centuries-old scene a garishly coloured notice announces that it is the '*Heure à transistor jazz*' but the women do not raise their heads to glance at it.

It is the picture I take with me in the Rouen bus, which runs up the left bank of the Seine through pleasant, uneventful country, with ducks on the green and lambs with pink ears in orchards of deeper pink apple blossom. Somewhere around Pont Audemer I glimpse a war memorial depicting a soldier apparently putting the bayonet in, only he has no bayonet. French war memorials are an art in themselves, if an occasionally unfathomable one. It is hard to imagine what can be the common philosophy that leads one village to commemorate its dead with the figure of France mourning for her children, another with a defiant Gallic cock.

After Pont Audemer the road begins to climb. I am listening, drowsily, to a pair of elderly passengers behind me complaining about the difficulty of getting decent reception of the third TV chain when the view opens out dramatically on the left. We are looking down on the Seine Valley. The river, here, is broad and steely as a shield, its banks lined with factories and oil refineries sending out puffs of steam, and rags of orange flame and smudges of dark smoke. If you look up from that monument to modern industrialisation you see a monument of another sort, the ruined castle of Robert the Devil. The fact that the Devil's existence as a historic personage is about as firmly established as that of Robin Hood does not detract from the romantic quality of the site. Lest anything should be lacking, the authorities have provided a waxwork museum, as well as clock golf. Something for everybody.

22   AT THE LAST big roundabout on the western approaches to Rouen the roads are convoluted like Celtic ornament into loops and curves and true lovers' knots. In the centre, an emerald in a complicated setting, is a grass plot on which an elderly couple are grazing a guinea pig in a woolly jacket. It is so warm that he might be happier if he were allowed to cast his clout, but it is still a heartening sight. People who exercise guinea pigs in the roaring middle of a traffic junction can domesticate any environment; one feels confident that the *Rouennais* will be able to rise above whatever further and yet more intensive development in the Seine Valley the future may bring, even though there are nightmare prophecies of a built-up area all the way from here to Paris.

It is not that industry is anything new to a city which has been a trade crossroads for 2,000 years and an Atlantic port for 500 — in 1550 Rouen staged what is claimed to have been Europe's first colonial exhibition — but that the rationalisation of post-war planning has, paradoxically, made it more conspicuous, at least in the distant view. Rouen suffered twice during the Second World War, by fire in 1940, when the town was occupied by the Nazis, by bombardment during 1944. It was not until August of that year that it was liberated by Canadian troops. The result was that the area between the cathedral and the Seine was virtually destroyed. It had been a district of ancient houses and old established industry, the Rouen where Charles Bovary, as a naïf young medical student come up from the country, looked down from his fourth-floor window on summer evenings on a *quartier* that recalled 'a mean little Venice', where workmen squatting on the banks of the river laved their arms in the water that flowed yellow and blue and violet beneath its bridges, and, from poles sticking out from the roofs of lofts, hanks of cotton dried in the breeze. Rather more than a century earlier the cotton had been the basis of a different era of industrial expansion. Spinning and weaving were among the city's earliest industries, first of wool and linen, from the sheep grazed and the flax grown on the clay lands of the *pays de Caux*, later, during the boom of the sixteenth century, of silks and cloth of gold and silver also. The cotton is reputed to have been the result of a happy accident. According to the story, until the beginning of the eighteenth century it was used only for making wicks for candles. Then a wealthy merchant, finding himself overstocked, decided to turn some of his surplus into cloth and was rewarded by the kind of success that followed the introduction of jeans into America. As it happened, the Rouen cotton also was dyed blue.

Now the industry, not textiles only, but oil, and chemicals, and paper, and rubber, and metallurgy among a good deal else, has been brought together in a zone well clear of the town, and the area near the river on the right bank has been rebuilt as a modern city whose architects were at some pains to reconcile it with the cathedral and the rest of the old town with which it made one entity. Over the river, as on the heights north of the Seine, there was no such frame of reference. The contemporary blocks rise one behind the other, neither better nor worse than most of their kind, but dismaying when you look down from one of the vantage points above the city, to find that your eyes are drawn from the inner towers and spires to the surrounding white cliffs.

Once down in the old town it is easy enough to forget them and be more impressed by how much has survived through 500 years and more, whether the half-timbered houses that overhang the narrow streets or the opulent Flamboyant Gothic of the church of St. Maclou, or the bell named *Cache Ribaud*, cast in 1260, which still rings curfew from the belfry, itself dating from the fourteenth century, of the *Gros Horloge*. Yes, I know that, these days, *horloge* is a feminine noun, but at Rouen, for its title, they have stuck to an older, provincial fashion.

By English standards, France, and indeed the Continent generally, has odd ideas about bells and belfries (an island race, naturally, cannot be expected to see the situation from the opposite viewpoint). The intricate art of change-ringing has no place in French culture, perhaps because the dedicated team-work it demands is foreign to the native ethos. Instead, France has *carillons*, some of which play tunes on the quarters and many of which are occasionally used for concerts by the rather small number of virtuoso players. There are enthusiasts who travel the country to perform on well-known *carillons*. In consequence, peals, where they may exist, are not highly regarded. Up to the Revolution, St. Maclou had one of twelve bells. Since Normandy has a tradition of bell-founding, it was quite possibly a good one, but, as the local people say, a peal is not a *carillon*. Rouen had to wait until 1920 to acquire a *carillon* of twenty-nine bells, which, since then, at vast expense, has been increased to fifty-six, weighing together more than thirty tons. They are hung in the Butter Tower of the cathedral.

For years I thought that Butter Tower, the name given to the glorious south tower, Flamboyant Gothic at its most splendid, was analogous to 'wool church', indicating that the building had been financed from the wealth that came from the chief product of the region, and, heaven knows, relatively, there is as much butter in Normandy as there were ever sheep in East Anglia, but the truth is more subtle. The cost of the tower was met from the money paid by citizens in an age which had never heard of cholesterol for the privilege of eating butter in Lent, and the result is a justification for the system of indulgences.

The survival of the tower, as, indeed, of the whole cathedral today, is due, not as it is commonplace and imprecise to say, to a miracle, but to prodigies of human courage and determination. Its south side was pulverised in 1944, which threatened the fall of the entire roof, suddenly robbed of the support of its flying buttresses. One may concede an element of the miraculous in the fact that a shell which went through the roof of the sanctuary to bury itself in the ground before the altar failed to explode, but the crucial missile was that which tore open one of the four massive pillars supporting the central lantern tower, whose collapse would have brought down with it a great part of the cathedral. Disregarding all canons of safety, a team of workers at once went into the building and shored up the pillar. The task of restoration, which took twelve years, began within the next twenty-four hours. This is an incident of war which I have always found only slightly less moving than the story of the councillors of Rotterdam, who, after the savage bombing of 1940, met in the smoking ruin of their city to plan the Rotterdam of the future, the city we know today. Less because, in 1944, the *Rouennais* at least knew that they were nearing the end of a war in which they were on the winning side, whereas the indomitable Dutch were going down into the dark for an unspecified period.

That peace also has its hazards is driven home when I go on to look again at the building which many first-time visitors to Rouen take, quite understandably, for a second cathedral, the Abbey Church of Saint-Ouen, built by Benedictines over three centuries, starting in 1315. It is in fact slightly larger than the cathedral, and architecturally its equal, but at this moment more than one young ash tree is sprouting from its West Front. They are a sign, not that the authorities undervalue their architectural treasures, but that the Ministry of Cultural Affairs, one of whose divisions is responsible for the upkeep of public buildings, could spend three or four times its budget, whatever that budget might be at any given time, and still not keep up with the enormous task, quite apart from the fact that the number of men qualified for some of the work involved is limited.

The cemetery surrounding the church is gay with see-sawing children, elderly men playing *boules* and *lycéens* swinging straps of books basking in the sun and talking endlessly. Despite so much assurance of human well-being, it still brings one to the matter which is at the heart of every British visit to Rouen. Up to now I have let myself be distracted from it by pleasant trivia, like the way the roaring post-war prosperity of the city finds expression in Ideal Home displays in the windows of furniture stores, including such refinements as a caramel brown bath, or a confectioner whose window says all that can be said about the rite of *dragées*. *Dragées* are the sugared almonds, in colours far more varied than the traditional pink, white and blue, without which no baptism, First Communion or wedding is complete. I have never heard that they are distributed at funerals, though there seems no good reason why not. Here they are made up into bouquets and posies and buttonholes, menu holders and place markers, as well as being packed into bags and boxes and triangular pokes for distribution to guests.

Less trivial is the illustration given by the rue du Gros Horloge of what a successful pedestrian street should be, and why the shopping precincts included in British new towns, as in some French, so often fail in their aim. Like its equivalents in cities as disparate as Verona and Copenhagen, the rue du Gros Horloge succeeds because it is not too wide, it offers temptations for pleasant dallying, signalled by the smell of roasting coffee, and it has fun shops — records and paperbacks and pop-gear — as well as elegant shops. It drives home the lesson that, even when the problem of cross draughts has been solved, a supermarket in a waste of concrete will not do.

But now I am in the cemetery among the assorted bits of sculpture, which include a statue of Rollo the Viking, the first

Duke of Normandy, and a copy of the Runestone of Tellinge, set up in the tenth century, which was presented to Rouen by the Carlsberg Foundation of Copenhagen in 1911 to mark the thousandth anniversary of the founding of the Duchy. Near the entrance a tablet records that, on this spot, Joan of Arc was pressed and deceived into signing an act of retraction of all her claims. The abjuration was brief; five days later the Maid withdrew it and went steadfastly to the fire, but the ignoble ceremony which secured it was crueller than the stake in the Old Market Place where, not so long ago, an Archbishop of Canterbury spent a moment bowed in recollection. It is no use telling oneself, with the support of ranks of historians, that the betrayal of Joan of Arc was a Quisling job rather than an English plot.

'Why did you burn Joan of Arc?' an eight-year-old French boy, in the last quarter of the twentieth century, asks the English *au pair* girl who has been wondering why he seemed so standoffish.

And, absurdly but inescapably: 'Why did we burn Joan of Arc?' British visitors to Rouen are still apt to ask themselves. Apart from being so unworthy, it was so silly. Don't make martyrs is the cardinal rule for any campaign which involves combating a people as well as an army, and here was a martyr whose fame has grown rather than diminished over five and a half centuries.

A French friend of a certain age has a vivid recollection of her beatification in 1909, which was followed, in 1920, by her canonisation and naming as the patron of France. The subject, naturally, was discussed among the little girls at Catechism, and my friend, aged about ten at the time, was absorbed and worshipping. So devoutly worshipping that she began to have twinges of conscience which finally led her, during confession, to say that she was guilty of something really serious. It came out in a rush. She knew one ought to love God more than anybody or anything else, but *'mon père*, I'm afraid I love Joan of Arc more than God, and I can't help it'. She remembers to this day the rather odd, spluttering cough that preceded the *cure*'s assurance

that there was not the slightest cause for worry, that God understood very well that Joan of Arc was bound to be more appealing to little girls than He was.

The reparations, of course, did not have to wait until the
canonisation. In 1456, twenty-five years after her death, and
three after the campaign which she had inspired had gathered
such momentum that England had lost all her French possessions except Calais, another trial, held in the Archbishop's palace,
resulted in Joan's complete rehabilitation. There was something
else to come. Joan of Arc's memorial chapel in Rouen Cathedral
contains her statue and a replica of her sword, which is laid
before the altar. There are two later additions. One is a memorial
tablet to the British troops who died in the war of 1914–18. The
other is a modern stained-glass window presented by the English.

23

AMIENS, TOO, HAS a tower. I recall the fact as I stand at the window of the train that is taking me there for a last glimpse of the Butter Tower. The Amiens tower is 104 metres tall, just short of twice the height of the *Colonne de la Grande Armée* which, in 1804, Napoleon set up at Boulogne to commemorate the camp from which he proposed to invade England. Or rather, which he began to set up, for his column got no farther than the plinth, just as his invasion force never set sail; it was not completed until the reign of Louis Philippe. After the Second World War, during which it was badly damaged, members of the Legion of Honour — who else, since Napoleon was the founder of their Order — raised a subscription to pay for repairing it. It is made of marble, and if you have the strength to climb 265 steps and have picked a clear day you can see the white cliffs of Dover from the top, which is more than Napoleon did. The tower at Amiens is made of reinforced concrete, by now, inevitably, a little dingy, and what you see from the glassed-in *terrasse* at the summit, to which a lift will take you, is a prospect of beetroot and battlefields on a darkling plain that extends, by way of the Low Countries and Pomerania, all the way to Western Siberia. In fact, I remember finding it quite exhilarating at Novosibirsk, where so much flatness made one's head spin, but the intermediate stretches do not stir me, any more than does the Amiens tower, much as one applauds the thought behind it. The tower was intended to be a signal of modern Amiens, as the cathedral is the signal of the old town, and building as a gesture has a Renaissance magnificence which one can only welcome in a utilitarian age.

If my ideas about a not exactly defined area which I think of vaguely as 'the north of France' are at best highly subjective, at worst, largely inaccurate as well as unjust, at least I can plead that they are shared by a great many of the French themselves. There are some whose feelings about the region were fixed for ever by one winter of military service in the Ardennes, others whose abstract of 'the north' is made up of smudged skies and the mean terraces of the mining belt, which extends approximately from Valenciennes (another place once known as the Athens of the North) to Bethune, an area which claims the attention of the rest of France only when it is the background for a strike or a more than usually titillating murder. I am conscious of my own inconsistency in sharing that general attitude while loving marine Flanders, which I cannot feel to be French at all, finding Amiens depressing but Abbeville extremely *sympathique*, regarding Arras with horror, but placing St. Quentin, which is equally industrialised, at least at the top of the second division of my favourite French towns.

Like most of their kind, the stereotypes have an element of truth, though they do not give enough place to the industrial farming, with its immense acreages of corn as well as sugar beet. The farmers here are not *paysans* but big businessmen, who may have a helicopter at the back door as well as a Citroën at the front, not to speak of a formidable lobbying power when agricultural subsidies are under discussion. Even those who love the area would admit that the climate of the Ardennes is rough, and only the spirit of the inhabitants, who have the virtues traditional in mining communities, can ennoble the *corons*, or courts of small brick houses in the black belt. What adds to the lowering effect is that this is an industrial area which is having its troubles, here declining, there in process of more or less difficult reconversion. The coalfield is being run down; the textile trade centred around Lille was traditionally the province of small, family firms, which, even without the competition of man-made fibres, would have been faced with the need to concentrate after the Second World War; the area lacks what are usually called modern industries, that is, the manufacture of consumer goods, with cars at their head. There are, too, curious little pockets of social backwardness, whether it is expressed in the odd commune with no piped water supply, young mothers who still believe that a necklace of amber beads will prevent their infants from having convulsions or the kind of malnutrition that comes from a diet consisting mainly of bacon and potatoes, which are unexpected in an area which is not remote.

Sixty per cent of Amiens was wiped out during 1940–4. Today the town is a mixture of old and new, with the new, as exemplified by the tower, predominating around the station, and giving me no sort of joy as I set off for the cathedral. The shopping street which is the first part of the route is an open-air *discothèque*, and a twenty-four hour one, I am ready to believe. Unless I am suffering an optical illusion, a shop window is offering a woman's dress at ten francs. Set between two pâtisseries, there is an advertisement about the treatment of *cellulite*, which, if I have properly understood my women's pages, is a local deposit of fatty tissue afflicting about three-quarters of the women in France. A challenge, you might say. À propos of absolutely nothing, it comes into my mind, reeling as it is from the sound of electric guitars bouncing off the walls, that Amiens was the town where St. Martin, when he was garrisoned here, cut his horseman's cloak in two with his sword to give one half to a shivering beggar.

There would be a case for dedicating the cathedral to him

instead of to Notre-Dame; there could still be that miraculous Golden Virgin over the South Door, golden no longer, but, like the equally famous Smiling Angel on the West Porch of Reims, gracious in an almost social manner. Ruskin, with all respect, called her the *Picard soubrette*, and you can see what he meant. Never was there a more absolute contrast than that between the Golden Virgin and the *Beau Dieu*, beautiful, indeed, but in an impersonal, inexpressive manner, which is the central figure of the West Front. One could spend a morning studying that façade, preferably with the help of opera glasses, and the afternoon delighting in the sixteenth-century carving of the oak choir stalls. There are 110 stalls, and the thousands of figures adorning them range from the Book of Genesis to scenes from the daily life of Amiens 450 years ago. The thought of how easily the lot could have gone in the devastation of 1940 makes you catch your breath and realise afresh the meaning of the word 'irreparable', but, like St. Paul's, Notre-Dame d'Amiens stood among the ruin that surrounded it. If only they would clean it, as Notre Dame de Paris has been cleaned, even though the removal of the grime might bring frightening revelations of what the atmosphere of an industrial city has done to the stone.

The logical next step is the secular cathedral, which, I cannot help feeling, would be a far more worthy signal of modern Amiens than that tower, the *Maison de Culture*, one of the most notable of the genre, opened by André Malraux in 1966 and well used since. Here the architect has conquered, instead of being conquered by his ferro-concrete, lightening it with glass and bronze panels. Three floors, with sliding partitions making possible a large variety of rooms round a central core of one theatre-cum-concert-hall seating 1,100 and another seating 300, ensure the most flexible use of space. This month's programme includes Karl Böhm directing the Orchestre de Paris in Schubert's Second and Ninth Symphonies, a debate on current threats to the biological balance of the oceans, a jazz concert with François Gain, who was soloist for Duke Ellington and his Swingers, and some days devoted to Chile — with the cathedral it is enough to redeem Amiens. I am still saying '*Vive* Malraux!' over a dispiriting lunch at the station buffet, where the menu seems to consist of sausages and whiting and it is hard to decide whether the pervading smells of chips and vinegar are generated on the spot or are drifting in from streets redolent of them.

They are dispelled in the afternoon. I spend it wandering along the towing path of the Canal de la Somme which links Amiens with Abbeville and the sea, and, on the landward side, with the Canal du Nord and so, by a series of links, with both Lille and Dunkerque. The whole of this part of Northern France is seamed with waterways; they are four times more dense than in the rest of the country. On the last leg of their journey, André and Julien, with their uncle, worked their passage on board a barge that was making the trip from Dunkerque to the neighbourhood of Phalsbourg by way of the canal from the Marne to the Rhine. Nowadays the canals of the Nord will take 350-ton barges and the 'main road' from Denain to Dunkerque is on the European gauge, which allows the passage of 1,350 tons.

What I want to see, however, is not the barges, which are no novelty when you live in Paris, but the *hortillonages*, the 300 hectares of market gardens occupying the low-lying ground beside the Canal de la Somme and its *rieux*, or side canals, black earth like that of the Fens of East Anglia, intensely fertile and immune from drought. Once down the steps leading from the side of one of the bridges you might be in another hemisphere. The towpath is almost rural. There are moorhens and the odd mallard, and, overhead, a kestrel quartering the closely cultivated patchwork that is lit here and there by the flash of greenhouse glass. All along the canal bank there are bright little houses, individual to a degree and set back in deep gardens, where flowers have their chance as well as vegetables. A narrow *rieu* divides them from the towing path; approach is by footbridges passing over it, some of them intricate to the point of fantasy, with the front gate on the seaward or canal side. A pair oar is out on the main canal, and in the side ones you can see, though rarely, the black punts, with high bows, like poor man's gondolas, which the market gardeners use to carry their produce to the *Marché sur l'Eau*. I had heard of this water market before ever I came to Amiens, and was fascinated by the idea of the loaded black punts being poled in the early morning to their moorings just below the cathedral.

An elderly woman leaning over her gate to survey the canal tells me that, these days, the water market is not what it used to be. There was a time when all the growers took their own vegetables in their own punts, and sold them directly, but now, what with the tax, and the rent of mooring, and the generally rising costs, fewer and fewer small men still carry on as individuals. Most of them grow for wholesalers who collect their stuff. One of those who is still holding out is a woman — she indicates a garden farther down the path where, in passing, I had noticed a girl bunching spring onions.

But then, the woman goes on, nothing is what it used to be. The elections? Oh, they are all the same. Still, she intends to vote, though who for it would take a tin opener to get out of her, but after she has been to the polling booth she intends to stay at home for the day. It will be safer.

This reminds me so much of the people who, not so long ago, went about saying that if the last of de Gaulle's referenda went against him you should try to get your wife and children out of Paris, that my belief in a central agency whose business it is to float such scares at election times is reinforced. I cannot give the idea all my attention because the woman is talking about the iniquity of family allowances. The government spends far too much on them and people nowadays expect everything to be put into their mouths. She herself brought up four children without any family allowances and she doesn't see why others should not do the same. It does not seem the time or the place to suggest that the inspiration of France's generous system of family allowances is demography rather than philanthropy — making two Frenchmen grow where otherwise only one would have grown — and, even if I made the point, by her canons, the harmful effect on the moral fibre of parents would be just the same.

In spite of her depressing account of the water market, I do get up at crack of dawn to see it. True, it takes place beside the canal, but there is not a punt in sight, only vans which seem to be loaded chiefly with lilac and rhubarb and pot plants. The expedition is worth it, nevertheless, because it gives me another chance, and by a different light, of seeing the West Front of the cathedral and saluting the Golden Virgin.

The hotel porter who carries my bags to the station is a Turk who makes up for his lack of French with a particularly happy smile — or is it only the effect of very white teeth in a dark face? Still, if he came to Western Europe in one of the regimented gangs of Turkish immigrants and has got off the conveyor belt into a job in a quite decent hotel with considerable tipping potential, he has something to smile about. It means, perhaps, that instead of going home with his mates at the end of a nine months' contract, he hopes to settle, adding one more ingredient to the rich stewpot of this part of France, where, I remember, two of the model figures in the window of a men's outfitters which I passed yesterday were black.

24   THE EXTENSIONS TO Dunkerque's man-
made harbour are designed to take tankers and mineral carriers
up to 300,000 tons, a suitable climax to the development of a
port whose trade tripled between 1959 and 1969, to give it third
rank in France after Marseille and Le Havre. Also it will add
another attraction to the 'technical tourism' which is said to be
having a growing vogue. At Dunkerque addicts can already enjoy
conducted tours of Usinor's massive ironworks, which are virtually on the shore, beside the basin for mineral carriers, and BP's
refinery, similarly placed for the tankers.

Having myself little taste for iron and petrol, so little, indeed,
that I have mad, atavistic moments of wondering whether the
world might not have been a more agreeable place if neither had
been discovered, I turn away to the right where, on the other
side of the Canal des Wateringues, the endless beach begins.
Sand and sea are grey under a grey, muffled sky that presses
down on the banal buildings of a resort that never had any *chic*
or even any amusingly outrageous vulgarity. Boys on motorbikes

are roaring along the gleaming flats. When the season starts there will be sand-yachts to obstruct them. Now there are only family games of football, and people striding out briskly with their dogs in that Saturday afternoon access of moral energy when one vows that, at last, one's life is to be made anew.

There are a few surfers gliding rather inexpertly in the shallows, and, crossing them, two men are struggling to get a rubber dinghy out against the incoming tide. Just so, in May and June 1940, the files of British and French troops waded out to that crazy fleet that brought 350,000 of them back to England. It is impossible to relate this infinitely commonplace strand with what French guide books call 'the hell of Dunkerque' and English 'the miracle of Dunkirk'. This is living memory, but already it is as remote as Agincourt, where the dead, French and English together, were bundled into a common grave, one layer in the humus of history that lies so thick over this north-east corner of France, which echoes with the bugles of six centuries of war. At Cassel, thirty kilometres south of here, there are buried 2,000 British soldiers who died in a desperate rearguard action against a Panzer division during the retreat to Dunkerque. Away to the south-east, 20,000 French were left on the field at Crécy, where was heard for the first time in Europe the cannon fire which was to swell through the courtly battles of the seventeenth and eighteenth centuries to the barrages of 1914–18. The obscene slaughter of that war is commemorated by various large-scale monuments rising like ships above the far horizons of these plains. It is an area that breeds soldiers as well as burying them. Pétain, de Gaulle and General Leclerc, the liberator of Paris, were all born in the *Nord*.

Failure to relate the beach to its past means that, at last, I can relate it to the town. When one thought of the evacuation, it was impossible to believe that anything lay behind the buildings of that promenade which was so grossly inappropriate a backcloth for it. Four-fifths of what did was destroyed; surprisingly, the rebuilding has produced an authentic Flemish town where the surviving buildings live in harmony with the new, largely because few of the latter are excessively high. There is always an exception, and this very day has seen the opening of a new hotel whose twenty-one floors above ground level have 128 rooms and fifty-eight *appartements de grande luxe*, but the norm is decent, three-storey blocks of flats whose verandahs are painted in different colours. Even the wide central square, typical of Flanders, which might have been a desert, for an open-air assembly hall is the kind of townscape that mellows slowly, already has a feeling of community. The variety and the human scale of the façades surrounding it, and the good-humoured relish with which the townspeople are enjoying what is by now a sunny Saturday afternoon both contribute. We are far enough east here to have left behind the nervy vivacity, at its most intense in Paris, which, in France, gives drama and importance to buying 250 grammes of butter. In its place is something heartier — heavier also, undeniably — and less abrasive, typified by the women whose dress fittings are on an average two, and sometimes three sizes larger than their Paris equivalents, settling comfortably in a *pâtisserie*, their shopping bags disposed at their feet, all taking milk in their tea in the English fashion and all eating at least two cream cakes.

Jean Bart looks down on them from his pedestal in the centre of the *place*. This is his town, as St. Malo is Duguay-Trouin's. His career as one of France's licensed pirates of the seventeenth and eighteenth centuries was equally notable and I like greatly his reply to Louis XIV, when the king received him personally to say: 'Jean Bart, I have appointed you Squadron Commander.' 'Well done, Sire!' said Jean Bart. He does not sound the kind of man to have dabbled with music, which makes it the more odd that the tune which marks the quarters from a square brick tower in the centre of Dunkerque is known as the '*Cantate de Jean Bart*'. The statue, splendidly rhetorical, is by David d'Angers, who worked during the first half of the nineteenth century, producing among much else the pediment of the Paris *Panthéon*.

I dismiss as idle curiosity the idea that it might be fun to stay the night at the twenty-one-storey tower hotel just to see what it is like. I know perfectly well what it will be like, for one *hôtel de grande luxe* is even more like another than one *hôtel de la gare* is like the next down the line. Also, funds will not run to such frivolities, and I have planned to spend the night at Lille. The route there runs through Armentières, whose name rings in the first half of the twentieth century like something out of Homer. As the train enters the town over the Nieppe bridge, you see one of the most striking monuments to the victims of the Resistance in the whole of the *Nord*; as it leaves, it passes between the cemeteries of 1914–18, where the acres of crosses marking the graves of the British dead alternate with the yellow light of colza fields.

Perversely, I have always liked Lille, rather in the fashion that I like Milan and Manchester, when there are grounds for not doing so. It is big and black and bustling, the smell of *frites* rises like incense from every street corner and it is the only place I know where people eat mussels with chips, which I cannot see as other than an unholy alliance. It is hard to think of a more improbable birthplace for General de Gaulle, even if the address, No 9 rue Princesse, did something to redeem the situation, until you learn the town's history. Lille was one of the seats of the Dukes of Burgundy. It has suffered eleven sieges, among them engagements like that of September 1792, when the citizens proved as staunch as the military were gallant. On that occasion it was the mayor who, invited by the Austrians to surrender, replied that the townspeople had just renewed their vow to be faithful to the Nation and, if need be, to die for her. 'We are not perjurers.' Wars were gentlemanly in those days. The Austrian commander, impressed by such courage, raised the siege.

It is more surprising that, in the last two of the eleven sieges, those of 1914 and 1940, the town should again have been granted battle honours — true, it was during the first months of the respective wars. In the first, when Prince Rupert of Bavaria refused the sword of the French Col. de Pardieu, 'in testimony to the heroism of the French troops', 4,000 reservists, with a stiffening of Spahis, had held out for three days against six Bavarian regiments. In the second about 40,000 French troops stopped six German divisions and Rommel's tanks, again for three days.

I suspect that my partiality owes something to a sentimental memory of my first visit to Lille. It involved an official luncheon at which I was seated next to an Anglophile *notable*, who recalled his memories of the German Occupation in the First World War. He was a small boy at the time, and, on their way to school each morning, he and his friends passed a column of British prisoners. 'We had sandwiches of bread and lard for lunch in our satchels. We used to give half every day to the soldiers, and sometimes they would give us a regimental button. I have the buttons still.'

He took one of the tiny Union Jacks which, with the French blue, white and red, decorated the table, looked at me inquiringly as he said : 'Have I the right?' and stuck it in his buttonhole.

Sentiment apart, what is engaging about Lille is the hearty good nature with which its citizens enjoy themselves. It is one of the rather rare provincial towns where people do not go to bed early, and it has a good line in those lusty, northern *kermesses,* with their vast eating and drinking and their element of the grotesque, expressed in Lille, as in a number of Flemish towns, by the parading of huge plaster figures of legendary giants, which are so different from Mediterranean carnivals.

This evening the streets are brilliant with sky-signs that hint at Piccadilly; on virtually every block one can buy *frites*, or frankfurters, or *bratwurst*, or *moules* with vinegar, and everybody is on the town. More, they seem to be less chasing pleasure than positively enjoying themselves, whether they are solid burghers, or Algerian and African immigrants, or little girls of fourteen, still so newly-fledged that they go to the cinema or to suburban dance halls in pairs rather than with boy friends. The heartiness extends to the brasserie where I have dinner, which is full of family parties with children, all taking a simple pleasure in their night out and all conveying an openhearted welcome to strangers. There is butter on the table; the wonderful coffee — we are a stone's throw from Belgium where the coffee is the best in Europe — comes up with cream and biscuits, the apple tart is melting, but, from an excess of generosity it may be, the *escalope viennoise* is served with brown gravy as well as lemon and anchovy and chopped egg. As always in the east, the beer is superb, and surely, all over Saturday night Lille, where it is flowing in cascades, there must be people drinking far too much of it, but either, from long training, they have learned to carry it home quietly, or, conversely, they do not go home till morning, for, when I trek back to my hotel around eleven, the streets are a monument to public order.

The Sunday morning train going south is half empty. I share a compartment with a girl in a green shirt with one of those Clouet faces that still persist in France and a neat, middle-aged woman with a hearing aid who never raises her eyes from her book. The heat is turned up to stifling point and there seems no way of reducing it. I sit in a daze or a doze, dividing what little attention I can muster between the landscape through which we are passing and today's issue of the *Journal de Dimanche*, which has a gripping article about life at the Élysée as it awaits the new incumbent, whoever he may be. The best cloth, for the most brilliant banquets, is 125 metres long and embroidered with stars and swords in gold thread. On it are laid thirty pieces of glass and silver for each place. Among the thousands of items in the reserve, there is a 450-piece enamel service taken from Goering. It might be interesting to establish the provenance of some of the treasures in the Royal or Presidential residences of many countries, though not, of course, in any spirit of condemnation, since it is known that acquisition from defeated enemies becomes looting only when it is practised on a small scale by other ranks.

There is more green than I remembered on the fringe of Lille, before we strike through the centre of the black belt. There are pitheads at Ostricourt, pylons at Douai, webbing the sky with patterns like a Paul Klee drawing, a glimpse of tractors on wagons and Citroëns straight off the assembly line being loaded on to transporter lorries. Then we come out into a land of huge fields of corn and beetroot and small houses with gardens where the rhubarb is doing nicely and the lettuces are set out in orderly rows. There is a glimpse of the triple towers, cathedral, belfry and church, at Cambrai, of the river and the canal around St. Quentin, of the lantern tower at Laon.

Crépy, just before we reach Laon, teases me with a memory which I do not succeed in pinning down until the train is sliding into the station at Reims. It is a totally unremarkable village, except for the fact that, in 1918, it was here that the Germans installed 'Big Bertha', trained on Paris. On March 29th, one of Bertha's shells fell on the church of St. Gervais and St. Protais, near the Hôtel de Ville, killing one hundred of the congregation assembled there for the Good Friday rites and injuring many others.

8—TFOF * *

25

WHY, I WONDER, should Reims on a Sunday morning remind me of Edinburgh? Precisely, not Reims itself, which feels gayer than any Covenanting Sabbath I have experienced, but the atmosphere of this rather elegant bar, which is as douce, in the Scottish rather than the French meaning of the word, as a teashop in Princes Street. It derives chiefly from two gentlewomen in hats who are seated opposite me. They are blooming in late middle age, and Raeburn would have enjoyed painting them. The illusion is so compelling that one half expects them to be nibbling shortbread, but in fact they are having a drink before lunch, and what they are drinking is not the wine of the country, champagne, but beer, which they are sipping thoughtfully as though it were dry sherry. So are almost all the other customers, except for a fat woman at a window table and myself, who are drinking coffee. Only from one corner, occupied by a man and two women, comes that heady pop which is the most expensive noise in the world. Is one to deduce that 'the wine of kings' is pricing itself out of the home market? It was

Edward VII, when Prince of Wales, who was credited with saying that he would rather have a bath of champagne than the Order of the Bath; and Henry VIII was an addict, so were a long line of French monarchs and several Popes.

To some extent it is, and deliberately so, taking the home market in the broader sense of France, not Reims, which is one of the two chief centres of the champagne trade, the other being Épernay. Success has its problems, and, during recent years, the trade has been experiencing success different in kind, not simply in degree, from that it enjoyed in the days when the Widow Clicquot, prototype of women in big business, gained a flying start in the Russian market by getting a shipload of her champagnes through as early as 1814, when the Empire had collapsed and peace was not assured, but Talleyrand, at the Congress of Vienna, was finding champagne to be a valuable adjunct to diplomacy. Then, as for most of the next century and a half, the market was a limited one, esoteric and international. Champagne, like diamonds and sables and, later, Rolls-Royce cars, had a place in mythology rather than in catalogues of consumer goods; it was a symbol of supreme quality as much as a wine. That kind of demand could be met without difficulty by the vineyards running in a strip, one hundred kilometres long and one kilometre wide, along the Côte des Blancs, the Valley of the Marne and the Montagne de Reims, which produce the best champagnes. With the age of affluence, the demand increased sensationally. New vineyards were planted; more and more growers began to improve their profits by keeping back a portion of their crop to make their own champagne, which they sold direct to the consumer.

In such a situation, the danger was not that producers would resort to adulteration, but that they would be tempted to exhaust the soil of their vineyards by overproduction, or to take short cuts in the long and complicated process of production — champagne is essentially a 'made' wine. By the beginning of the 1970s, when the trade started pricing up its wares to restrain demand, one danger had become a reality. Quality champagne spends three years maturing in vaults, many of Gallo-Roman origin, tunnelled in the low, chalky hills that form the eastern escarpment of the plateau of the Ile de France. So, for every bottle sold, there should be three in store. In 1972–3 there were only 2.75. This was eating the seed corn; the relief of the merchants was genuine when, in 1973, the higher prices caused home sales to drop by 3.5 per cent.

Many occasional drinkers in Britain might be hard put to it to name more than six or seven of those merchants; probably few Frenchmen could list many more than a dozen. In round figures there are 140, but more than half the total sales are made by the ten biggest houses, Moët-Hennessy, Mumm, Piper-Heidsieck, Pommery, Taittinger, Veuve Clicquot, Lanson, Roederer, Bollinger and Krug. Naming a 'best' among them would be invidious, but Krug and Bollinger, both relatively small houses, are renowned for their faithfulness to traditional methods and their refusal to truckle to what is supposed to be 'the taste of the customer'. The point is, which customer? Krug are on record as saying : 'Our aim is to please a certain number of devotees, not to make a trifling product (*un produit de frivolités*).'

It would be wrong to think of the odd 130 merchants who make the lesser half of the sales, many of whom, like almost all the great houses, are growers also, as frugal peasants. The price of champagne is reflected in the price of land in the area, which has been making between 400,000 and 600,000 francs a hectare. From only one hectare a grower, in a year, may realise 40,000 francs before tax. With six or eight hectares, a size which, in many parts of France, would make him a struggling smallholder, he is a rich man. If he chooses to use some of his grapes to make his own champagne, its quality will depend very largely on the extent to which he co-operates with his neighbours to obtain a variety of *crus*. Champagne is a blended wine whose excellence — when it is excellent — derives from careful selection of the *crus* which go into it. Veuve Clicquot's executives spend the first three months of each year daily testing the products of the previous harvest, in order to classify and blend them into a vintage that conforms with the 'house style'. Krug's *Private Cuvée* contains forty-nine different wines and Mumm's *Cordon rouge* thirty-five. In each case the details of the blending are a secret closely guarded by the house.

One cannot help wondering how much the present boom in champagne depends on the froth and bubble : perhaps the only way to resolve the question is to establish who buys the *natures* like the red Bouzy and Mareuil, and the white Cramant, which are non-effervescent. Originally there was no froth and very little bubble. The wine drunk by Henry VIII and Henri IV of France was no more than faintly *petillant*. It was a seventeenth-century Benedictine, Dom Perignon, cellarer of the Abbey of Hautvillers, who exploited its natural tendency to sparkle by perfecting the process of double fermentation. The head that makes it necessary to wire the cork down is produced by the careful addition of sugar and yeast in the spring after the harvest. During their subsequent three years in the vaults, the bottles are regularly turned one-eighth of a circle and tilted ever more steeply, so that the deposit which the wine throws gathers round the cork and can be expelled. The man who does the tilting and turning is called a *remueur*, and when he knows his job, which demands a four-year apprenticeship, he can handle 30,000 bottles in a day. After all that you get the pop which represents the peak of conspicuous consumption.

These are impious thoughts, typical of one whose favourite drink is not champagne and who, of the champagnes, prefers the *natures*. Equally irreverent is my wonder that, during the eight centuries for which French kings, with rare exceptions, have been sacred in Reims Cathedral — Hugh Capet was the first and Charles X the last of them — neither the trade, nor the burghers, nor whoever was France's equivalent of the Duke of Norfolk, whose job it was to arrange coronations, managed to find an official place for champagne in the ceremony. It is particularly surprising when you consider all that was involved in the proceedings, which remained unchanged from the twelfth century to the nineteenth. They began with two bishops walking in procession to the archiepiscopal palace to haul the king symbolically from the bed on which he was symbolically asleep, to take him to the cathedral, and included the release of a flight of doves and a salvo of musketry — but surely not the latter in the twelfth century? — inside it. Provision for some kind of symbolic sousing or sprinkling would have crowned champagne as an authentically royal wine, instead of which the trade had to be content with the vastly increased business which the coronations brought to the town. In an indirect way they still do. Near the cathedral is a drugstore displaying not just magnums, but Jeroboams and Methuselahs — eight bottles — towards which, at this moment, a group of well-fleshed German tourists, fresh from what, judging from the guide books which most of them are carrying, has been a comprehensively documented tour of the cathedral, are moving purposefully.

The building itself stops the vein of flippancy like a tap, an effect it never fails to have on me.

Clocher de Chartres, nef d'Amiens,
Choeur de Beauvais, portail de Reims

runs the old tag, and the richness of the West Front, recently cleaned, like that of Notre-Dame de Paris, is incomparable. The church is like an enormous reliquary, sumptuous with sculpture and ornament that never becomes over-ornate. There is an extra grace in that, artistically, the Champagne region is Sienese rather than Florentine. The parallel must not be applied too strictly, in spite of the almond eyes which are common to both, but it does give some indication of the gentle gaiety you find in religious imagery here, exemplified by the famous Smiling Angel who welcomes visitors at the West Door, one in spirit with Amiens's Golden Virgin and blithely unconscious of her mutilated hands.

That half of what one sees is restoration, if not reconstruction, is unimportant. Time has treated much of the carving harshly, but not as mercilessly as the bombardments of the First World

War, which wrecked the cathedral. The restoration took twenty years, by which time the second was imminent. Happily it brought no further damage. Old and new have grown into an organic whole, so that what you look at is the most harmonious as well as the most remarkable Gothic cathedral in France. The interior startles one by its simplicity : it seems devoid of ornament until your eye takes in the luxuriance of the nave capitals and the saints in their niches on the inner face of the West Porch. It is the longest nave in France, over 138 metres, and one of the loftiest; only Beauvais, Metz and Amiens surpass it in height. Room enough under these arches for the doves to wheel and the salvoes to rattle, nobility enough in the austerely perfect proportions of this interior for even the most moving of all the sacrings it has seen, that at which Joan the Maid watched Charles VII kneel before the altar to be anointed with holy oil from the *Sainte Ampoule* and have the crown of Charlemagne placed on his head. She took her standard into the cathedral. It was not customary, but when she was criticised for doing so she said that since it had endured the fight it was only just that it should see the glory.

That ceremony was more than the crowning of a king. It was Lacordaire who said that France was born of an act of faith on a battlefield, that act being the baptism of Clovis at Reims in AD 498. What Joan witnessed almost 1,000 years later was the rebirth of her country.

I had meant, as I always do mean when I am in Reims, to go to see the room at No. 10 rue Franklin Roosevelt, where Eisenhower had his HQ and the German capitulation was signed on May 7th, 1945, but once again I do not, this time because the two kinds of history will not mix. Instead, I stroll along the tree-shaded *cours*, where a fair is going on in a rather lackadaisical fashion, as far as the Porte Mars, a splendid third-century Roman arch, then find my way to a far different church, which commemorates the next most improbable convert after Clovis to have been baptised at Reims. Foujita, the Japanese painter who was a member of the school of Paris (he was born in Tokyo, but never went back there to live once he had found Montmartre) had a mystical experience in the Abbey Church of St. Remi at Reims which led to his conversion and baptism in the cathedral. To show his gratitude he determined to build a chapel, and, for him, building meant more than financing the operation. He himself drew up the plans for Notre-Dame de la Paix, which is never called anything other than the Chapelle Foujita, he designed the wrought-iron and the stained-glass, he was constantly on the spot to supervise the craftsmen. He kept the decoration of the walls for himself; the Romanesque style had been chosen for the chapel partly because its arches would give more space for frescos. Foujita knew nothing of the technique of fresco, but, at the age of eighty, he learned it, and *fresco buono* at that, the true art of painting in the wet plaster, which calls for a swift hand and allows no second thoughts. The New Testament scenes, which resulted, line the walls of the chapel. Foujita, like some Renaissance painters, has put himself into one of them; with his friend, Rene Lalou, he is to be seen kneeling among the crowd at the Crucifixion. The fact that I do not greatly care for his frescos in no way diminishes my pleasure in Foujita's achievement. He even managed the time of his death competently, staying alive long enough to finish his work but not so long as to risk any effect of anti-climax. He died in 1968, at the age of eighty-two.

The next morning is frustrating. I had planned to spend it seeing the birthplace of the greatest public servant Europe has known, and, in so describing him, I am not forgetting either Robert Cecil or, in another age and genre, Edwin Chadwick, who did more than any other single person to make Victorian England grasp the concept of public health. Colbert was the son of a cloth merchant of Reims, and took the bourgeois virtues implanted by such a background with him when he entered the service of Louis XIV, in a climate unpropitious for the qualities of justice, prudence and temperance. He took much else beside. Whether you look at the encouragement he gave to French industry, or a realised project like the Canal du Midi, or the development of the Bibliothèque Nationale in his time, you find evidence of a creative good sense whose works live after it.

But in Colbert's native town there is no birthplace to be found, only a statue which is what the North would call 'nobbut'. Such sense as I have myself suggests that the house must have been one of the 1,000 in Reims destroyed during 1914–18. I try to console myself with the thought that Colbert, who hated spending money unnecessarily, though he was ready to supplement public funds from his own pocket in what he thought was a righteous cause, would not have wished to see its upkeep being a burden on either the rates or the finances of the National Monuments. Perhaps one might see as a post-dated memorial to his spirit of enterprise the commercial innovations which Reims has introduced during the present century. Since 1948 it has been the launching pad successively of the self-service store, the *'supermag'* and, latest, the *'hypermarché'*; with a sales area of more than 2,500 metres and parking space *en suite*. Love them or hate them, all three are now part of the fabric of French life, and are subtly changing a style of living that has been constant for generations.

Would Colbert have hated them because of their threat to small craftsmen, and because many of their employees have a dog's life, and because of the ease with which, if they want to, they can take their customers for a ride? Or would he have loved them for the ingenuity of their methods of attracting customers — some have cinemas and bowling alleys; most have cafeterias; Nancy has an all night *hyper* that sells playing cards and whodunnits, iced champagne for insomniacs and hot croissants for early risers — and their almost unlimited potential?

I am pondering the question while looking at a window display of those 'jokes' which are timeless and international, rubber spiders, and sneeze powder, and blots of ink, reaching their peak, or nadir, with dog dirt (Made in France) and vomit (Made in Germany) when I realise that, technically, I have come to journey's end. Reims was the last stop which André and Julien made on their tour. Then the city, as it had done in

233

Colbert's day, still lived largely by the wool industry; the brothers bought there a warm blanket for an old woman who had helped them on their way when they were starting on their travels. They did not see the cathedral and it goes without saying that they had no truck with the champagne.

All we are told of what happened when they left Reims is that, after a weary week ('*une semaine de fatigue*') they came at last to Alsace-Lorraine, their barge taking them to within a few kilometres of Phalsbourg. For me, that week, or as much of it as proves necessary, will be spent in three pilgrimages.

26 THE JAPANESE GIRL is wearing jeans and holding up a miniature Tyrolean pipe.

'Did General de Gaulle smoke one like this?' she asks the proprietor of the souvenir shop at Colombey-les-Deux-Églises.

'Often,' the proprietor assures her. 'And three packets of cigarettes a day.'

If that last is true, the General must have lapsed badly in his later years, for he once said that he had managed to give up cigars and cigarettes by telling everyone around him that he had stopped smoking, after which he could not start again.

The proprietor turns to me. 'We voted the right way here on Sunday. We voted for Giscard. Without the General the UDR is *foutu*.'

Sunday was the first round of the Presidential elections. Before the end of the evening we knew that the UDR's candidate, Jacques Chaban-Delmas, a Gaullist with impeccable Resistance credentials and an outlook which, during his term as Prime Minister, proved to be sufficiently progressive to alarm a large

235

section of his own party, had been knocked out. Sunday's run-off is between Valéry Giscard d'Estaing, technocrat and man of today, or even tomorrow, unquestionably brilliant if dubiously aristocratic — his noble particle is not accepted in the most exigent circles — and François Mitterand, leader of the Left. Mitterand is the man who, against all expectations, deprived de Gaulle of a first-round victory in the 1965 Presidentials. He, too, has a distinguished Resistance record; now that Pierre Mendès-France is no longer in the lists he is perhaps the most interesting politician in the country.

Gaullism died on Sunday, then, but will de Gaulle, in this place, ever be dead? Since his burial, that ceremony from which he excluded the great and tacitly invited the whole of France, the 'people' for whom he professed a mystical respect, with which went a disregard verging on contempt for the individuals who comprised it, Colombey has been growing steadily more like Lourdes. It seems only a question of time before people will be touching for King's Evil on the General's tombstone.

This shop provides a foretaste. Look where you will, you see likenesses of him, in two dimensions and in three, in wood, in pottery, in plastic, in bronze and brass and textile, in uniform and in plain clothes, on ashtrays and vases and plates and cups and saucers, as brush-holder or book-end or paper-weight, as a plaque, as a bust, as a statuette, in a bottle like a sailing ship and in a glass globe which, when shaken, envelopes the Saviour of France in a blizzard. There is even a shelf of books by or about him in a village with a population of less than 400, where, in the ordinary way, you would hardly expect to find reading matter more demanding than popular magazines. The effect is hypnotic. When I leave I find I have bought a key ring adorned with a Cross of Lorraine, whether out of *politesse* to the shopkeeper or as an act of piety I cannot be certain.

Some of this, of course, started during the General's lifetime. Any President of the Republic, even when he is not a national hero, is a centre of popular attention; M. Pompidou, when he was on holiday, or spending a weekend at his country house, could count on crowds and cameras at the church door when he and his wife went to mass. At Colombey the phenomenon was on a different scale. Motorists would take the village in during a tour of the Champagne; on Sunday mornings, busloads of trippers debouched on to the *place* before the church, firstcomers finding a seat inside for a nearer view of de Gaulle, whose family pew, by a chance which one would not have dared to dream of, was between the banner of Joan of Arc and a stained glass window of St. Louis.

Colombey has been classed by the *Beaux Arts*, which means that there can be no unauthorised building to disturb the harmony of its good stone houses, with their red-tiled roofs and borders of pansies, but it will never again be as de Gaulle described it, a peaceful, frugal village where nothing had changed through the years. The world has come in, even if the cows do still pass along the main street morning and evening for milking. Prosperity began modestly, with the arrival of journalists and the *gendarmes* assigned to a President of the Republic who, between them, started the local café on the road to a new success. Now, bars and restaurants, and a couple of hotels are thriving, and a new *gendarmerie* has been built. A detachment will continue to be stationed here as long as Madame de Gaulle lives at La Boisserie, hidden behind its trees along the road leading from the church which is named after her husband.

The house was enlarged and improved after de Gaulle became President of the Republic, but it remained an unpretentious residence for a head of state. On the other hand, it was exactly the kind of place to suit a prudent but not penurious Army officer looking for a country house midway between Paris and the Eastern frontier, which, later, would be a retreat for his years as a half-pay colonel. That was de Gaulle's situation in 1934, the year in which he bought it, when he commanded the 507th Armoured Regiment, garrisoned at Metz. The house, like the surrounding park, was run down, but the outlook was noble, a sweeping half circle of unpopulated landscape (*'Cent quatre-vingts degrés sans une maison et sans un promeneur.'*):

it was obviously a good buy. The property was on the classic invasion route but, during the war, it suffered nothing worse than being requisitioned as a billet for German officers. They had vacated it before the arrival of General Leclerc, who stopped to liberate La Boisserie during his triumphant advance from Paris to Strasbourg.

There would be no possibility of making La Boisserie a place of pilgrimage even without the protective *gendarmes*. During his lifetime, in or out of office, de Gaulle contrived to lead there the life of a private gentleman. No more colourful details about him became known outside than that he had had one room consecrated for the celebration of mass on occasions when he did not wish to go outside to church, that when he had a haircut he gave the barber who came to La Boisserie once a month from the neighbouring town of Chaumont a fifty franc note in an envelope, that he refused to have any of his poultry killed for the table. He died there a wholly private death at the end of a retirement of unexampled dignity, slumping over the card table on which he had set out his evening game of patience, and so escaping that 'shipwreck' of old age which he had so dreaded. Even the local doctor and the local priest did not arrive in time to see him alive. Other than his wife, the witnesses of his last moments, and those who prepared him for his burial, were the two household servants, both elderly women, and the chauffeur who had been in the General's service for twenty-five years, and almost certainly saved his life by his presence of mind in accelerating violently when the car in which de Gaulle was travelling was raked by gunfire during the assassination attempt at Petit Clamart.

The centre of the cult is the small churchyard where, as long before his death as January 1952, de Gaulle had left instructions that he was to be buried in the grave 'where my daughter, Anne, lies already, and where, one day, my wife will rest.' Anne was the General's dearly loved handicapped daughter. At her death, at the age of twenty, her father is recorded as saying : 'Now she is like other girls.'

The tomb is a plain cross of white stone. On the left, where blue and white violas are growing in a stone bowl, a tablet reads: 'Anne de Gaulle 1928–48.' The flowers on the right are pansies, their deep colour something between brown and purple, and the inscription is: 'Charles de Gaulle 1890–1970.' It was Châteaubriand who said that mausoleums are for little men; great men need only a tablet and a name.

For the first weeks after the burial the grave was piled high with flowers and less conventional, but sometimes more moving tributes. Once a child left one of the toy storks which are the emblems of Alsace. Finally, at Madame de Gaulle's request, which may be seen as one more instance of separating the public persona of her husband from the private, they were transferred to the wrought-iron mission cross in the centre of the church-yard. Now it is there that pilgrims lay their offerings before going on to stand before the grave for a few moments of recol-lection. The heap can scarcely have diminished in size, or in the variousness of its composition, since that early period. There are dreadful ceramic flowers, a wreath of carnations 'from the 507th Regiment of Tanks to its CO', a wooden cross from the blood donors of Talange in the Moselle, a plaque from the former hostages of Colombey, a tribute to the Great Defender of the French language from the Free Walloons of Bierges, in Belgium. Filling up the interstices are the tributes of the un-known, the *muguet* of May, and knots of wildflowers from children who have been brought to stand here so that, later, they shall have a memory which may turn out to be their first aware-ness of history. Holy places are like this. So, around *Toussaint*, is the grave of Edith Piaf in the cemetery of Père Lachaise in Paris, which is not a disrespectful comparison but an indication of how diverse are the ways in which one can reach the heart of a people.

The national memorial might be in a different universe. This is the enormous Cross of Lorraine, paid for by national subscrip-tion, which has been set up on 'the mountain', a hill just outside the village, to look out over a landscape which has already been made safe against spoilation. The taxi runs between meadows dreamy with dandelion clocks, then sets me down in the car park at its foot. Beyond this point, no cars, no transistors, no picnics, no dogs running loose. One has an absurd feeling that one should go up barefoot like the pilgrims at Croagh Patrick, or on one's knees, as at the Scala Santa in the Lateran Palace. The path curves up the side of the hill, with benches at intervals for those who may be overcome by years or emotion, and, as one mounts, a noble landscape opens out below. De Gaulle called it a country of huge, blurred, wistful horizons, of wood and meadow, ploughland and mournful fallow (*'vastes, frustes et triste horizons, bois, prés, cultures et friches mélancoliques'*). It may seem like that in the autumn of the year, or the autumn of a life. Today, in the spring wind and sunshine, it is the very reverse, clear and bright and well-farmed, a land for tranquil happiness outside of history.

The memorial cross is appalling. Faced with it I realise that, against the evidence of any number of illustrations and descriptions, I had been expecting something as native to the country as the rough stones of the memorial on the Ile de Sein. Instead there is this artefact of granite blocks, interspersed apparently with glass, though here observation may have been led astray by repulsion. Aesthetically it is on a level with the objects in the souvenir shop, while being gargantuan: when it is floodlit as, final horror, it regularly is, you could see it from Constantinople. For the General, who, in the sealed testaments which, years before his death, he deposited with his son, Philippe, and his closest collaborator, Georges Pompidou, repudiated any idea of a national funeral, and refused in advance all distinctions, dignities and decorations, it seems the ultimate outrage.

Saddened, I lower my eyes, to find some consolation. The handling of the space round the memorial is perfect. Intensely green turf alternates with granite paving, and, as on the grave in the churchyard, there are two tablets. That on the left reads:

'Il existe un pacte vingt fois séculaire entre le grandeur de la France et la liberté du monde.'

that on the right :

'En notre temps, la seule querelle qui vaille est celle de l'homme. C'est l'homme qu'il s'agit de sauver, de faire vivre et de développer.'

At least they let him write his own epitaph. It would be a rash follower who took on the task. By chance, the perfect one was spoken by Françoise Giroud, later to become France's first Minister for Women.

Would de Gaulle have twenty lines in the history textbooks of tomorrow, she was asked in an interview. No, replied Madame Giroud. One. 'Saved the honour of France on June 18th, 1940.' She added : 'Who, in the autumn of his years, wouldn't settle for as much ?'

27   THE TAXI-DRIVER says he used to work for Peugot. He was on the assembly line.

'Doing the same movement, eight hours a day, five days a week, for three years. It was a job for a robot, not a man.'

He came to Neufchâteau because his wife had the *Buffet de la Gare* there. It fitted in very well with the taxi, and now nothing is going to make him budge.

'I wouldn't live in Paris for anything. It's no life. The young ones want to be away there, of course. They're better off in the country if only they realised, but you can't tell them anything these days. All the same, I'd have loved to do the things they do now and live the way they live. There wasn't the chance in our day. We didn't have the money, or the free time, and even if we had, we wouldn't have dared.'

He sounds wistful rather than resentful; this is not rancour but middle age sighing at the sight of 'the young in one another's arms, birds in the trees', half in envy, half out of the knowledge that, even while it looks, time is sweeping them away with the whirling leaves, as it has swept away the young ones who, five and a half centuries ago, came to this spot to dance under the fairy tree.

We are standing on the terrace below the basilica which has been built on the hillside of *le Bois Chenu*, above Domrémy, looking over the green valley of the Meuse, here as candid as a trout stream. At the trial of Jeanne d'Arc, her prosecutors, charging her with sorcery, suggested that the voices which had sent her on her mission did not come from St. Michael, St. Margaret and St. Catherine, but from the fairies in the tree at *le Bois Chenu*, where, like the rest of the young people from Domrémy, she used to go to play and picnic. That was what the girls in the village said, Jeanne replied. She had told them then that it was not true. She did not believe in fairies. I have an entirely imaginary picture of her as a sturdy, commonsensical child of twelve, the age at which she first heard her voices, clinching the matter by telling the other children that *le Bois Chenu* was part of her father's property, and he wouldn't have fairies on his land. Jacques d'Arc owned twenty hectares of meadow and woodland, which made him, by village standards, a man of substance. Jeanne was not the poor shepherdess she is so often said to have been, though she may occasionally have tended the sheep on the family farm.

The fairy tree was destroyed during the Thirty Years' War. Now there is a fine beech growing on what is presumed, or hoped, to be the same spot. It was planted in 1881. So was the basilica, though, long before that, *le Bois Chenu*, associated as it was with the odious and ludicrous sorcery charge, had seen a first act of reparation. At the time of Jeanne's rehabilitation, a chapel called *l'ermitage de Notre-Dame de La Pucelle* had been built beside the fairy tree; the tower of the present church occupies its site. The bronze statues of the Maid's parents, Jacques d'Arc and Isabelle Romée, and the histrionic group of Jeanne listening to the voices of her three saints are acts of modern piety rather than medieval expiation; perhaps one will

243

be forgiven for wishing they had planted some more beech trees instead.

The basilica is in another class, not so much architecturally, though, as pilgrimage churches built during the past century go, it might be a great deal worse, but because, as at shrines in Italy where the prayers of centuries have left a patina that makes the haberdashery irrelevant, the sense of its purpose is so strongly conveyed. The tourist who stops here from idle curiosity, or, on a more sophisticated level, to see how the frescos recording Jeanne's campaign, which decorate the church, compare with that older record, the Bayeux Tapestry, are liable to be jerked into a different frame of mind by the austerity of the crypt. The first thing that catches your eye there is a tablet commemorating the day, August 23rd, 1921, when Foch came to hear mass and make his communion in thanksgiving to God and Sainte Jeanne d'Arc for victory. The crypt is dedicated to *Notre Dame des Armées*, and, in its stillness, mass is said daily for soldiers, living and dead, and for the country. An inscription beside the kneeling figure of Jeanne at its entrance recalls her wish : 'Build chapels where they will pray for soldiers who have died for their country'. The glass and paintings and mosaics of the basilica itself have little to add to this experience, but it is worth going up to it nevertheless for the sake of the Staircase of Peace, with its curving, wrought-iron balustrade bearing the arms of the cities through which Jeanne passed during her campaign.

The souvenirs are down in Domrémy; true, they lack the variety and exuberance of those at Colombey-les-Deux-Églises. This village street, too, is classed, but the regulations allow a shop selling postcards, metal figures of Jeanne, on foot and on horseback and in several sizes, and plates with pictures of the Basilica. There is also an Hotel de la Pucelle, with a modest eight bedrooms. The birthplace is opposite the hotel. Whether it is authentic or not depends on how much restoration one considers compatible with authenticity, but the point is unimportant beside the truth that, if it was not exactly in this house that Jeanne d'Arc was born, it must have been in a house exactly like this.

Four low-ceilinged little rooms, with thick walls and small windows, a loft above, a huge hearth surmounted by the arms of Lorraine, a floor of stone rather than beaten earth, evidence that this was the house of a rich peasant — they are all so true in spirit as to make nonsense of the hagiography that holds the dim room leading to the store cupboard to have been Jeanne's bedroom, or says that she wanted to sleep on the floor in order to give her bed to the poor.

The history of the building is known. It remained in the Arc family until 1586, after which it passed through several hands until the beginning of the eighteenth century, when it was bought by a man named Jean Gérardin. A hundred years later, in 1814, Jean Gérardin the fourth, who was then in occupation, was offered a large sum for the house by an Englishman. It was the period of the collapse of the Empire, when once more the English, this time allied with the Russians and the Prussians, were attacking France. The country was in confusion, cash, one would have thought, was a more valuable asset than property. Gérardin refused to part with the house. Four years later he sold it to the Department of the Vosges for only 2,500 francs, on condition that he was allowed to stay under his own roof during his lifetime as custodian of what was already regarded as a national shrine.

Since the Second World War the Department has established an admirable small museum, separated from the house by a stream. Over the door is the pediment of the original chapel of *le Bois Chenu*, and inside a statue of Jeanne in armour, kneeling in prayer, which is believed once to have been in the chapel, though it was transferred to the museum from the niche over the doorway of her birthplace — the statue now there is a reproduction.

The village church, whose square tower rises on the other side of the house, is still more evocative. Its orientation was changed early in the nineteenth century, and there has been a certain amount of restoration, but the font is that in which Jeanne was baptised, the holy water stoup at the entrance is that in which she dipped her fingers, the statue of St. Margaret backed against a pillar is that before which she prayed, in the low-vaulted choir, with the other children of Domrémy, she made her First Communion.

The whole building is as heavy with fact as the comprehensively documented museum nearby. Is there another European nation that has as its patron not a myth, but a historic personage? And which does that nation really venerate, the saint — who, it is worth remembering, was canonised for being obedient to the call of God, not for delivering France from her enemies — or the brilliant and victorious young leader, as Britain, or the British Navy, venerates Nelson? I think of the building near the Basilica of *le Bois Chenu*. It is a Carmelite convent which honours the secondary patron of France, a young woman who died at the age of twenty-three, after an ordeal hardly less agonising, if far different from, that of Jeanne d'Arc. At the time of her death, in 1897, Thérèse Martin, St. Thérèse of Lisieux, was an unknown nun in a provincial convent; less than twenty years later, and before her canonisation, the French soldiers of the First World War had spontaneously adopted her as their patron.

The paradox puzzles me on the drive back. Are there in the annals of history or the calendar of saints two more improbable patrons for a people who are by nature rational and sceptical rather than mystical?

In Neufchâteau it is suddenly cold. There are tales of a flake or two of snow having drifted down this morning and I am thankful for the wood fire in the dining room, where the chef is going through the full performance of operating a *grille au charbon de bois*. He piles the fire high with logs, pushing glowing pieces under the grill; a piece of beef turns on the spit, then a knife flashes to divide it into enormous steaks for a couple in early middle age at the other side of the room. They are casual and expensive, he in a blue, open-necked shirt and a cashmere *pull*, she with emerald-green trousers and beautifully cut silver hair. There is an air about them of fast cars, and winter sports, and *résidences sécondaires*. Here is late twentieth-century France typified, and it makes me add 'elegant', and 'hedonistic', and 'worldly' to 'rational' and 'sceptical'. How do you relate them and all they stand for to Jeanne hearing her voices, and the little Carmelite in her obscure cloister?

I give it up, settling instead for pleasure in 'the drunkenness of things being various', and go up to my room before the couple are anywhere near the end of their steaks.

28

THERE WAS ONLY one concentration camp on French soil. Struthof is 800 metres up in the Vosges, on the northern slopes of a hill, the rocher Louise, which was a favourite winter sports resort for the people of Strasbourg, fifty kilometres to the north-west. When work on the camp was started, in May 1941, the temporary huts for the 300 prisoners who laid out the permanent site, carrying up the building materials on their backs from the valley below, were set up beside the hotel which had welcomed the skiers.

Today Struthof is maintained as a memorial to all the French men, women and children who died in the Nazi concentration camps, the tomb which the nation has made for those who have no known burial place, those who went out by the chimney of the crematorium or whose all but fleshless bones were piled in nameless charnel heaps. The road up from Rothau, on a typical May morning, is enchanting, with jubilant birds and the sun catching the light green of the beech leaves that flicker here and there among the conifers.

My driver tells me that he lived at Rothau through the Occupation : he was the chauffeur for the Germans at the camp. A collaborationist? By no means. Then, as now, he was the village taxi-driver, and refusing duty because a fare was a Nazi, particularly when he carried a gun, would have been a wholly pointless kind of resistance. Even without that job, he would have known a good deal about prison camps. In the 1914–18 war his father spent two years in a German 'hostage' camp. He only lived a year after he came home. In this last war his brother was in Neuengamme for eighteen months. When he came out he weighed only thirty-three kilos. (Neuengamme, about as ill-reputed as Struthof, was in the north, near Lübeck.)

Thin people lasted better than fat in the camps, the driver goes on. And the best prospects for survival were the prisoners who were there for a reason. It didn't matter what kind of reason. Resistance workers, and Communists and Christians alike, they held on when innocents pulled in during a raid, those who said, 'Why me? I haven't done anything,' gave up very quickly.

Down in Rothau things were not so bad, except when the Nazis started reprisals against the families of boys of seventeen who vanished into the Resistance to escape being called up into the German Army, or deported. The Occupying troops, other than the SS, were quite 'correct'. As he says that, I remember a Dutch colleague, who lived through the war years as a school-boy in Rotterdam, saying that a military Occupation was always more supportable than a civil one. The chief trouble at Rothau had been that the people were forbidden to speak French. 'And we didn't know any other language,' says the driver. (The village is just west of the *patois* line.) Also, anybody who wore a beret was likely to have it knocked off his head, as being 'too French'.

He pulls up before the main gate of the camp. It has been preserved as it stood from 1941 to 1944, heavily barred and wired, as has the double fencing of the perimeter. During those three years the fence was electrified, there were searchlights and machine guns in the watchtowers and tracker dogs in the kennels near the gate. There was only one escape from Struthof, says the driver, and that was not a business of tunnelling under the fence, but a superb stroke of audacity. An Alsatian prisoner got hold of the Commandant's uniform and, with three or four comrades, drove out in a car with the guard presenting arms. They made a clean getaway and joined, or rejoined, the Resistance.

He himself had been the first man from Rothau to enter the camp after it had been evacuated. 'The Nazis had left it as tidy as though they had intended to come back in the morning.'

The monument, necropolis rather than cenotaph, for an unknown prisoner is buried beneath it, is just inside the gate, a rising spiral of white stone on whose convex side is carved a skeletal figure, representing the thousands who starved and died in the camps. The spiral, we are told, represents the flame of the crematorium and also the idea of boundless liberty. Symbolism being so personal, it is statement of fact rather than criticism to record that, for me, the triangular curve, whose distant view suggests a sail, whose near view can seem obtrusive against the august background of hills, does not speak of the experience of the camps. One would be inclined to say that nothing could, if it were not for the *Memorial de la Déportation* on the point of the Ile de la Cité in Paris, a catacomb whose iron bars, urns of ashes and walls scrawled with the messages of the unconquered dead seldom fail to still the chatter of even the most unaware groups of visitors.

From the gate the site extends downhill in broad terraces, each hacked out of the rock by the prisoners. There were huts on each level; two have been left as specimens. The unforgettable memorial is at the bottom of the slope, behind the crematorium. The Pit of Ashes today is lined with green turf. Over it a rough cross, no more than two sticks at right angles, looks down at another cross blocked out in pansies above which is written: *Honneur et Patrie*, below: *Ossa Humiliata*.

Our guided party includes a Canadian family, husband, wife and two small children.

'Helga,' says the young husband, 'd'you notice, you don't hear a bird or anything in this place?'

In fact, in the wood backing on to the Pit of Ashes, a thrush is shouting its head off against an accompaniment of twittering finches, but perhaps, to this place, you bring your own climate. I recall a priest, a former prisoner, whom I met on my only other visit to Struthof. It was an official occasion and he was wearing a double row of medals on his cassock. The worst thing of all, he had said, looking round a hut which was identical with the one in which he had spent months, was not the starvation, and the slavery, and the beatings, and the perpetual imminence of death. It was the feeling that the whole world had gone mad.

There should be nightmares after a day like this, but I sleep sweetly enough in the little hotel at Rothau, after two French workmen who keep their berets on, three Germans and myself have dined in the red-papered bar-cum-restaurant, which finds room for a refrigerator, an outsize coffee grinder and a piano, as well as a rather unexpected plaque of Saint-Germain-des-Prés, some white tulips past their best and a quantity of ersatz forsythia stuck into a trunk of silver birch. Only in the morning do I have a moment of panic, waking to an illusion that the room is suffused with the cold, hideous blue which was the colour of the interior of the prison hut. It continues to obsess my visual memory as a tune may obsess one's aural memory.

POSTLUDE

RETURNING TO PHALSBOURG gives me something of the sense of
homecoming that it had for André and Julien. The non-stop
cyclorama of the past six weeks has made permanence hard to
realise, but here is eternity. Marshal Mouton is steadfast on his
pedestal and the newsagent's black cocker is still sitting dead
centre of the shop entrance, with customers walking round him
in acknowledgment that it is his doorstep. At the hotel Madame
recognises me and gives me the same room. Last time she was
tending pots of polyanthus, now it is geraniums, but that is
continuity, not change. There is time before dinner to go round
the municipal museum, where, along with regional costumes and
an impressive collection of Service uniforms, there is a copy of
Le Tour de la France used by Adolphe Bergen (born 1867) at
the *École primaire*, Paris, Georges Bergen (born 1909) at the
École primaire, Argenteuil, and Charles Bergen (born 1915) at
the *Collége de Saverne*. In the morning the jam is still Madame's
superb home-made apricot and the market stalls are still piled
high with cauliflowers as white as curd.

But if there is relief at returning, their is poignancy about departing. The two brothers and their uncle left Phalsbourg to settle in France, pausing on their way through Paris to see the sights. I am leaving France, pausing in Paris to make my farewells. It is painful to find, once there, that, in all but body, I have already left. The new tenants are installed in my flat; the roof lent by a kindly friend, which enables me to stay for these last days, is in the alien territory of the Right Bank; I am no longer a taxpayer and I do not know the grocer. Silently, inexorably, the gates have swung shut in my face, from a resident I am become a tourist among tourists.

If I were still in the *quartier* the valedictory rites would have devised themselves; here, disorientated, *depaysée*, one's reactions have become incoherent. Between meetings with scattered friends I stray in a disorganised fashion among the places which, in their different ways, have symbolised France for me. One day it is the groined roof of *St. Sévérin* and the seething, polyglot streets around it, redolent wth the cooking smells of half the nations of Europe, Asia and Africa, another, the prow of the Ile de la Cité, where I drink Bourgeuil, and eat a sandwich of *rillettes* while looking out at the statue of Henri IV, sitting his horse for ever on the Pont Neuf. In the Louvre, when I go for a last look at the Avignon *Pietá* and Watteau's *Gilles*, I almost think I have encapsulated the essence of a nation and a people when I hear a father, rosy with beef and Beaujolais, say to his blonde small daughter, aged perhaps ten: 'Fragonard, 1732 to 1806 — remember!' but it will not quite do.

Nor will the red and blue and green sails of the toy boats on the pond in the Tuileries, where the cock pigeons puff and trail their tails, and children strapped in the saddles of their donkeys, creep at the pace of a State funeral up and down the alley beside the rue de Rivoli, or even the vista that takes the eye, direct as an arrow, from the inner court of the Louvre, between the Chevaux de Marly to the dead centre of the Arc de Triomphe.

On the last day, defeated, I stop looking for significance and decide to occupy a free morning by going up to Montmartre. I get off the bus in the place Blanche, and walk up the rue Lepic towards the piled, preposterous meringues of the Sacré Coeur, then, on an impulse — if you are a tourist, why not behave like one — start toiling up the endless steps to the dome. The climb, like all of its kind, is laborious, claustrophobic, with a moment about halfway up when you wonder why you ever started, and different from any other I know in having another moment of pure terror when, from the reeling height of the *Galerie des Vitraux*, you look down on to the whole interior of the basilica.

Then we are out on the *Galerie des Colonnes*; after the constricted dimness, the sense of light and release is like an explosion; on this bright day the view extends for fifty kilometres in every direction.

One looks from the centre, where the Seine threads the city like a river in an Italian painting, to the distances, back to the centre to pick out the familiar domes and towers, then out again. Southward, the view shades into the blue-green of the *Forêt de Fontainebleau*, to the north the grimy plain of Saint Denis, with 300 different industries crammed into its few kilometres, lies between Montmartre and the sombre basilica that was the burial place of the kings of France. To the east, the city is flanked by the open space of the *Bois de Vincennes*: westward, the mineral landscape of the new business quarter beyond *La Défense* thrusts up its tower blocks.

Why look for elements that will symbolise the whole? Here is the whole at one's feet. Here is France, ordered and anarchic, Jansenist and profligate, archaic and *avant garde*, changing under one's eyes and eternally immutable, magnificent and maddening and incomparable.

Il y a longtemps que je t'aime,
Jamais je ne t'oublierai.

La Marche à la suite des Deux Enfants